Consumption Tax Trends 2018

VAT/GST AND EXCISE RATES, TRENDS AND POLICY ISSUES

OECD

BETTER POLICIES FOR BETTER LIVES

This work is published under the responsibility of the Secretary-General of the OECD. The opinions expressed and arguments employed herein do not necessarily reflect the official views of OECD member countries.

This document, as well as any data and any map included herein, are without prejudice to the status of or sovereignty over any territory, to the delimitation of international frontiers and boundaries and to the name of any territory, city or area.

Please cite this publication as:
OECD (2018), *Consumption Tax Trends 2018: VAT/GST and Excise Rates, Trends and Policy Issues*, OECD Publishing, Paris.
https://doi.org/10.1787/ctt-2018-en

ISBN 978-92-64-30902-9 (print)
ISBN 978-92-64-30903-6 (pdf)

Consumption Tax Trends
ISSN 1562-8752 (print)
ISSN 1999-0979 (online)

Revised version, March 2019
Details of revisions available at: *http://www.oecd.org/about/publishing/Corrigendum_Consumption_Tax_Trends_2018.pdf*

The statistical data for Israel are supplied by and under the responsibility of the relevant Israeli authorities. The use of such data by the OECD is without prejudice to the status of the Golan Heights, East Jerusalem and Israeli settlements in the West Bank under the terms of international law.

Corrigenda to OECD publications may be found on line at: *www.oecd.org/about/publishing/corrigenda.htm*.

Foreword

This is the twelfth edition of *Consumption Tax Trends*, a biennial OECD publication. It presents cross-country comparative data relative to consumption taxes in OECD member countries, as at 1 January 2018. Tables using data from the *National Accounts* and data on tax revenue from *Revenue Statistics 2018* are updated up to and including 2016. Price levels for fuel oils are updated as at 4th Quarter 2017 from *Energy Prices and Taxes - Quarterly Statistics* issued by the International Energy Agency. The country data for the report have, for the most part, been provided by delegates to the Committee on Fiscal Affairs' Working Party N°9 on Consumption Taxes. The exchange rates used to convert national currencies into US dollars (USD) are average market rates for 2017 taken from the OECD *Monetary and Financial Statistics*, except for Tables 3.A.5 where market rates for 2016 are used as taxes and prices refer to the year 2016; and 2.A.5 and 2.A.8 where the Purchase Power Parity (PPP) rates for GDP are used as they provide for a better comparison of the value of VAT relief thresholds (PPP rates for GDP 2017 are extracted from the OECD Statistics Database).

This publication illustrates the evolution of consumption taxes as instruments for raising tax revenue and, sometimes, to influence customer behaviour. It identifies and documents the large number of differences that exist in respect of the consumption tax bases, rates and implementation rules while highlighting the features underlying their development. It looks, in particular, at revenue and policy trends and developments in the Value Added Tax/Goods and Services Tax (VAT/GST) area (referred to as "VAT" in this publication). It notably presents an updated estimate of the VAT Revenue Ratio (VRR) for OECD countries, providing an indicator of the loss of VAT revenue as a consequence of exemptions and reduced rates, fraud, evasion and tax planning. It provides an update on the implementation of the OECD International VAT/GST Guidelines as the international standard for the application of VAT to cross-border trade in services and intangibles and, in particular, on the implementation of the recommended rules and mechanisms for the efficient and effective collection of VAT on digital sales.

Chapter 1 summarises trends in consumption taxes and their main features. It shows the evolution of consumption tax revenues between 1965 and 2016 and looks in some more detail at the challenges of applying VAT to international trade, and at policy responses particularly in the context of cross-border online trade. Chapter 2 describes the key features of VAT regimes in OECD countries, i.e. tax rates, exemptions, specific restrictions to input tax credit, registration and collection thresholds, and special tax collection methods. It also considers the recent evolutions concerning the struggle against VAT fraud. It finally describes how the VAT Revenue Ratio (VRR) provides an indicator of the effect of exemptions, reduced rates and non-compliance on government revenues and explains how it is calculated and should be interpreted. Chapter 3 describes the main features of excise duties and their impact on revenue, customer behaviour and markets. It shows the detailed excise tax rates on beer, wine, alcoholic beverages, tobacco, and mineral oil products in OECD countries. It also provides an estimate of the total tax burden in a pack of cigarettes in OECD countries. Chapter 4 describes the main features of vehicle taxes and their use for influencing customer behaviour. It provides detailed information on taxes on sale and registration of vehicles and recurrent taxes.

This publication was prepared under the auspices of the Working Party N°9 on Consumption Taxes of the Committee on Fiscal Affairs. It was written by Stéphane Buydens of the OECD Centre for Tax Policy and Administration (CTPA).

Acknowledgements

Acknowledgements are due to: David Bradbury (Head, Tax Policy and Statistics Division); Piet Battiau (Head, Consumption Taxes Unit), Kurt Van Dender (Head, Tax and Environment Unit); Michelle Harding (Head, Statistical Analysis Unit); Florens Flues (Tax Economist), Michel Lahittete (Statistician), Emmanuelle Modica (Statistician/Analyst), Michael Sharratt (Website and Database Developer), Marie-Aurélie Elkurd (Assistant), Karena Garnier (Assistant), and Alexandra Le Cam (Assistant), CTPA; Mariano Berkenwald, International Energy Agency; Professor Walter Hellerstein (Distinguished Research Professor & Francis Shackelford Distinguished Professor in Taxation Law, University of Georgia).

The OECD's Centre for Tax Policy and Administration wishes to gratefully acknowledge the invaluable contributions to Consumption Tax Trends of Michel Lahittete who passed away in July 2018.

Table of contents

Tables

Figures

Executive Summary

Consumption taxes generally consist of *general taxes on goods and services* ("taxes on general consumption"), consisting of value-added tax (VAT) and its equivalent in several jurisdictions (goods and services tax, or GST); sales taxes, and other general taxes on goods and services; and *taxes on specific goods and services*, consisting primarily of excise taxes, customs and import duties, and taxes on specific services (such as insurance premiums and financial services).

Consumption taxes accounted for 30.6% of total tax revenues in OECD countries in 2016, on average. While the share of all taxes on consumption (taxes on general consumption plus taxes on specific goods and services) as a percentage of total tax revenue has remained relatively stable since 1975, the composition of consumption taxes has fundamentally changed. Over time, OECD countries have relied increasingly on taxes on general consumption. Since 1975, the share of these taxes as a percentage of GDP in OECD countries has increased considerably from 4.1% to 7.0%. They presently raise 20.8% of total tax revenue on average, compared with 13.4% in 1975. VAT has become the largest source of taxes on general consumption, accounting on average for 6.8% of GDP and 20.2% of total tax revenue in OECD countries in 2016. While revenues from taxes on general consumption fell between 2005 and 2009, as a consequence of the global economic crisis, they have now returned to the pre-crisis levels largely due to the rise in standard VAT rates in many countries. In contrast to this increase, revenues from taxes on specific goods and services, the bulk of which are excise taxes, have fallen over time as a percentage of GDP (from 4.6% in 1975 to 3.3% in 2016) and as a percentage of total tax revenue (from 17.7% in 1975 to 9.8% in 2016).

Key trends

- VAT revenues are stabilising at a high level in OECD countries at 6.8% of GDP and at 20.2% of total tax revenue on average (excl. the United States which do not have a VAT system).
- Standard VAT rates in the OECD reached a record level of 19.3% on average in 2015 and have remained stable since. Ten OECD countries now have a standard VAT rate above 22%, against only four in 2008. The average standard rate of the 23 OECD countries that are members of the European Union (21.8%) is significantly above the OECD average.
- Countries are increasingly implementing or considering base broadening measures to raise additional revenue from VAT, notably by increasing reduced VAT rates and/or narrowing their scope in line with OECD recommendations, although movements in opposite direction are also observed.
- Most OECD countries have implemented or announced measures for the effective collection of the VAT on the ever-rising volume of online sales to private consumers by offshore vendors, in line with the International VAT/GST Guidelines and the

BEPS Action 1 Report. This increasingly includes reforms to ensure the effective collection of VAT on the importation of low-value goods from online sales, which continues to grow particularly rapidly with increasingly important effects on revenues and competitiveness. Australia was the first OECD country to implement reform to collect GST on low-value imports as of July 2018, in line with BEPS Action 1 guidance, and New Zealand and the EU have announced the implementation of similar reform as from October 2019 and 2021 respectively.

- Many countries are considering or have already announced and/or implemented reform to enlist online marketplaces and other digital platforms in the collection of VAT on e-commerce. This can include the requirement for these platforms to collect and remit the VAT on behalf of online vendors and/or enhanced reporting and information sharing requirements. The OECD is developing work to support these reforms.
- Countries are increasingly implementing measures to enhance compliance and reduce the vulnerability of VAT regimes to fraud. This includes alternative collection mechanisms such as domestic reverse charge and split-payments in sectors that are particularly vulnerable to fraud; real-time VAT invoice reporting and electronic data transmission requirements; and enhancing the international administrative cooperation in the area of VAT.
- Excise duties are increasingly used to influence consumer behaviour. For example, the total tax burden on cigarettes is now above 50% of the consumer price in almost all OECD countries and has reached 80% or more in 8 countries.

Key findings

Many OECD countries continue to apply reduced VAT rates to a broad range of products such as basic essentials, pharmaceuticals and healthcare services, cultural and sporting events, etc. to pursue equity or other non-distributional goals (e.g. supporting cultural objectives, promoting locally supplied labour-intensive activities or correcting environmental or other externalities). This notwithstanding evidence that reduced rates are not an effective tool to achieve redistribution or to pursue the other non-distributional goals as mentioned above. They also continue to make considerable use of exemptions to pursue distributional objectives (such as exemptions for basic health, charities and education) and for activities that are considered hard to tax (for example, financial services).

The VAT Revenue Ratio (VRR) for OECD countries suggests that there is still potential for additional revenue by improving the performance of VAT. The VRR provides a comparative measure of how exemptions and reduced rates affect tax revenues and countries' ability to secure effectively the potential tax base for VAT. It measures the difference between the VAT revenue collected and what would theoretically be raised if VAT was applied at the standard rate to the entire potential tax base in a "pure" VAT regime. Across the OECD, the unweighted average VRR has remained relatively stable at 0.56 in 2016, compared to 0.55 in 2015, meaning that 44% of the potential VAT revenue is not collected. Although the VRR has to be interpreted with care and tax base erosion may be caused by a variety of factors, this VRR estimate suggests that there is significant potential for raising additional revenues by improving VAT systems' performance.

The share of excise duties in total tax revenue has been subject to a long decline since 1975, when they accounted for 10.5% on average, compared to 7.8% in 2016. Excise duties are increasingly used to influence consumer behaviour, in particular to reduce pollution through taxes on motor fuels and improve health by heavier taxation of tobacco products.

Car taxation is increasingly used to influence customer behaviour and encourage the use of low polluting vehicles. In 2018, more than three quarters of OECD member countries take environmental or fuel efficiency criteria into account when determining the level of taxation for the purchase or use of vehicles.

Chapter 1. Key Consumption Tax Trends and Figures

This chapter describes the relative importance of consumption taxes as a source of tax revenues and the main features of these taxes. It shows the evolution of consumption tax revenues between 1965 and 2016. It describes the functioning of value added taxes (VAT) and of retail sales taxes (in the United States) and the main characteristics of consumption taxes on specific goods and services. It looks in some more detail at the application of VAT to international trade, more particularly at the challenges of applying VAT to cross-border trade and at the International VAT/GST Guidelines that the OECD has developed as the global standard to address these challenges.

1.1. Introduction

Consumption taxes account for approximately one third of the total taxes collected in OECD countries. They have two common forms: taxes on general consumption (value added taxes and retail sales taxes) and taxes on specific goods and services (mainly excise duties).

Since the mid-1980s, VAT[1] (also called Goods and Services Tax – GST) has become the main consumption tax both in terms of revenue and geographical coverage. VAT is designed to be a tax on final consumption that is broadly neutral towards the production process and international trade. It is widely seen as a relatively growth-friendly tax. Many countries have sought to raise additional revenues from VAT, rather than from other taxes, as part of their fiscal consolidation strategies in the aftermath of the global financial and economic crisis. Many developing countries have introduced a VAT during the last two decades to replace lost revenues from trade taxes following trade liberalisation. Some168 countries operate a VAT today (see Annex A), including 35 of the 36 OECD member countries, the only exception being the United States although most states within the US employ some form of retail sales tax. VAT raises approximately a fifth of total tax revenues in the OECD and worldwide.

The global spread of VAT along with increasing VAT rates plus the rapid globalisation of economic activity and the strong growth of the digital economy, which have resulted in an increased interaction between VAT systems, have raised the profile of VAT as an increasingly important policy issue for an increasing number of countries. The application of VAT to cross-border trade, particularly trade in services and digital trade, was flagged as a particularly challenging issue needing an urgent international response by tax authorities worldwide over recent years. In contrast with existing international standards for the taxation of income such as the OECD Model Tax Convention and the Transfer Pricing Guidelines, there was no internationally agreed framework for the application of VAT to cross-border trade. This led to increasing uncertainty and complexity for tax authorities and businesses and to growing risks of double taxation and unintended double non-taxation. This was a matter of special concern with respect to international trade in services and intangibles, which has grown particularly strong over the last decades notably as a consequence of the strong growth of the digital economy. The OECD's Committee on Fiscal Affairs (CFA) developed the *International VAT/GST Guidelines* in response to the strong international call for a global standard on VAT design and operation. These Guidelines present a set of internationally agreed standards and recommended approaches for the consistent application of VAT to international trade, with a particular focus on trade in services and intangibles. Their main objective is to reduce the uncertainty and the risks of double taxation and unintended non-taxation that result from inconsistencies in the application of VAT in a cross-border context. The *International VAT/GST Guidelines* were developed through an inclusive process, with the active involvement of international organisations and jurisdictions beyond the current OECD membership and with intense consultation of the business community. They were endorsed as a global standard by over one hundred countries, jurisdictions and international organisations at the OECD Global Forum on VAT in November 2015. They were adopted as a Recommendation by the Council of the OECD in September 2016. This Recommendation is the first OECD legal instrument in the area of VAT. Work by the OECD is now focusing on complementing these Guidelines with implementation guidance, and on measures for the effective, efficient and internationally consistent collection of VAT on digital trade.

Whilst VAT was first introduced about 60 years ago, excise duties have existed since the dawn of civilisation. They are levied on a specific range of products and are assessed by reference to various characteristics such as weight, volume, strength or quantity of the product, combined in some cases with *ad valorem* taxes. Although they generally apply to alcoholic beverages, tobacco products and fuels in all OECD countries and beyond, their tax base, calculation method and rates vary widely between countries, reflecting local cultures and historical practice. Excise duties are increasingly being used to influence consumer behaviour to achieve health and environmental objectives.

This chapter first provides an overview of the statistical classification of consumption taxes (Section 1.2) and shows the evolution of consumption tax revenues between 1965 and 2016 (Section 1.3). It then describes the geographical spread of VAT (Section1.4) and outlines the main features of VAT design (Section 1.5). This is followed by a high-level description of the main design features of retail sales taxes (Section 1.6) and of the main characteristics of consumption taxes on specific goods and services (Section 1.7). This chapter then looks in some more detail at the challenges of applying VAT to cross-border trade in services and intangibles and at the International VAT/GST Guidelines developed by the OECD as the global standard to address these challenges. It also looks at the available options for collecting VAT on cross-border trade in low value goods (Section 1.8).

1.2. Classification of consumption taxes

In the OECD classification, "taxes" are confined to compulsory, unrequited payments to general government. According to the OECD nomenclature, taxes are divided into five broad categories: taxes on income, profits and capital gains (1000); social security contributions (2000); taxes on payroll and workforce (3000); taxes on property (4000); and taxes on goods and services (5000) (OECD, 2018[1]).

Consumption taxes (Category 5100 "Taxes on production, sale, transfer, leasing and delivery of goods and rendering of services") fall mainly into two sub-categories:

- *General taxes on goods and services* (5110 "taxes on general consumption"), which includes value added taxes (5111), sales taxes (5112) and other general taxes on goods and services (5113).
- *Taxes on specific goods and services* (5120) consisting primarily of excise taxes (5121), customs and import duties (5123) and taxes on specific services (5126, e.g. taxes on insurance premiums and financial services).

Consumption taxes such as VAT, sales taxes and excise duties are often categorised as *indirect taxes* as they are generally not levied directly on the person who is supposed to bear the burden of the tax. They are rather imposed on certain transactions, products or events (OECD Glossary of Tax Terms). They are not imposed on income or wealth but rather on the expenditure that the income and wealth finance. Governments generally collect the tax from producers and distributors at various points in the value chain, while the burden of the tax falls in principle on consumers assuming that it will be passed on to them in the prices charged by suppliers.

1.3. Evolution of consumption tax revenues

On average, consumption taxes produced 30.6% of the total tax revenue and accounted for 10.3% of the GDP in the OECD member countries in 2016 (unweighted average, see

Annex Table 1.A.1). Approximately two thirds of revenue from consumption taxes is attributable to taxes on general consumption and one third to taxes on specific goods and services (see Annex Table 1.A.2 and Annex Table 1.A.3).

Figure 1.1. Average tax revenue as a percentage of aggregate taxation by category of tax, 2016

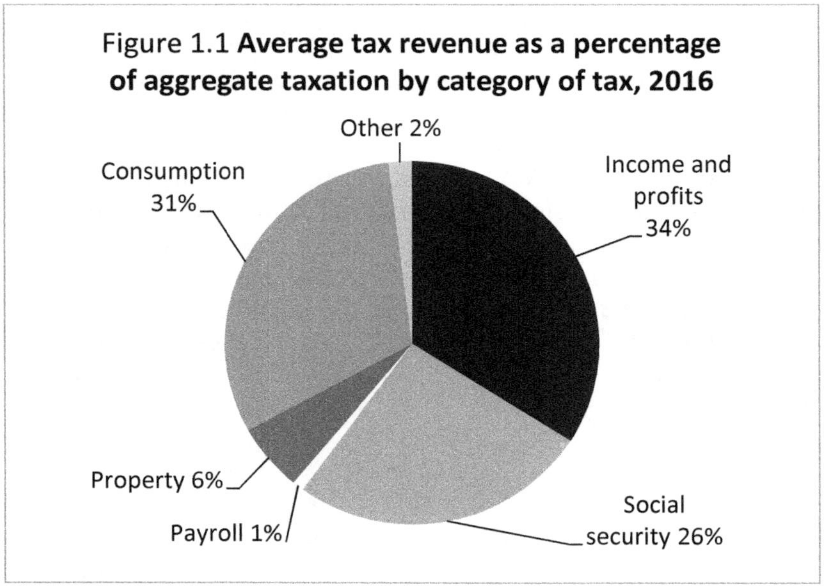

Source: Adapted from (OECD, 2018[1]) *Revenue Statistics 2018*, OECD Publishing, Paris.

StatLink https://doi.org/10.1787/888933889989

Annex Table 1.A.2 presents revenues from taxes on general consumption as a percentage of Gross Domestic Product (GDP) and as a percentage of total taxation in 2016. These taxes include VAT, sales taxes and other general taxes on goods and services. These ratios vary considerably between countries both in percentage of GDP and of total taxation. In Australia, Mexico, Switzerland, and the United States, taxes on general consumption account for less than 4% of GDP while they account for more than 9% in Denmark, Estonia, Finland, Hungary, Israel, New Zealand and Sweden. Revenues from those taxes account for less than 15% of total taxation in Australia, Canada, Italy, Japan, Switzerland and the United States and for more than 29% in Chile, Hungary, Israel and New Zealand. Taxes on general consumption account for more than 20% of total taxation in 20 of the 36 OECD countries, with an OECD unweighted average of 20.8%.

Over the longer term, OECD member countries have relied increasingly on taxes on general consumption. Since 1965, the share of these taxes as a percentage of GDP in OECD countries has more than doubled, from 3.2% to 7.0% in 2016. They accounted for only 11.9% of total tax revenue in OECD countries in 1965 compared to 20.8% in 2016.

VAT is now the largest source of revenue from taxes on general consumption in OECD countries, on average (see Annex Table 1.A.4). Revenues from VAT as a percentage of GDP slightly increased from 6.6% in 2005 to 6.8% in 2016 on average while they remained stable at 20.2% as a share of total taxation over the same period.

VAT is now operated in 35 of the 36 OECD countries, the United States being the only OECD country not to have adopted a VAT. In 1975, thirteen of the current OECD member countries had a VAT (see Table 2.A.1 in Chapter 2). Greece, Iceland, Japan, Mexico, New Zealand, Portugal, Spain and Turkey introduced VAT in the 1980s while Switzerland followed shortly afterwards. Central European economies introduced VAT in the late 1980s and early 1990s, often based on the European Union (EU) model in anticipation of their future EU membership. Australia implemented a VAT ("Goods and Services Tax – GST) in 2000.

While the global financial and economic crisis had an effect on consumption tax revenues, which fell between 2005 and 2009, they have generally returned to the pre-crisis levels, largely due to the rise in standard VAT rates in many countries during and in the aftermath of the crisis (21 of the OECD member countries raised their standard rate between 2009 and 2014 – see Chapter 2).

The share of VAT in total tax revenues in the 35 OECD countries that operate a VAT shows a considerable spread, ranging from 12-13 % (Australia, Canada, Japan, Switzerland) to 26-27% (Estonia, Latvia, Lithuania) and to 29.8 % in New Zealand and 41.2 % in Chile (see Figure 1.2 and Annex Table 1.A.4). VAT produces 15% or more of total tax revenues in 30 of the 35 OECD countries that operate a VAT and it exceeds 20% of total taxation in 20 of these countries.

Figure 1.2. Value added taxes (5111) as percentage of total taxation in 2016

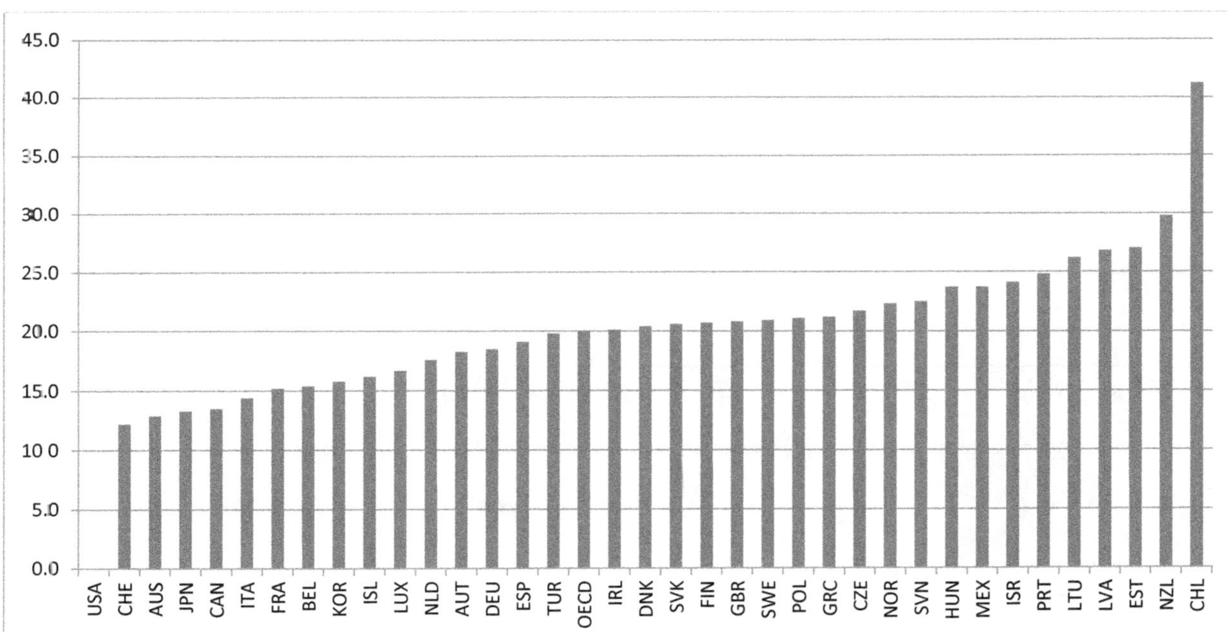

Source: Adapted from (OECD, 2018[1]) *Revenue Statistics 2018*, OECD Publishing, Paris.

StatLink https://doi.org/10.1787/888933890008

Annex Table 1.A.3 shows that revenues from taxes on specific goods and services, the bulk of which are excise taxes, have decreased steadily as a percentage of GDP between 1975 (4.6%) and 2010 (3.3%) and have remained stable on average since then. The evolution of the share of taxes on specific goods and services in total taxation has followed the same pattern and decreased from 17.7% in 1975 to 9.8% in 2016 on average. The share of taxes on specific goods and services in total tax revenues fell in 25 OECD countries in increased in 7. Excise taxes are discussed in greater detail in Chapter 3.

As a result, the composition of consumption taxes has fundamentally changed over time. The substantially increased importance of VAT has effectively balanced the diminishing share of taxes on specific goods and services (see Figure 1.3). Only Turkey still collects a significant part of its revenues by way of taxes on specific goods and services, i.e. 22.2% of its total tax revenue against an OECD average of 9.8%.

Figure 1.3. Share of consumption taxes as percentage of total taxation 1968-2016

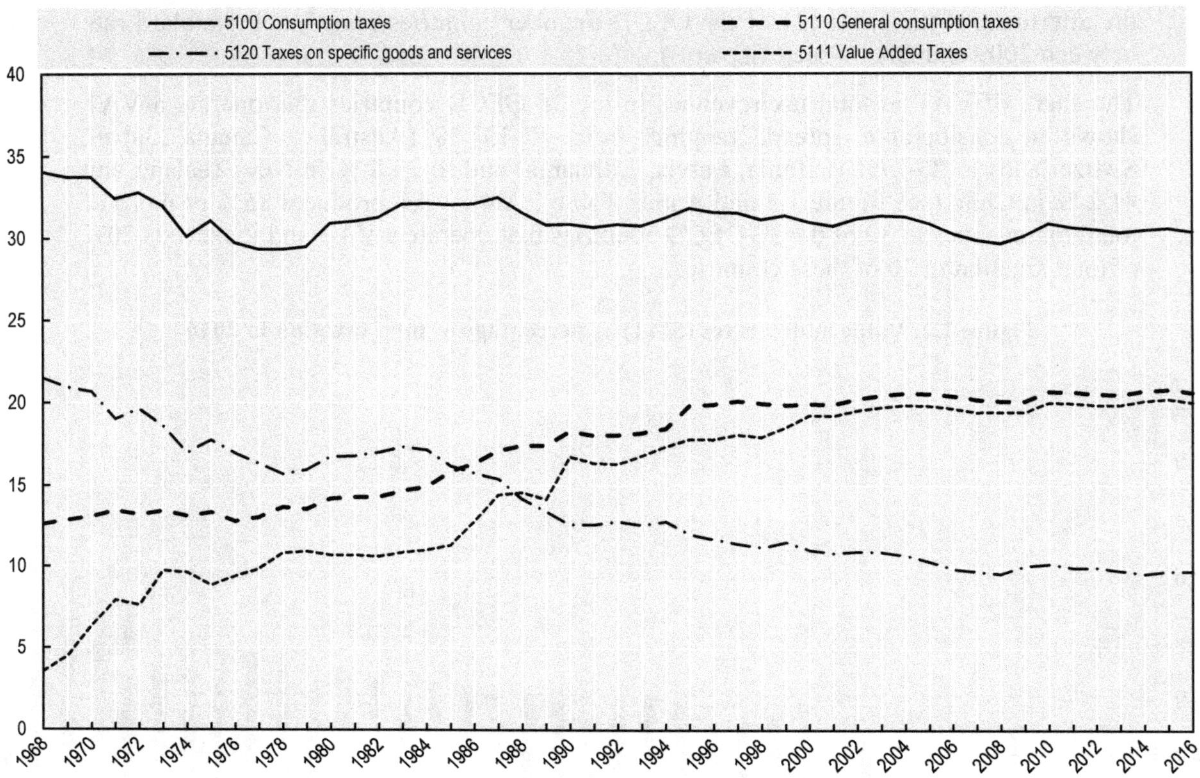

Source: Adapted from (OECD, 2018[1]) *Revenue Statistics 2018*, OECD Publishing, Paris.

StatLink https://doi.org/10.1787/888933890027

Figure 1.3 and Figure 1.4 show the evolution of the tax structure or tax mix in OECD countries between 1965 and 2016. Tax structures are measured by the share of major taxes in total tax revenue. On average, taxes on personal income (personal income tax and social security contributions) increased slightly over this period, representing together about 50% of total tax revenue in 2016. With a share of about 20%, VAT is the third largest source of tax revenue for OECD countries on average, ahead of corporate income taxes, payroll and property taxes. The share of corporate income taxes remained relatively stable, reaching 9% of total tax revenue in 2016.

Figure 1.4. Evolution of the tax mix

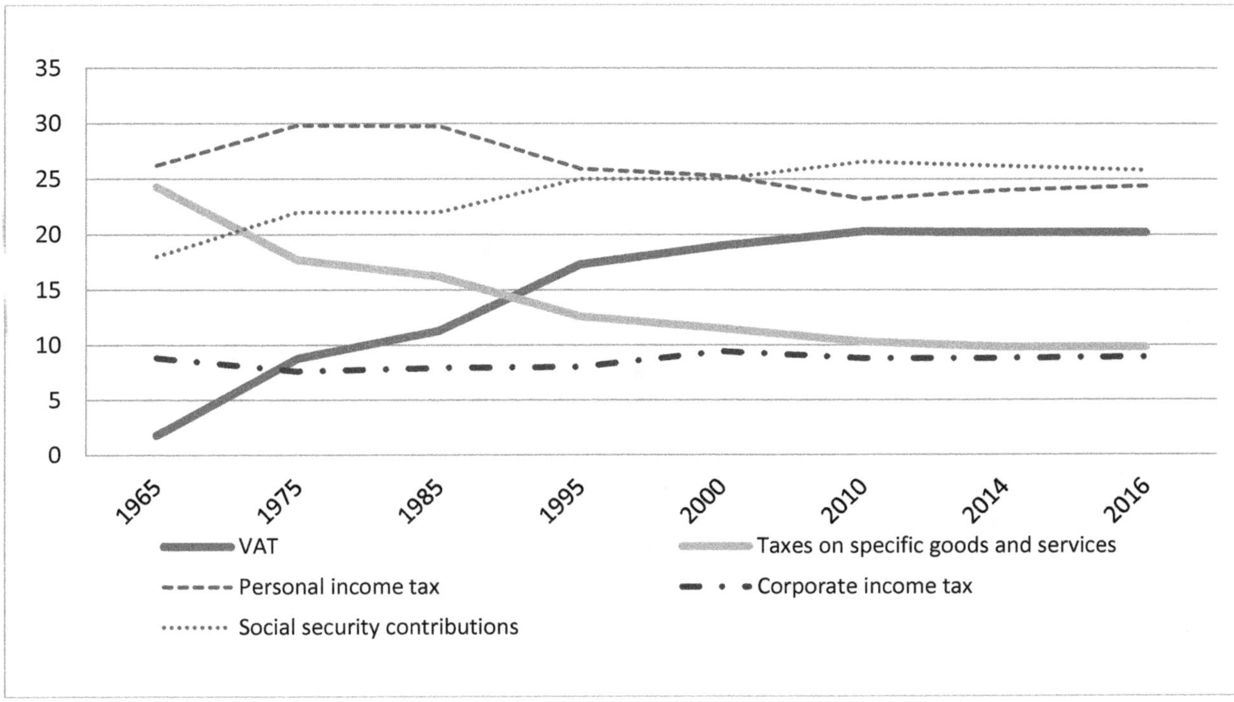

Source: Adapted from (OECD, 2018[1]) *Revenue Statistics 2018*, OECD Publishing, Paris.

StatLink https://doi.org/10.1787/888933890046

1.4. Spread of VAT

The spread of VAT has been among the most important developments in taxation over the last half century. Limited to less than 10 countries in the late 1960s, it is today an important source of revenue in 168 countries worldwide (see Figure 1.5 and Annex A).

The domestic and international neutrality properties of the VAT have encouraged its global spread. Many developing countries have introduced a VAT during the last two decades to replace lost revenues from trade taxes following trade liberalisation. In the EU, VAT is directly associated with the development of its internal market. The adoption of a common VAT framework in the EU was intended to remove the trade distortions associated with cascading indirect taxes that it replaced and to facilitate the creation of a common market in which member states cannot use taxes on production and consumption to protect their domestic market or to gain a competitive advantage compared to other member states. A VAT is operated in 35 of the 36 OECD countries, the only exception being the United States.

Figure 1.5. Countries with VAT 1960 - 2018

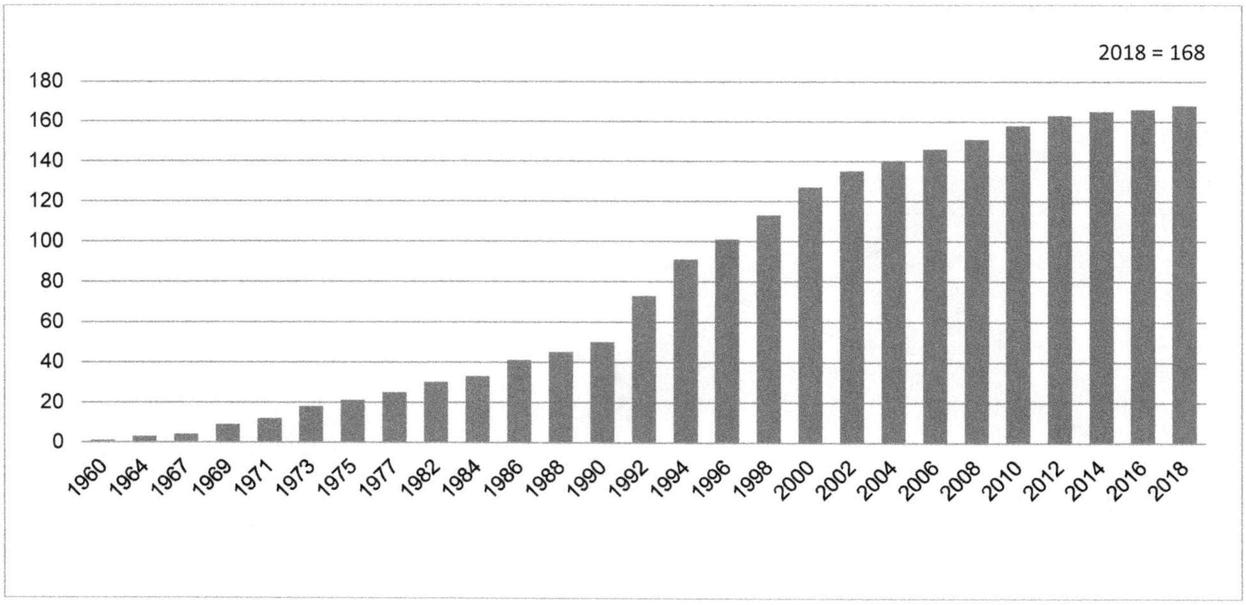

Source: (Fabiola Annacondia IBFD, 2018[2])

StatLink https://doi.org/10.1787/888933890065

1.5. The main features of VAT design

Although there is a wide diversity in the way VAT systems are implemented, the VAT can be defined by its purpose and its specific tax collection mechanism. The *OECD International VAT/GST Guidelines* (OECD, 2017[3]) provide an overview of the core features of VAT, which are summarised below.

1.5.1. A tax on final consumption

VAT is a broad-based tax on consumption by households as, in principle, only private individuals, as distinguished from businesses, engage in the consumption at which a VAT is targeted. In other words "*businesses buy and use capital goods, office supplies and the like - but they do not consume them in this sense*" (Hellerstein, 2010[4]) In practice, however, many VAT systems impose VAT burden not only on consumption by private individuals, but also on various entities that are involved in non-business activities.

From a legal and practical standpoint, VAT is essentially a transaction tax. In "real life" things can be consumed in many ways. Some can be consumed fully and immediately (like a taxi ride); some can be bought and fully consumed later (like a sandwich); some can be consumed over a longer period of time (like a desk or a subscription to an on-line database). However, VAT does not actually tax such material consumption. Rather, it aims at taxing the sale to the final consumer through a staged payment process along the supply chain.

VAT is collected by businesses through a staged process but, since it is a tax on final consumption by households, the burden of the VAT should not rest on businesses, except when they acquire goods, services or intangibles for private consumption by their owners or their employees.

It can be argued, however, that the economic burden of the VAT can lie in variable proportion on business and consumers. Indeed, the effective incidence of VAT, like that of any other tax, is determined not only by its formal nature but also by market circumstances, including the elasticity of demand and the nature of competition between suppliers. (Ebrill et al., 2001[5])

1.5.2. The staged collection process

The central design feature of a VAT, and the feature from which it derives its name, is that the tax is collected through a staged process on the value added at each stage of production and distribution. Each business in the supply chain takes part in the process of controlling and collecting the tax, remitting the proportion of tax corresponding to its margin, i.e. on the difference between the VAT imposed on its taxed inputs and the VAT imposed on its taxed outputs. Businesses collect VAT on the value of their outputs from their customers and are entitled to deduct the tax they have paid on purchases and must account and remit the difference (or receive a refund from) to the tax authorities. In this respect, the VAT differs from a retail sales tax ("RST"), which taxes consumption through a single-stage levy imposed in theory only at the point of final sale.

This mechanism reflects the central design feature of the VAT as a tax collected by businesses through a staged payment process coupled with the fundamental principle that the burden of the tax does not rest on businesses but on final consumers. This requires a mechanism for relieving businesses of the burden of the VAT they pay when they acquire goods, services or intangibles.

There are two main approaches for operating the staged collection process:

- Under the ***invoice credit method*** (which is a "transaction based method"), each trader charges VAT at the rate specified for each supply and passes to the purchaser an invoice showing the amount of tax charged. The purchaser is in turn able to credit that input tax against the output tax it charges on its sales, remitting the balance to the tax authorities and receiving refunds when there are excess credits. This method is based on invoices that could, in principle, be cross-checked to pick up any overstatement of credit entitlement. By linking the tax credit on the purchaser's inputs to the tax paid by the purchaser, the invoice credit method is designed to discourage fraud.
- Under the ***subtraction method*** (which is an "entity based method"), the tax is levied directly on an accounts-based measure of value added, which is determined for each business by subtracting the VAT calculated on allowable purchases from the VAT calculated on taxable supplies.

Almost all jurisdictions that operate a VAT use the invoice-credit method. In the OECD, only Japan uses "credit subtraction VAT", where the VAT on taxable sales (output tax) is calculated by multiplying the total taxable sales by the VAT rate while the amount of deductible input VAT is calculated by extracting the VAT from the total VAT inclusive amount of purchases as recorded in the business's purchase records (including purchase from exempt suppliers such as unregistered small businesses so that there is no incentive to purchase from taxable businesses, but excluding exempt supplies such as financial services). The VAT-liability is calculated on an annual basis, except for certain businesses which can elect for quarterly accounting periods (e.g. exporters that are eligible for VAT refunds). There is no requirement to issue VAT invoices; businesses are required to document their VAT liability and this documentation can include invoices.

1.5.3. Neutrality

The staged collection process, whereby tax is in principle collected from businesses only on the value added at each stage of production and distribution, gives to the VAT its essential character in domestic trade as an economically neutral tax. The full right to deduct input tax through the supply chain, except by the final consumer, ensures the neutrality of the tax, whatever the nature of the product, the structure of the distribution chain, and the means used for its delivery (e.g. retail stores, physical delivery, Internet downloads). As a result of the staged payment system, VAT "flows through the businesses" to tax supplies made to final consumers.

Where the deductible input VAT for any period exceeds the output VAT collected, there is an excess of VAT credit, which should in principle be refunded. This is generally the case in particular for exporters, since their output is in principle free of VAT (i.e. exempt with right to deduct the related input tax) under the destination principle, and for businesses whose purchases are larger than their sales in the same period (such as new or developing businesses or seasonal businesses). These are especially important groups in terms of wider economic development, so it is important that VAT systems provide for an effective treatment of excess credits to avoid the risk that VAT introduces significant and costly distortions for these groups of business. At the same time, however, the payment of refunds evidently can create significant opportunities for fraud and corruption. It is important therefore that an effective refund system is administered properly, supported by a well designed and operated risk based compliance strategy and by a comprehensive audit strategy (Ebrill et al., 2001[5]).

When the right to deduct input VAT covers all business inputs, the final burden of the tax does not lie on businesses but on consumers. This is not always the case in practice, as the right to deduct input tax may be restricted in a number of ways. Some are deliberate and some result from imperfect administration (see Chapter 2).

Restrictions to the deduction of input VAT result in particular from the application of VAT exemptions. When a supply is VAT-exempt, no VAT is charged on the supply and the supplier is not entitled to deduct the related input VAT. Many VAT systems apply exemptions for social (health, education and charities), practical (financial services, insurance) or historical (immovable property, land) reasons.

Another set of restrictions to the right of deduction of input VAT relates to purchases used, or deemed to be used, for the private consumption of the owners of a business, or of its employees or clients (e.g. cars and entertainment).

Chapter 2 of the OECD's *International VAT/GST Guidelines* presents the key principles of VAT-neutrality and a set of internationally agreed standards to support neutrality of VAT in international trade.

1.6. Main design features of Retail Sales Taxes

A retail sales tax is a tax on general consumption charged only once on products at the last point of sale to the end user. In principle, only consumers are charged the tax; resellers are exempt if they are not final end users of the products. To implement this principle, business purchasers are normally required to provide the seller with a "resale certificate," which states that they are purchasing an item to resell it, or with equivalent evidence that the business will fulfil whatever tax obligations it may have (*e.g.* a so-called "direct pay" permit, which is analogous to the "reverse charge" concept). The tax is charged on each item sold to purchasers who do not provide such a certificate or equivalent evidence. The retail sales tax covers not only retailers, but all businesses dealing with purchasers who do not provide a resale or other evidence signifying that no tax is due (e.g. a public body or a charity, unless specific exemption applies).

The basis for taxation is the sales price. Unlike multi-stage cumulative taxes and like the VAT, this system allows the tax burden to be calculated precisely and it does not in principle discriminate between different forms of production or distribution channels. In practice, however, at least in the United States, the failure of the retail sales tax to reach many services and the limitation of the resale exemption to products that are resold in the same form that they are purchased, or are physically incorporated into products that are resold, leads to substantial taxation of business inputs.

In theory, the final outcomes of VAT and retail sales tax should be identical: they both ultimately aim to tax final consumption of a wide range of products where such consumption takes place. They also both tax the consumption expenditure i.e. the transaction between the seller and the buyer rather than the actual consumption. In practice, however, the end result is somewhat different given the fundamental difference in the way the tax is collected. Unlike VAT where the tax is collected at each stage of the value chain under a staged payment system (see Section 1.5 above), sales taxes are collected only at the very last stage i.e. on the sale by the retailer to the final consumer. The latter method has significant disadvantages: the higher the rate the more pressure is placed on the weakest link in the chain – the retailer, especially numerous small retailers; all the revenue is at risk if the retailer fails to remit the tax and the audit and invoice trail is poorer than under a VAT, especially for services; there are inevitably troublesome "end-use exemptions"; and revenue is not secured at the easiest stage, that is at the time of importation and this can be crucial for many developing countries. As a result, a single point resale sales tax is efficient at relatively low rates, but is increasingly difficult to administer as rates rise (Smith and Tait, 1990[6]).

The United States is the only OECD country that employs a retail sales tax as the principal consumption tax. However, the retail sales tax in the United States is not a national tax. Rather, it is a subnational tax imposed at the state and local government levels. Currently, 45 of the 50 States as well as thousands of local tax jurisdictions impose broad-based retail sales taxes. In general, the local taxes are identical in coverage to the state-level tax, are administered at the state level and amount in substance simply to an increase in the state rate, with the additional revenues distributed to the localities. Retail sales taxes are complemented in every state by functionally identical "use" taxes imposed on goods purchased from out-of-state vendors, because the state has no power to tax out-of-state "sales" and therefore imposes a complementary tax on the in-state "use" (Hellerstein et al., 2014[7]).

Combined state and local sales tax rates vary widely in the United States, from 1.76% (Alaska), 4.35% (Hawaii) and 5.42% (Wisconsin) to 10.02% (Louisiana), 9.46% (Tennessee) and 9.41% (Arkansas). Five states do not have a state-wide sales tax (Alaska, Delaware, Montana, New Hampshire, and Oregon and of these, only Alaska generally allows localities to charge local sales taxes and Montana permits special taxes in local resort areas (Walczak Jared and Drenkard Scott, 2018[8]). These rates are much lower than the applicable VAT rates in OECD countries (except Canada, Japan and Switzerland). This is due to two main factors: the compliance risks associated with the sales tax collection method (see above) and the competition between jurisdictions (see below).

Retail sales and use taxes in force in the United States are subject to significant competitive pressure, especially in the context of interstate and international trade. Prior to the US Supreme Court's decision in *South Dakota v. Wayfair, Inc.* (June 2018), Supreme Court rulings prohibited states from requiring vendors to collect tax with respect to cross-border sales when they were not physically present in the purchaser's state. States were therefore unable effectively to collect use taxes with respect to cross-border sales from remote sellers, a problem that became increasingly significant with the advent of the Internet and online sales. In *Wayfair*, the Court overruled the physical-presence requirement for enforcing tax collection obligations on remote vendors as "unsound and incorrect," and it sustained a South Dakota statute imposing such obligations on remote vendors whose annual sales into the state exceeded USD 100 000 or who annual engaged in 200 or more separate transactions in the state. In place of the physical-presence nexus rule for requiring remote vendors to collect tax on sales to in-state customers, the Court adopted a nexus rule that looks to whether the taxpayer tax collector "avails itself of the substantial privilege of carrying on business" in the state based on its "economic and virtual contacts" with the state.

Although the general standards the Court articulated in *Wayfair* provide little concrete guidance to state tax administrators and state tax advisors as to the nature and level of "economic and virtual" contacts that will satisfy constitutional nexus norms for remote sellers, the Court did identify several features of the South Dakota statute that, in its view, were designed to prevent undue burdens upon interstate commerce and thus may provide guidance to the states in designing their tax enforcement regimes in the future. First, the nexus statute provided a safe harbour for those who transact only limited business in the state. Second, the statute did not apply retroactively. Third, South Dakota was one of more than 20 states that have adopted the Streamlined Sales and Use Tax Agreement (SSUTA - available at www.streamlinedsalestax.org), which "standardizes taxes to reduce administrative and compliance costs." As the Court elaborated: "It requires a single, state level tax administration, uniform definitions of products and services, simplified tax rate structures, and other uniform rules. It also provides sellers access to sales tax administration software paid for by the State. Sellers who choose to use such software are immune from audit liability." It remains to be seen how this general standard will be implemented in the future, but as of December 2018, 32 states had already adopted legislation or administrative guidance imposing tax collection obligations on remote vendors based on thresholds analogous to those sustained by the Court in *Wayfair*, and more than half these states are already members of SSUTA, a number that is likely to increase in the future. It is also worth noting that the US Congress possesses the ultimate power (regardless of pre-existing judicially created nexus rules) to prescribe the terms under which remote vendors must collect tax on cross-border sales and could approve proposed legislation authorising states to require such collection if they have adopted SSUTA or similar measures to ease compliance burdens for vendors.

1.7. Main characteristics of consumption taxes on specific goods and services

In the OECD nomenclature, taxes on specific goods and services (5120) include a range of taxes such as excises, customs and import duties, taxes on exports and taxes on specific services. Consumption Tax Trends focuses on excise duties only.

A number of general characteristics differentiate excise duties from value added taxes:

- They are levied on a limited range of products.

- They are not normally due until the goods enter free circulation, which may be at a late stage in the supply chain.
- Excise charges are generally assessed by reference to the weight, volume, strength or quantity of the product, combined in some cases, with *ad valorem* taxes.
- Consequently, and unlike VAT, the excise system is characterised by a small number of taxpayers at the manufacturing or wholesale stage (although, in some cases they can also be levied at the resale stage).

As with VAT, excise taxes aim to be neutral internationally. As the tax is normally collected when the goods are released into free circulation, neutrality is often ensured by holding exports under controlled regimes (such as bonded warehouses) and certification of final export (again under controlled conditions) by Customs. Similarly, imported excise goods are levied at importation although frequently the goods enter into controlled tax-free regimes until released into free circulation.

Excise taxes may cover a very wide range of products like salt, sugar, matches, fruit juice or chocolates. However, the range of products subject to excise has declined with the expansion of taxes on general consumption. Excise taxes on alcohol, tobacco and hydrocarbon oils continue to raise significant revenues for governments (see Chapter 3).

There has been a discernible trend in recent decades to ascribe to these taxes characteristics other than simply revenue-raising. A number of excise duties have been adjusted with a view to discouraging certain behaviours considered harmful, especially for health reasons. This is particularly the case for excise duties on tobacco and alcohol whose rates have increased over time with the aim of reducing consumption of these products. The structure of certain excise duties has also gradually changed to encourage more responsible behaviour towards the collective welfare, especially the environment. This is the case for taxes on fuels, cars and other products which produce environmentally harmful emissions.

Such a trend can be regarded as a change in tax policy of governments. Governments have long been conscious that the tax system has an influence on the decisions of firms and individuals. They know the impact of the tax system on employment, business formation and expansion, and consumption patterns but have generally considered behavioural responses by taxpayers undesirable. In other cases, changing behaviour, e.g. to reduce pollution or discourage consumption of products considered harmful to health, can be a policy objective, along with revenue raising. Environmentally related taxes, although they are often not levied for environmental reasons alone, are effective instruments for pursuing environmental objectives (see Chapter 3).

1.8. VAT and international trade - The destination principle

The overarching purpose of the VAT as a levy on final consumption coupled with its central design feature of a staged collection process lays the foundation for the core VAT principles bearing on international trade. The fundamental issue of economic policy in relation to the international application of the VAT is whether the levy should be imposed by the jurisdiction of origin or destination. Under the destination principle, the tax is fully levied on the final consumption that occurs within the taxing jurisdiction. Under the origin principle, the tax is levied in the various jurisdictions where the value is added. The key economic difference between the two principles is that the destination principle places all firms competing in a given jurisdiction on an even footing whereas the origin principle places consumers in different jurisdictions on an even footing.

The application of the destination principle in VAT achieves neutrality in international trade. Under the destination principle, exports are exempt with refund of input taxes (that is, free of VAT) and imports are taxed on the same basis and at the same rates as domestic supplies. Accordingly, the total tax paid in relation to a supply is determined by the rules applicable in the jurisdiction of its consumption and therefore all revenue accrues to the jurisdiction where the supply to the final consumer occurs.

For these reasons, there is widespread consensus on the destination principle, which is actually the international norm. It is sanctioned by the World Trade Organisation rules and it is one of the key principles on which the OECD's *International VAT/GST Guidelines* are grounded.

Sales tax systems, although they work differently in practice, also set out to tax consumption of goods, and to some extent services, within the jurisdiction of consumption. Exported goods are usually relieved from sales tax to provide a degree of neutrality for cross-border trade. However, in most sales tax systems, businesses do incur some irrecoverable sales tax and, if they subsequently export goods, there will be an element of sales tax embedded in the price.

The application of the destination principle is not without its own difficulties. First, as already noted, the usual way of implementing this principle for VAT involves exemption of exports, which means that goods and services circulate free of tax in cross-border trade. The possibilities of fraud are evident. Second, although most of the rules currently in force are generally intended to tax supplies of goods and services within the jurisdiction where consumption takes place in application of the destination principle, practical means of implementing this intention are diverse across countries. This can, in some instances, lead to double taxation or unintended non-taxation and create uncertainties for both business and tax administrations. The adoption of the OECD International VAT/GST Guidelines responds to these challenges (see below).

1.8.1. Implementing the destination principle

While the destination principle has been widely accepted as the basis for applying VAT to international trade, its implementation is nevertheless diverse across jurisdictions. This can lead to double taxation or unintended non-taxation and to complexity and uncertainty for businesses and tax administrations.

In order to apply the destination principle, VAT systems must have a mechanism for identifying the destination of supplies. Because VAT is generally applied on a transaction-by-transaction basis, VAT systems contain "place of taxation" rules that address all transactions, building on "proxies" that indicate where the good or service supplied is expected to be used by a business in the production and distribution process (if the supply is made to a business) or consumed (if the supply is made to a final consumer).

The following paragraphs provide a concise overview of the mechanisms for identifying the destination of a supply, focusing on supplies of goods first and then on supplies of services.

1.8.2. Application of the destination principle to the cross-border trade in goods

The term “goods” generally means “tangible property” for VAT purposes. The VAT treatment of supplies of goods normally depends on the location of the goods at the time of the transaction and/or their location as a result of the transaction. The supply of a good is in principle subject to VAT in the jurisdiction where the good is located at the time of the transaction. When a transaction involves goods being moved from one jurisdiction to another, the exported goods are generally “free of VAT” in the origin’s jurisdiction (and are freed of any input VAT via successive businesses’ deductions of input tax), whilst imports are subject to the same VAT as equivalent domestic goods in the importing jurisdiction. The VAT on imports is generally collected at the same time as customs duties, although in some countries collection is postponed until declared on the importer’s next VAT return. Deduction of the VAT incurred at importation, in the same way as input tax deduction on a domestic supply, ensures neutrality and limits distortions in relation to international trade.

Within the European Union, which abolished internal customs barriers and tax frontiers in 1993, the system of intra-Community delivery (free of VAT in the Member State of origin) and intra-Community acquisition (taxed in the Member State of destination) for business-to-business supplies allows the application of the destination principle even in the absence of customs procedures.

Many VAT systems apply an exemption for the importation of relatively low value goods. These exemptions are generally motivated by the consideration that the administrative costs of bringing these low value items into the customs and tax system were likely to outweigh the revenue gained. Most OECD countries currently apply such a VAT relief arrangement, with thresholds varying widely across countries, from USD 11 in Denmark to USD 300 in Mexico. From 1 July 2018 Australia collects GST on the sale of imported goods below AUD 1000 through a vendor collection system and collects GST above AUD 1000 through border processes (see Table 2.A.10). However, 20 out of these countries belong to the EU where legislation (Directive 2006/112/EC) provides that member states must exempt from VAT the import of goods whose value does not exceed EUR 10, and are permitted to grant an exemption for imported goods with a value of more than EUR 10 but not exceeding EUR 22. All EU member states that are members of the OECD have opted for the higher threshold of EUR 22, except Denmark that applies the lower threshold of EUR 10 and France and Poland where there is no threshold for goods imported on mail order. This exemption in the EU does not apply to tobacco or tobacco products and alcoholic products. Outside the EU, two OECD countries (Chile and Turkey) do not apply any threshold and tax all imports of goods regardless of their value.

The exemptions for low value imports have become increasingly controversial in the context of the growing digital economy. This was one of the findings of Action 1 of the OECD/G20 Base Erosion and Profit Shifting (BEPS) project, on *Addressing the Tax Challenges of the Digital Economy* (OECD, 2014[9]). At the time when most low value import relief provisions were introduced, internet shopping did not exist and the level of imports benefitting from the relief was relatively small. In recent years, however, many countries have seen a significant and rapid growth in the volume of low value imports of physical goods from online sales on which VAT is not collected. This results in potentially unfair competitive pressures on domestic retailers who are required to charge VAT on their sales to domestic consumers and in decreased VAT revenues. It also creates an incentive for domestic suppliers to relocate to an offshore jurisdiction in order to sell their low value goods free of VAT. The report on Addressing the Tax Challenges of the Digital Economy recognised that the difficulty lies in finding the balance between the need for appropriate revenue protection and avoidance of distortions of competition, which tend to favour a lower threshold, and the need to keep the cost of collection proportionate to the relatively small level of VAT collected, which favours a higher threshold. The report observed that tax authorities could be in a position to remove or lower the exemption threshold for imports of low value goods, if they were able to improve the efficiency of processing such low value imports and of collecting the VAT on such imports. The report then outlines and assesses the main available approaches for a more efficient collection of VAT on the import of low value goods, which may allow governments to reduce or remove the VAT exemption thresholds, should they decide to do so. The report explores models for collecting import VAT that would limit or remove the need for customs authorities to intervene in the VAT collection for imports that are not subject to customs duties (noting that most countries apply a de minimis threshold for customs duties, which is often higher than the VAT exemption threshold). This is expected to lower the cost of collection of VAT on low imports considerably.

Australia implemented reform to collect GST to imports of low-value goods as of 1 July 2018. The GST relief for imports of goods with a value of AUD 1 000 or less supplied by foreign vendors to Australian final consumers was subject to a new vendor collection mechanism from that date. Foreign vendors that supply more than AUD 75 000 of taxable goods, to consumers in Australia per year, as well as any supplies of inbound digital products and services made to Australian consumers are now required to register for GST in Australia and charge the tax on their sales to final consumers in Australia. The GST on the sale of these goods is mostly collected from these foreign vendors through a simplified registration-based collection regime, in line with OECD guidance. The threshold of AUD 75 000 is the same as the local registration threshold, below which Australian businesses are relieved from the collection of the GST. It aims to relieve small foreign vendors for whom the compliance cost of registering and remitting the GST on their goods sales to Australian consumers, from the requirement to do so. Goods purchased from abroad via an online marketplace are considered to have been supplied by this online marketplace – this marketplace is required to collect and remit the GST.

New Zealand has announced the introduction of a similar offshore supplier registration model to collect GST on imported low value goods from 1 October 2019.

A similar trend can be observed in the EU. EU member states adopted the so-called VAT e-commerce package in December 2017, with a view to enhancing and simplifying VAT compliance for online businesses. One of the key measures included in this package is the removal of the VAT exemption for imports of low-value goods (i.e. goods worth not more than EUR 22) from outside the EU as of 2021 (European Commission, 2017[10]). From that date, non-EU vendors will have the option to charge and collect the VAT on distance sales of imported goods to EU consumers, from their EU customers at the point of sale, and to declare and pay this VAT through the EU's online digital portal (One Stop Shop; OSS). These goods will then be exempt from VAT at importation, allowing a fast release at customs. If non-EU vendors do not opt for this import One Stop Shop regime, import VAT will be collected from customers by the customs declarant (e.g. postal operator, courier firm, customs agents) which will pay it to the customs authorities via a monthly payment rather than on a transactional basis. These new rules will apply to distance sales of goods by non-EU vendors with a value of EUR 150 or below. Imports of goods above the EUR 150 (customs) threshold will still require a full customs declaration. Where such distance sales are facilitated by electronic marketplaces, it will be the marketplace operator that will be liable for the VAT on these sales. This requirement will include sales of goods that are already being stored by non-EU vendors in warehouses (so-called "fulfilment centres") within the EU, which have been increasingly used to sell goods fraudulently without VAT to consumers in the EU.

The EU VAT e-commerce package further includes a range of measures to simplify intra-EU e-commerce in both services and goods (European Commission, 2017[7]).

Switzerland is also implementing VAT reform to level the playing field between domestic and foreign companies. New rules for determining the requirement for companies to register for Swiss VAT were introduced as of 2018 – these are now based on global turnover instead of only Swiss turnover. Foreign suppliers of goods and (certain) services are now liable to register for VAT in Switzerland and to collect the tax on supplies to Swiss customers when their global taxable turnover exceeds CHF 100 000. The second major reform targets foreign (online) vendors selling low-value goods to Swiss consumers. Currently, VAT on imports is only levied if the VAT amount exceeds CHF 5. The low VAT rates of 2.5% and 7.7% imply that goods up to a value of CHF 200 (taxable at 2.5%) and CHF 65 (taxable at 7.7%) can be imported VAT-free. To remove the competitive disadvantage from this regime for domestic retailers, foreign vendors selling goods to consumers in Switzerland for a total amount of at least CHF 100 000 will be required to register and remit the VAT on these sales in Switzerland, as from 1 January 2019.

1.8.3. Application of the destination principle to the cross-border trade in services and intangibles

The VAT legislation in many countries tends to define a "service" negatively as "anything that is not otherwise defined", or to define a "supply of services" as anything other than a "supply of goods". While this generally also includes a reference to intangibles, some jurisdictions regard intangibles as a separate category. For the purposes of this section references to "services" include "intangibles" unless otherwise stated.

A wide range of proxies can be used by VAT systems to identify the place of taxation of services, including the place of performance of the service, the place of establishment or actual location of the supplier, the residence or the actual location of the consumer, and the location of tangible property (for services connected with tangible property, such as repair services). Many systems use multiple proxies before the place of taxation is finally determined and may use different rules for inbound, outbound, wholly foreign, and wholly domestic supplies (Cockfield et al, 2013).

In the European Union, the determination of the "place of supply" (i.e. the place of taxation) depends on the status of the customer receiving the service and the nature of the service supplied. Supplies of services between businesses (B2B supplies) are in principle taxed at the customer's place of establishment (or at the fixed establishment of the customer to which it is provided), implementing the destination principle for both supplies within the EU and with customers in third countries. On the other hand, supplies of services to final consumers (B2C supplies) are still, in principle, taxed at the supplier's place of establishment. This latter rule does not reflect a will to apply the "origin principle" to B2C supplies but rather the historical reality that most services were consumed where they were provided and it was technically difficult to provide services at a distance to final consumers. There are, however, many exceptions aiming at aligning the place of taxation with the place where consumption is likely to take place. These exceptions include notably the services connected with immovable property (taxed where the property is located); services relating to cultural, artistic, sporting, scientific, educational, entertainment etc. (taxed at the place where they are physically carried out) and the B2C electronically supplied services, that are taxed where the customer resides (since 2003 for services provided by non-EU suppliers and since 2015 also for EU suppliers).

To facilitate compliance by non-EU suppliers, the EU member states created an online digital portal ("Mini One Stop Shop"), allowing these suppliers to register at a distance in only one member state and account in this member state for the VAT due in all the member states of the EU where their customers are located.

Although the EU model for determining the place of supply applies to the 28 Member States of the Union and to a number of other countries such as Norway, Switzerland, and Russia, it is not the international norm. A number of countries (e.g. Australia, Canada, New Zealand, Singapore, South Africa) have adopted different models. While the EU model is based on an approach by category of supplies, where a "place of supply" (which is also the place of taxation) is determined for each category according to its nature and the status (business or consumer) of the customer, other models systematically apply a series of proxies for place of consumption or use to all kinds of services. Such systems work in steps: first a connection with the country is established (e.g. the supplier or the customer are established there; the service is performed or can be acquired there). Then, a number of proxies are applied to determine the actual place of taxation, e.g. a connection with a tangible property; the customer location and/or residence; the location of the person to whom the services are delivered or who uses the service.

For example, in New Zealand (which adopted the GST in 1986) the place of taxation for supplies made by non-residents is generally presumed to be outside New Zealand, except when the service is performed in New Zealand or supplied to a customer who is resident in New Zealand and the recipient is either a final consumer or a registered business who has agreed to have the transaction treated as being made in New Zealand. In contrast, the place of taxation for supplies by residents is presumed to be New Zealand, unless the supply is a zero-rated export of services. These services include international transport and related services; services physically performed outside New Zealand; services supplied to a non-resident who is outside New Zealand at the time the services are performed; services directly in connection with land or goods located outside New Zealand and supplies in relation to intellectual property rights for use outside New Zealand. From 1 October 2016, New Zealand applies GST to supplies of services and intangibles made by non-resident suppliers to final consumers who are usually resident in New Zealand (see section below).

In Australia (which adopted GST in 2000), supplies are taxable (unless GST-free) in Australia and the GST collected through the supplier when the supplies are "connected with Australia". Supplies made through an Australian based business or performed in Australia for a final consumer are connected with Australia. To prevent GST applying to services not consumed or used in Australia, the Australian GST law includes broad, proxy-based zero-ratings ("GST-free") similar to those used in New Zealand. The Australian GST rules were amended as from 1 July 2017, to make supplies of services and intangibles made by non-residents to final consumers who are residents of Australia generally taxable unless the GST-free provisions apply.

The different ways in which the VAT systems have attempted to bring consumption within the scope of the tax during the second half of the 20th century and the new interactions between national VAT systems have become increasingly problematic as volumes of cross-border trade in services and intangibles were growing. VAT systems have experienced considerable difficulties in determining where services are deemed to be consumed, to monitor these transactions and to ensure collection of the tax, particularly where businesses sell services in jurisdictions where they do not have a physical presence. In the absence of adjustment, from a government's viewpoint there is a risk of under-taxation and loss of revenue, or distorting trade through double taxation; from a business viewpoint, there are large revenue risks and high compliance costs.

The OECD developed the *International VAT/GST Guidelines* (hereafter "the Guidelines") as the international standard for applying VAT to cross-border trade in services and intangibles, to minimise the risks of double taxation and unintended double non-taxation resulting from mismatches between national VAT systems.

1.8.4. The International VAT/GST Guidelines

The OECD released its completed Guidelines in November 2015 at the third meeting of its Global Forum on VAT, where these Guidelines were endorsed as the international standard for the application of VAT to the international trade in services and intangibles by over 100 countries, jurisdictions and international organisations. These Guidelines were subsequently adopted as a Recommendation by the Council of the OECD in September 2016 (OECD, 2017[3]). This is the first OECD legal instrument in the area of VAT.

The Guidelines present a set of global standards and recommended approaches for the consistent VAT treatment of international transactions, focusing in particular on trade in services and intangibles. Thy include chapters on the principle of VAT neutrality and its implementation in practice, and on the implementation of the destination principle for allocating the taxing rights on cross-border supplies of services and intangibles. For business-to-business supplies the Guidelines establish that, the taxing rights on cross border supplies of services and intangibles are to be allocated to the jurisdiction where the business customer has located its permanent business presence. For business-to-consumer supplies, the Guidelines recommend that the taxing rights over "on-the-spot supplies" be allocated to the jurisdiction in which the supply is physically performed; and that the taxing rights over all other supplies and services be allocated to the jurisdiction in which the customer has its usual residence. These include remote supplies of services and digital products over the Internet (e.g. apps, streaming of music and movies, online gaming) by foreign suppliers. The Guidelines recommend that these foreign suppliers be required to register and remit VAT in the jurisdiction of taxation and that countries implement a simplified registration and compliance regime to facilitate compliance for non-resident suppliers. They finally recommend that the taxing rights be allocated to the jurisdiction where immovable property is located when they are closely connected with such property.

The Guidelines do not aim at providing detailed prescriptions for national legislation. Jurisdictions are sovereign with respect to the design and application of their laws. Rather, the Guidelines seek to provide guidance to jurisdictions in developing national legislation with a view to facilitating a coherent application of national VAT systems to international trade, taking into account their specific economic, legal, institutional, cultural and social circumstances and practices.

These Guidelines are now being complemented with guidance and technical standards to support their coherent implementation and application (implementation packages). A first report on "Mechanisms for the effective collection of VAT/GST" was delivered in 2017.

(OECD, 2017[11])This report provides further detailed practical guidance to support the implementation of the rules and mechanisms for the efficient and the effective collection of VAT on inbound digital services from offshore suppliers, as recommended in the International VAT/GST Guidelines and in the 2015 Final Report on Action 1 "Addressing the Tax Challenges of the Digital Economy" of the BEPS project. Work by the OECD is now focusing on possible approaches for enlisting online marketplaces and other digital platforms in the collection of VAT on e-commerce, to support and coordinate country reform in this context.

Table 2.A.8 presents a broad overview of the approaches adopted by OECD countries for collecting VAT on cross-border supplies of services and intangibles from foreign suppliers (i.e. on “inbound supplies”). This overview shows that the EU rules determine the place of taxation for cross-border supplies of services and intangibles (i.e. transactions with non-EU member states) in principle by reference to the customer’s location (for Business-to-business supplies - B2B) and to the customer’s usual residence (for Business-to-Consumer supplies - B2C). The VAT on inbound supplies is collected through a reverse charge mechanism, for B2B supplies, and through a simplified vendor registration and compliance regime (“Mini One Stop Shop”) for B2C supplies of telecommunication, broadcasting and electronic services. This regime is operated by the 23 OECD member countries that belong to the EU (Austria, Belgium, Czech Republic, Denmark, Estonia, Finland, France, Germany, Greece, Hungary, Ireland, Italy, Latvia, Lithuania, Luxembourg, Netherlands, Poland, Portugal, Slovak Republic, Slovenia, Spain, Sweden and the United Kingdom). Ten other OECD countries use (some variation of) the customer location (usual residence, head office, etc.) as the main proxy for determining the place of taxation for cross-border supplies of services and intangibles (Australia, Canada, Iceland, Israel, Japan, Korea, New Zealand, Norway, Switzerland and Turkey). Most OECD countries make a distinction between B2B and B2C supplies for determining the place of taxation as well as for determining the mechanism to collect the VAT on inbound supplies. The tax status of customers in this context is generally determined on the basis of the presence of a VAT registration number or on the basis of the customer’s business tax identification number. Two countries (Japan and Korea) distinguish between B2B and B2C supplies on the basis of the nature of the services provided. In these countries, services that are considered to be generally used by final consumers such as provision of e-books, digital newspapers, music, videos, games, etc. are deemed to be B2C services while others are considered B2B supplies. Some countries do not systematically distinguish between B2B and B2C supplies (Canada, Chile, Mexico).

Most OECD countries apply a reverse charge mechanism to collect VAT on inbound B2B supplies of services and intangibles. In Australia, Canada and New Zealand this mechanism only applies when the customer has a limited right to deduct the input tax, and no tax is due when the customer has a full right to deduction. In Switzerland, the application of the reverse charge mechanism is limited to situations where the place of taxation is determined according to the customer's residence proxy. When the supply is taxed in Switzerland according to other proxies (e.g. the location of the immovable property to which the supply is connected), the reverse charge mechanism does not apply and the supplier must register and account for VAT. In addition, foreign suppliers that are registered in the Switzerland to account for VAT on their B2C supplies, must also account for their B2B supplies under that local registration and the reverse charge does not apply. In Korea, inbound B2B supplies are considered out of scope and no VAT is due on such supplies. In Iceland, inbound supplies of services are VAT exempt if the customer has a full right to deduction; where this is not the case the supplier must register for VAT in the country.

For B2C supplies, many OECD countries (31 of 35 countries, i.e. 23 EU member states, Australia, Iceland, Japan, Korea, New Zealand, Norway, Switzerland and Turkey) require the foreign supplier to register and account for VAT. A simplified registration and collection regime (without right to deduct input taxes in the taxing jurisdiction - "pay-only registration") applies in the vast majority of these countries (the option of standard registration is also available in most of these countries). Only two countries (Switzerland and Iceland) require the supplier to register under the standard regime (with the right to deduct the input tax incurred in the country). Japan and Switzerland require the supplier to appoint a tax agent in the country to account for VAT. Four countries (Canada, Chile, Israel, Mexico) operate a self-assessment regime that requires the private customer to remit the VAT on services and intangibles acquired from foreign suppliers.

Four among the countries requiring foreign suppliers to register to account for VAT on their B2C supplies (Iceland, Japan, New Zealand and Norway) do not impose such requirement when the turnover of the suppliers in the country is below a certain threshold. In these countries, the same threshold applies for both domestic and foreign suppliers.

Notes

[1] For ease of reading, all value added taxes will be referred to as VAT in this chapter.

References

Ebrill, L. et al. (2001), *The Modern VAT*, http://www.imf.org. [5]

European Commission (2017), *Modernising VAT for cross-border B2C e-commerce Proposal for a Council Directive*, http://www.consilium.europa.eu/en/press/press-releases/2016/05/25-conclusions-vat-action-plan/. [10]

Fabiola Annacondia IBFD (2018), "Overview of General Turnover Taxes and Tax Rates-January 2018", *International VAT Monitor*, Vol. 1. [2]

Hellerstein, W. (2010), *Interjurisdictional Issues in the Design of a VAT*, https://www.researchgate.net/publication/228153719. [4]

Hellerstein, W. et al. (2014), *Hellerstein, Stark, Swain, and Youngman's State and Local Taxation, Cases and Materials, 10th*, http://store.westacademic.com/Hellerstein_Stark_Swain_and_Youngmans_State_and_Local_Taxation_Cases_and_Materials_10_9780314286987.html. [7]

OECD (2018), *Revenue Statistics 2018*, OECD Publishing, Paris, https://dx.doi.org/10.1787/rev_stats-2018-en. [1]

OECD (2017), *International VAT/GST Guidelines*, OECD Publishing, Paris, https://dx.doi.org/10.1787/9789264271401-en. [3]

OECD (2017), *Mechanisms for the Effective Collection of VAT/GST where the supplier is not located in the jurisdiction of taxation*, OECD, Paris, http://www.oecd.org/tax/consumption/mechanisms-for-the-effective-collection-of-vat-gst.htm. [11]

OECD (2014), *Addressing the Tax Challenges of the Digital Economy*, OECD/G20 Base Erosion and Profit Shifting Project, OECD Publishing, Paris, https://dx.doi.org/10.1787/9789264218789-en. [9]

Smith, S. and A. Tait (1990), "Value Added Tax: International Practice and Problems.", *The Economic Journal*, Vol. 100/399, p. 269, http://dx.doi.org/10.2307/2233622. [6]

Walczak Jared and Drenkard Scott (2018), *State and Local Sales Tax Rates 2018 Key Findings*, Tax Foundation, https://taxfoundation.org/. [8]

Annex 1.A. Data on Tax Consumption

Annex Table 1.A.1. Consumption taxes (5100) as a percentage of GDP and total taxation

	Tax revenue as % of GDP					Tax revenue as % of total taxation				
	1975	2005	2010	2015	2016	1975	2005	2010	2015	2016
Australia	6.6	7.6	6.5	6.6	6.4	25.8	25.4	25.7	23.8	23.2
Austria	12.3	11.0	10.7	10.8	10.9	33.9	26.8	26.2	25.1	25.9
Belgium	10.1	10.1	10.1	10.1	10.2	26.0	23.3	23.8	22.5	23.2
Canada	8.1	7.8	7.0	7.0	7.1	26.0	23.7	22.5	21.5	21.8
Chile	..	10.1	9.4	10.3	10.3	..	48.7	48.2	50.8	51.1
Czech Republic	..	10.0	10.1	10.6	10.8	..	29.0	31.2	31.8	31.4
Denmark	12.0	15.1	13.8	13.3	13.6	32.6	31.4	30.8	28.8	29.5
Estonia	..	12.0	13.0	13.5	13.9	..	40.0	39.1	40.6	41.3
Finland	11.4	12.9	12.6	13.7	13.9	31.6	30.6	30.8	31.2	31.5
France	11.3	10.6	10.2	10.7	10.8	32.4	24.8	24.1	23.5	23.7
Germany	8.7	9.5	10.0	9.7	9.5	25.4	27.9	28.4	26.1	25.5
Greece	7.9	9.9	11.2	12.1	13.3	42.2	31.9	34.9	33.0	34.2
Hungary	..	14.2	15.6	16.6	16.2	..	38.8	41.8	42.9	41.3
Iceland	18.6	15.0	11.0	11.2	11.3	62.2	37.8	33.1	30.8	21.9
Ireland	12.4	10.6	9.0	6.8	6.9	44.4	36.2	33.3	29.4	29.7
Israel[2]	..	11.1	11.2	11.0	11.0	..	32.8	36.5	35.2	35.2
Italy	6.9	9.3	9.9	10.4	10.5	28.3	23.8	23.6	24.2	24.7
Japan	3.0	4.5	4.4	6.0	5.8	15.1	17.2	16.7	19.5	18.9
Korea	8.9	7.5	7.6	6.6	6.9	60.0	33.3	32.6	26.2	26.4
Latvia	..	11.2	10.6	11.5	12.1	..	39.9	37.7	39.2	39.7
Lithuania	..	10.7	11.2	11.2	11.3	..	36.5	39.7	38.6	37.8
Luxembourg	6.5	10.7	10.0	9.3	9.4	20.6	28.4	26.8	25.2	24.8
Mexico	..	4.2	4.7	6.0	6.3	..	37.1	36.7	37.9	38.1
Netherlands	8.5	10.0	9.8	9.7	10.1	22.5	28.6	27.4	26.3	26.3
New Zealand	6.8	10.8	11.2	11.5	11.3	22.8	30.0	37.1	36.3	35.7
Norway	14.2	11.1	11.0	11.0	11.5	36.6	26.1	26.2	28.6	29.7
Poland	..	12.1	12.1	11.2	11.7	..	36.8	38.6	34.6	35.1
Portugal	7.6	13.2	11.8	12.7	12.9	40.1	42.7	38.8	36.9	37.7
Slovak Republic	..	11.4	9.3	9.9	9.8	..	36.5	33.0	30.9	30.3
Slovenia	..	12.5	13.2	13.6	13.4	..	33.1	35.7	37.4	36.8
Spain	4.3	9.1	7.7	9.2	9.0	24.0	25.8	24.7	27.3	27.2
Sweden	8.8	11.8	12.2	11.7	11.9	22.7	25.3	28.2	27.1	27.0
Switzerland	4.6	5.4	5.3	5.1	5.1	20.6	20.3	19.9	18.7	18.4
Turkey	4.8	11.1	11.4	10.7	10.6	40.9	47.4	45.8	42.7	42.1
United Kingdom	8.1	9.4	9.5	10.2	10.2	23.7	28.8	29.4	31.8	31.1
United States	4.2	3.8	3.6	3.8	3.7	17.1	14.8	15.4	14.4	14.4
OECD unweighted average[1]	8.7	10.2	9.9	10.1	10.3	31.1	31.2	31.2	30.6	30.6

Notes:

1. The 2016 OECD average excludes the one-off revenues from stability contributions in Iceland

2. Israel: The statistical data for Israel are supplied by and under the responsibility of the relevant Israeli authorities. The use of such data by the OECD is without prejudice to the status of the Golan Heights, East Jerusalem and Israeli settlements.

Source: *Revenue Statistics 2018, OECD Publishing, Paris. DOI:* https://doi.org/10.1787/rev_stats-2018-en

StatLink https://doi.org/10.1787/888933889894

Annex Table 1.A.2. General taxes on goods and services (5110) as a percentage of GDP and total taxation

	Tax revenue as % of GDP					Tax revenue as % of total taxation				
	1975	2005	2010	2015	2016	1975	2005	2010	2015	2016
Australia	1.7	4.0	3.5	3.7	3.7	6.7	13.4	13.8	13.3	13.2
Austria	7.2	7.6	7.7	7.6	7.7	19.8	18.6	18.7	17.7	18.3
Belgium	6.3	7.0	7.0	6.8	6.9	16.2	16.2	16.4	15.1	15.5
Canada	3.9	4.8	4.3	4.5	4.6	12.5	14.8	14.0	13.8	14.0
Chile	..	7.8	7.5	8.3	8.3	..	37.8	38.5	40.8	41.2
Czech Republic	..	6.6	6.6	7.3	7.4	..	19.1	20.5	21.7	21.7
Denmark	6.4	9.7	9.4	9.1	9.4	17.5	20.2	21.0	19.8	20.4
Estonia	..	8.1	8.6	9.1	9.1	..	26.9	25.8	27.2	27.0
Finland	5.6	8.4	8.3	9.1	9.1	15.6	19.9	20.4	20.6	20.7
France	8.2	7.4	7.0	7.1	7.1	23.4	17.3	16.7	15.6	15.6
Germany	5.0	6.1	7.0	7.0	6.9	14.6	18.0	20.0	18.8	18.5
Greece	3.4	6.9	7.3	7.5	8.4	18.3	22.2	22.8	20.4	21.6
Hungary	..	10.2	11.1	11.9	11.6	..	28.0	29.7	30.8	29.6
Iceland	8.6	10.8	7.5	8.2	8.4	28.6	27.3	22.7	22.6	16.2
Ireland	4.1	7.3	6.0	4.6	4.7	14.7	24.7	22.2	19.7	20.1
Israel[2]	..	9.3	9.2	9.3	9.2	..	27.5	29.8	29.6	29.6
Italy	3.5	5.7	6.1	6.1	6.1	14.3	14.6	14.5	14.2	14.4
Japan	0.0	2.5	2.5	4.2	4.1	0.0	9.5	9.6	13.7	13.3
Korea	1.9	3.9	4.1	3.8	4.2	12.7	17.4	17.5	15.3	15.8
Latvia	..	7.4	6.7	7.8	8.3	..	26.4	23.7	26.8	27.2
Lithuania	..	7.5	7.8	7.8	7.9	..	25.8	27.5	26.9	26.5
Luxembourg	3.8	6.1	6.4	6.5	6.4	12.1	16.1	17.0	17.6	16.7
Mexico	..	3.3	3.8	3.8	3.9	..	29.3	29.4	23.9	23.7
Netherlands	5.4	6.7	6.7	6.5	6.8	14.4	19.2	18.7	17.6	17.6
New Zealand	2.7	8.6	9.3	9.5	9.4	9.0	23.8	30.7	30.2	29.8
Norway	8.0	7.7	7.8	8.2	8.7	20.5	18.2	18.6	21.4	22.4
Poland	..	7.7	7.6	7.0	7.0	..	23.2	24.2	21.6	21.1
Portugal	2.1	8.2	7.5	8.5	8.5	11.2	26.6	24.7	24.8	24.8
Slovak Republic	..	7.7	6.2	6.9	6.7	..	24.6	22.0	21.3	20.6
Slovenia	..	8.4	8.1	8.3	8.2	..	22.2	21.9	22.8	22.5
Spain	2.7	6.2	5.2	6.4	6.4	15.3	17.7	16.7	18.9	19.2
Sweden	4.7	8.6	9.3	9.1	9.3	12.0	18.5	21.5	21.2	21.1
Switzerland	2.0	3.6	3.4	3.5	3.4	8.7	13.6	13.0	12.6	12.4
Turkey	0.0	5.1	5.4	5.2	5.0	0.0	21.8	21.7	20.6	19.8
United Kingdom	3.0	6.0	6.0	6.8	6.8	8.9	18.4	18.7	21.2	20.8
United States	1.7	2.1	2.0	2.0	2.0	7.0	8.1	8.4	7.7	7.7
OECD unweighted average[1]	4.1	6.8	6.7	6.9	7.0	13.4	20.7	20.9	20.8	20.8

1. The 2016 OECD average excludes the one-off revenues from stability contributions in Iceland

2. Israel: The statistical data for Israel are supplied by and under the responsibility of the relevant Israeli authorities. The use of such data by the OECD is without prejudice to the status of the Golan Heights, East Jerusalem and Israeli settlements.

Source: *Revenue Statistics 2018, OECD Publishing, Paris. DOI:* https://doi.org/10.1787/rev_stats-2018-en

StatLink https://doi.org/10.1787/888933889913

Annex Table 1.A.3. Taxes on specific goods and services (5120) as a percentage og GDP and total taxation

	Tax revenue as % of GDP					Tax revenue as % of total taxation				
	1975	2005	2010	2015	2016	1975	2005	2010	2015	2016
Australia	4.9	3.6	3.0	2.9	2.8	19.1	12.0	11.9	10.4	10.0
Austria	5.1	3.3	3.1	3.2	3.2	14.0	8.1	7.5	7.4	7.6
Belgium	3.8	3.1	3.1	3.3	3.4	9.8	7.2	7.4	7.4	7.7
Canada	4.2	2.9	2.6	2.5	2.6	13.6	8.9	8.5	7.7	7.8
Chile	..	2.3	1.9	2.0	2.0	..	10.9	9.8	10.0	9.9
Czech Republic	..	3.4	3.5	3.4	3.3	..	9.8	10.8	10.1	9.7
Denmark	5.6	5.4	4.4	4.1	4.2	15.2	11.2	9.7	9.0	9.1
Estonia	..	3.9	4.4	4.5	4.8	..	13.1	13.3	13.4	14.3
Finland	5.8	4.5	4.3	4.7	4.8	16.0	10.7	10.4	10.6	10.8
France	3.2	3.2	3.1	3.6	3.7	9.0	7.5	7.4	7.9	8.1
Germany	3.7	3.4	2.9	2.7	2.6	10.8	9.9	8.4	7.3	7.0
Greece	4.5	3.0	3.8	4.6	4.8	23.9	9.6	11.9	12.4	12.4
Hungary	..	3.9	4.5	4.7	4.6	..	10.8	12.1	12.0	11.7
Iceland	10.1	4.2	3.5	3.0	2.9	33.6	10.6	10.5	8.2	5.7
Ireland	8.3	3.4	3.0	2.2	2.2	29.7	11.5	11.1	9.7	9.6
Israel[2]	..	1.8	2.1	1.8	1.8	..	5.3	6.8	5.6	5.6
Italy	3.4	3.6	3.8	4.3	4.4	14.0	9.2	9.1	10.0	10.3
Japan	3.0	2.0	1.9	1.8	1.7	15.1	7.7	7.2	5.8	5.7
Korea	7.0	3.6	3.5	2.8	2.8	47.3	15.9	15.1	10.9	10.5
Latvia	..	3.8	3.9	3.6	3.8	..	13.6	13.9	12.4	12.5
Lithuania	..	3.1	3.4	3.4	3.4	..	10.6	12.2	11.7	11.3
Luxembourg	2.6	4.7	3.7	2.8	3.1	8.4	12.3	9.8	7.6	8.1
Mexico	..	0.9	0.9	2.2	2.4	..	7.8	7.3	14.0	14.4
Netherlands	3.1	3.3	3.1	3.2	3.3	8.1	9.5	8.7	8.7	8.7
New Zealand	4.1	2.2	1.9	1.9	1.9	13.8	6.2	6.4	6.1	5.9
Norway	6.3	3.4	3.2	2.8	2.8	16.1	7.9	7.7	7.2	7.4
Poland	..	4.5	4.5	4.2	4.7	..	13.6	14.4	13.0	14.0
Portugal	5.5	5.0	4.3	4.2	4.4	28.9	16.1	14.1	12.1	13.0
Slovak Republic	..	3.7	3.1	3.1	3.1	..	11.9	10.9	9.5	9.6
Slovenia	..	4.1	5.1	5.3	5.2	..	10.8	13.8	14.5	14.2
Spain	1.6	2.8	2.5	2.8	2.7	8.7	8.1	8.0	8.4	8.0
Sweden	4.2	3.2	2.9	2.6	2.6	10.7	6.8	6.8	6.0	5.9
Switzerland	2.7	1.8	1.8	1.7	1.7	11.9	6.7	6.9	6.0	6.0
Turkey	4.8	6.0	6.0	5.5	5.6	40.9	25.5	24.1	22.0	22.2
United Kingdom	5.1	3.4	3.5	3.4	3.4	14.8	10.4	10.7	10.5	10.3
United States	2.5	1.7	1.7	1.8	1.7	10.0	6.7	7.0	6.7	6.6
OECD unweighted average[1]	4.6	3.4	3.3	3.2	3.3	17.7	10.4	10.3	9.8	9.8

1. The 2016 OECD average excludes the one-off revenues from stability contributions in Iceland

2. Israel: The statistical data for Israel are supplied by and under the responsibility of the relevant Israeli authorities. The use of such data by the OECD is without prejudice to the status of the Golan Heights, East Jerusalem and Israeli settlements.

Source: *Revenue Statistics 2018, OECD Publishing, Paris. DOI:* https://doi.org/10.1787/rev_stats-2018-en

StatLink https://doi.org/10.1787/888933889932

Annex Table 1.A.4. Value added taxes (5111) as a percentage of GDP and total taxation

	Tax revenue as % of GDP					Tax revenue as % of total taxation				
	1975	2005	2010	2015	2016	1975	2005	2010	2015	2016
Australia	0.0	3.9	3.4	3.6	3.6	0.0	13.1	13.4	13.0	12.9
Austria	7.2	7.6	7.7	7.6	7.7	19.8	18.6	18.7	17.7	18.3
Belgium	6.3	6.9	6.9	6.7	6.8	16.2	15.9	16.2	15.0	15.4
Canada	0.0	3.2	4.3	4.3	4.4	0.0	9.9	13.7	13.2	13.5
Chile	..	7.8	7.5	8.3	8.3	..	37.8	38.5	40.8	41.2
Czech Republic	..	6.6	6.6	7.3	7.4	..	19.1	20.5	21.7	21.7
Denmark	6.4	9.7	9.4	9.1	9.4	17.5	20.2	21.0	19.8	20.4
Estonia	..	8.1	8.5	9.1	9.1	..	26.9	25.7	27.2	27.0
Finland	5.6	8.4	8.3	9.1	9.1	15.6	19.9	20.4	20.6	20.7
France	8.1	7.2	6.8	6.9	6.9	23.1	16.7	16.1	15.2	15.2
Germany	5.0	6.1	7.0	7.0	6.9	14.6	18.0	20.0	18.8	18.5
Greece	0.0	6.7	7.1	7.3	8.2	0.0	21.5	22.0	20.0	21.2
Hungary	..	8.2	8.5	9.6	9.3	..	22.5	22.9	24.9	23.7
Iceland	0.0	10.8	7.5	8.2	8.4	0.0	27.3	22.7	22.6	16.2
Ireland	4.1	7.3	6.0	4.6	4.7	14.7	24.7	22.2	19.7	20.1
Israel[2]	..	7.5	7.5	7.8	7.5	..	22.3	24.4	25.0	24.1
Italy	3.4	5.7	6.1	6.1	6.1	13.7	14.6	14.5	14.2	14.4
Japan	..	2.5	2.5	4.2	4.1	..	9.5	9.6	13.7	13.3
Korea	0.0	3.9	4.1	3.8	4.2	0.0	17.4	17.5	15.3	15.8
Latvia	..	7.4	6.7	7.7	8.2	..	26.4	23.7	26.4	26.8
Lithuania	..	7.1	7.8	7.7	7.8	..	24.3	27.5	26.7	26.2
Luxembourg	3.8	6.1	6.4	6.5	6.4	12.1	16.1	17.0	17.6	16.7
Mexico	..	3.3	3.8	3.8	3.9	..	29.3	29.4	23.9	23.7
Netherlands	5.4	6.7	6.7	6.5	6.8	14.4	19.2	18.7	17.6	17.6
New Zealand	0.0	8.6	9.3	9.5	9.4	0.0	23.8	30.7	30.2	29.8
Norway	8.0	7.7	7.8	8.2	8.6	20.5	18.1	18.5	21.3	22.3
Poland	..	7.7	7.6	7.0	7.0	..	23.2	24.2	21.6	21.1
Portugal	0.0	8.2	7.5	8.5	8.5	0.0	26.6	24.7	24.8	24.8
Slovak Republic	..	7.7	6.2	6.9	6.7	..	24.6	22.0	21.3	20.6
Slovenia	..	8.4	8.1	8.3	8.2	..	22.2	21.9	22.8	22.5
Spain	0.0	6.2	5.2	6.3	6.3	0.0	17.7	16.6	18.9	19.1
Sweden	4.7	8.5	9.2	9.0	9.2	12.0	18.3	21.2	20.9	20.9
Switzerland	0.0	3.6	3.4	3.4	3.4	0.0	13.4	12.7	12.4	12.2
Turkey	..	5.1	5.4	5.2	5.0	..	21.8	21.7	20.6	19.8
United Kingdom	3.0	6.0	6.0	6.8	6.8	8.9	18.4	18.7	21.2	20.8
United States	0.0	0.0	0.0	0.0	0.0	0.0	0.0	0.0	0.0	0.0
OECD unweighted average[1]	3.1	6.6	6.5	6.7	6.8	8.8	20.0	20.3	20.2	20.2

1. The 2016 OECD average excludes the one-off revenues from stability contributions in Iceland.

2. Israel: The statistical data for Israel are supplied by and under the responsibility of the relevant Israeli authorities. The use of such data by the OECD is without prejudice to the status of the Golan Heights, East Jerusalem and Israeli settlements

Source: *Revenue Statistics 2018, OECD Publishing, Paris. DOI:* https://doi.org/10.1787/rev_stats-2018-en

StatLink https://doi.org/10.1787/888933889951

Annex Table 1.A.5. Tax structures in the OECD area[1]

	1965	1975	1985	1995	2000	2005	2010	2014	2015	2016
Taxes on income, profits and capital gains	35	37	37	34	35	34	33	33	34	34
Personal income tax	26	30	30	25	25	23	23	24	24	24
Corporate income tax	9	8	8	8	9	10	9	9	9	9
Social security contributions	18	22	22	25	25	25	27	26	26	26
Taxes on payroll	1	1	1	1	1	1	1	1	1	1
Taxes on property	8	6	5	5	5	5	5	6	6	6
Taxes on goods and services	38	33	34	34	33	33	33	33	33	33
General consumption taxes	36	31	32	32	31	31	31	31	31	31
VAT	2	9	11	18	19	20	20	20	20	20
Specific consumption taxes	2	2	2	2	2	2	2	2	2	2
Other taxes	0	1	1	1	1	1	1	1	1	0
Total	100	100	100	100	100	100	100	100	100	100

1. In 2016, Iceland received revenues from one-off stability contributions from entities that previously operated as commercial or savings banks and were concluding operations. The stability contributions aimed to liberalise the capital controls that were imposed following the 2007-08 crisis, while preserving Iceland's economic stability. The revenue from these contributions led to unusually high tax revenues for a single year. The one-off stability contributions raised nearly ISK 385 000 million, equivalent to 15.7% of Iceland's GDP in 2016. Iceland's tax-to-GDP ratio rose from 36.3% in 2015 to 51.6% in 2016, before dropping 13.9 percentage points to 37.7% in 2017 (provisional). Due to the exceptional nature of the stability contributions, they are not representative of trends in tax levels across OECD countries and have been excluded from the calculation of the OECD average, both for the average tax-to-GDP ratio and for the average tax structure, in 2016.

Source: *Revenue Statistics 2018, OECD Publishing, Paris. DOI:* https://doi.org/10.1787/rev_stats-2018-en

StatLink https://doi.org/10.1787/888933889970

Chapter 2. Value Added Taxes: Main Features and Implementation Issues

This chapter describes a selection of key features of VAT regimes in OECD countries, i.e. tax rates, exemptions, specific restrictions to input tax credit, registration and collection thresholds and the application of margin schemes. It is complemented with a technical discussion of the rationale and impact of reduced VAT rates.

2.1. Introduction

Although most VAT systems are built on the same core VAT principles (see Chapter 1), there is considerable diversity in the structure of VAT systems in OECD countries. This is notably illustrated by the variety of reduced rates, exemptions and other preferential treatments and special regimes that are widely used in OECD countries, often for equity or social objectives or for practical or historical reasons.

This chapter presents an overview of the VAT rate structures in OECD countries and their evolution between 1975 and 2018 (Section 2.2) and looks in some detail at the VAT exemptions that exist in these countries (Section 2.3). This is followed by an overview and analysis of the wide variety of special regimes used in OECD countries in the following areas: specific restrictions on the right to deduct VAT on specific inputs (Section 2.4), registration and collection thresholds (Section 2.5), and the application of margin schemes (Section 2.6). It also presents the VAT Revenue Ratio as an indicator of the effect of exemptions, reduced rates and non-compliance on VAT revenues (Section 2.7) and the measures taken by governments to combat VAT fraud and avoidance (Section 2.8).

2.2. The evolution of standard rates and reduced rates

2.2.1. Standard VAT rates have reached a plateau in recent years

The evolution of VAT rates can be divided into five periods. The first period between 1975 and 2000 has seen a progressive increase in VAT rates as countries implemented their VAT system. Between 1975 and 2000, the OECD average standard VAT rate rose from 15.6% to 18%.

During a second period, between 2000 and 2009, the standard rate of VAT remained stable in most countries, with 26 out of 35 countries maintaining a rate between 15% and 22%. As of 1 January 2009, only four countries had a standard rate above 22% (Denmark, Iceland, Norway and Sweden -see Annex Table 2.A.1).

The third period, between 2009 and 2014, was marked by a considerable increase in the standard VAT rate in many countries, often in response to financial consolidation pressures caused by the economic and financial crisis. VAT standard rate increases have played a key role in many countries' consolidation strategies, since raising additional revenue from VAT rather than from other taxes (such as income taxes) is often considered more effective (it generates immediate additional revenue) and less detrimental to economic growth and competitiveness than income taxes (OECD, 2010). Between January 2009 and December 2014, 23 countries raised their standard VAT rate at least once. These changes occurred principally in European Union (EU) countries (Czech Republic, Estonia, Finland, France, Greece, Hungary, Ireland, Italy, Latvia, Lithuania, the Netherlands, Poland, Portugal, Slovak Republic, Slovenia, Spain and United Kingdom) but also in some non-EU countries (Iceland, Israel, Japan, Mexico, New Zealand, and Switzerland). Two OECD countries lowered their standard VAT rate temporarily and then raised it again (Ireland and the United Kingdom). This evolution resulted in a hike of the unweighted OECD average standard VAT rate from 17.7% in January 2009 to an all-time record level of 19.3% on 1 January 2015. Ten OECD countries now operate a standard rate above 22% against only four in 2009.

The increases in standard VAT rates observed until the end of 2014 have not continued and it would appear that OECD countries have entered a new period of relatively stable standard VAT rates. Only two OECD countries increased their standard VAT rate between January 2015 and January 2018, i.e. Greece, and Luxemburg. Two OECD countries reduced their standard VAT rate, i.e. Iceland and Israel. The unweighted OECD average standard VAT rate has remained stable at 19.3% since 1 January 2015 (see Figure 2.1).

Figure 2.1. Evolution of standard VAT rates - OECD average 1976-2018

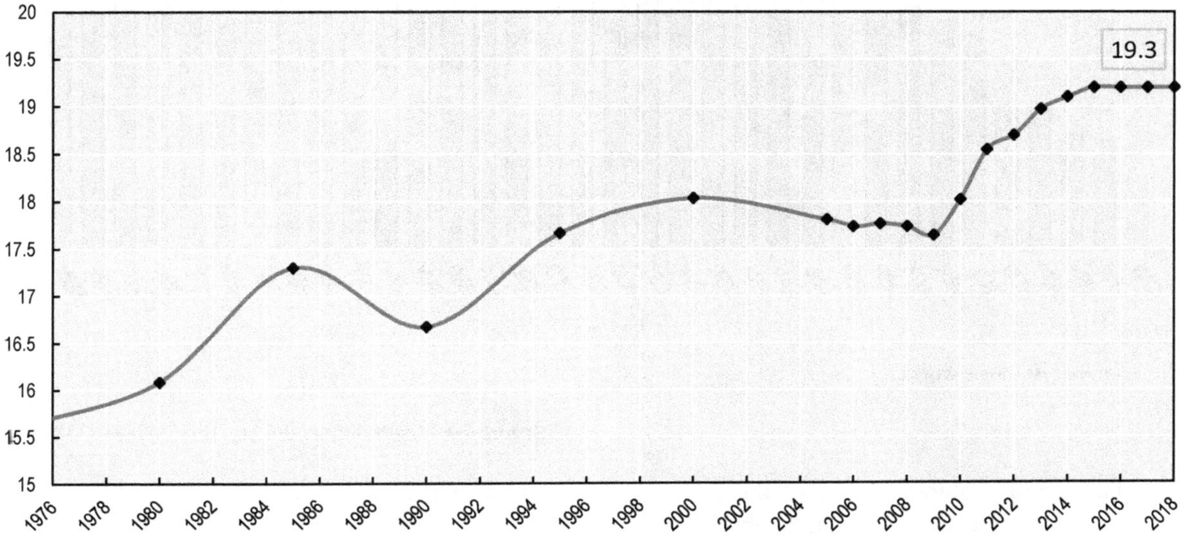

Note: OECD unweighted average.
Source: Author's calculation.

StatLink https://doi.org/10.1787/888933890141

Major differences in standard rates can still be observed among the OECD countries, with rates ranging from 5% in Canada (although most Canadian provinces levy sales taxes or Harmonised Sales Taxes alongside the Federal 5%), 7.7% in Switzerland and 8% in Japan to 25% in Denmark, Norway and Sweden and 27% in Hungary (see Figure 2.2).

Figure 2.2. Standard rates of VAT in OECD countries, 2018

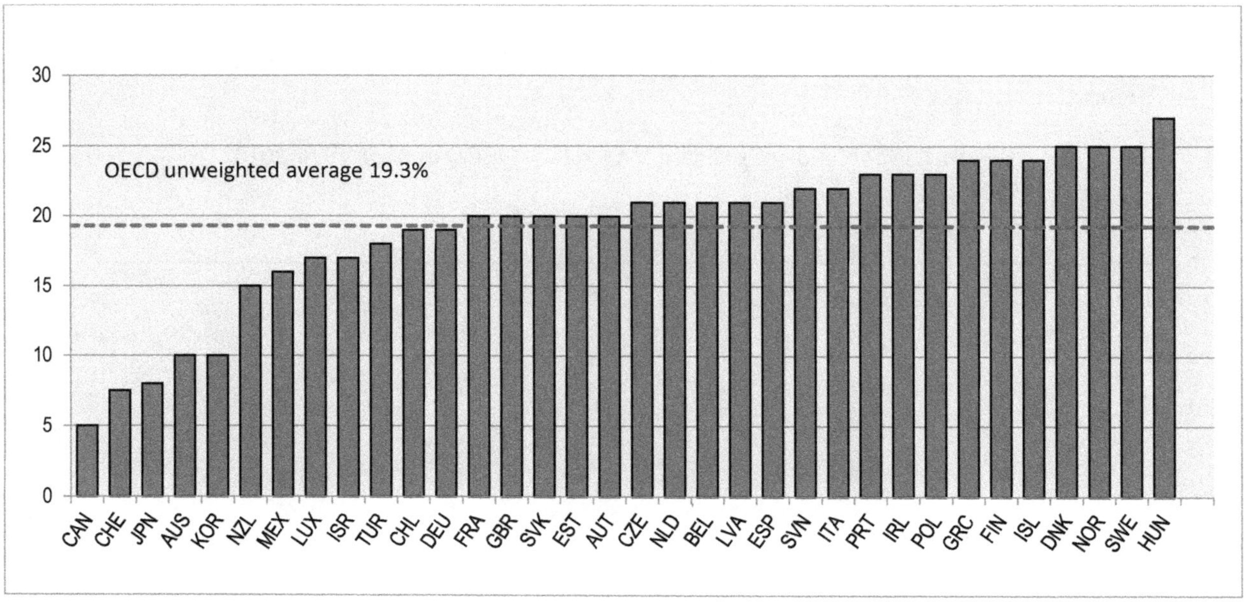

Source: Author's work.

StatLink https://doi.org/10.1787/888933890160

The average standard rate of the 23 OECD countries that are members of the EU is at 21.8%, which is significantly above the OECD average (19.3%). EU member states are bound by common rules regarding VAT rates (VAT Directive 2006/112/EC), which set the minimum level of the standard rate at 15%. Two reduced rates of not less than 5% may be applied to a restricted list of goods and services as well as to certain labour intensive services, and no rate can be higher than the standard rate. The European Commission has recently proposed that EU member states be given more flexibility in setting reduced rates (proposal COM(2018)20 final). According to this proposal, EU member states would be given the option to apply a third reduced rate (between 0% and 5%); and the complex list of goods and services to which reduced rates can be applied would be replaced by a new negative list to which reduced rates cannot be applied. This proposal is still under discussion - its adoption will require the unanimous agreement of all member states. For the time being, over 40 different standard and reduced VAT rates are being applied in the EU, often based on specific derogations granted to individual member states.

2.2.2. OECD countries continue to apply a wide variety of reduced VAT rates

Most OECD countries continue to apply a wide variety of reduced VAT rates and exemptions (see Annex Table 2.A.2 and Annex Table 2.A.3). With the exception of Chile and Japan, all OECD countries that have a VAT have one or more reduced rates to support various policy objectives. A major reason for the application of reduced rates is the promotion of equity. Countries generally consider it desirable to alleviate the tax burden on goods and services that form the larger share of expenditure of the lower income households (e.g. food, water). Countries also apply reduced VAT rates or exemptions to medicine, health, education and housing. Reduced VAT rates have also been used to stimulate the consumption of "merit goods" (such as cultural products) or promoting locally supplied labour-intensive activities (e.g. tourism) and correcting externalities (e.g. energy-saving appliances).

However, evidence suggests that exemptions and reduced VAT rates are not an effective way of achieving such objectives (OECD/KIPF, 2014[1]) and can be even regressive in some instances. Other measures, including through the income tax and the benefit system, tend to be more effective in addressing equity concerns and to pursue policy objective other than raising tax revenues. Reduced VAT rates that are implemented to support lower-income households (i.e. to address distributional goals) typically do have the desired progressive effect. For example, reduced rates for basic food provide in general greater support to the poor than the rich as a proportion of household income or expenditure. However, despite this progressive effect, these reduced VAT rates are a very poor distributive tool. Indeed, better-off households tend to benefit more in absolute terms from VAT reduced rates: their consumption of the tax-favoured goods and services is generally greater than that of poorer households as they tend to consume more, and more expensive products than poorer households. As regards preferential VAT provisions for employment, cultural and other non-distributional goals, research shows clearly that richer households benefit more, and often considerably so, than the lower-income categories of the population from VAT exemptions and reduced VAT rates in this context (e.g. on cultural products, restaurants, tourism and medicine).

Preferential VAT regimes such as reduced rates and exemptions (see Section 2.3) also tend to have an adverse effect on administrative and compliance costs and on compliance levels, and may create economic distortions (incl. tax cascading resulting from exemptions). A more effective policy to achieve distributional objectives is generally to reduce the scope for reduced VAT rates where possible and use measures that are directly targeted at increasing the real incomes of and public services for poorer households. Although these principles are well known, it is often difficult if not impossible to implement them in practice. The political economy obstacles to implementing such a reform (in particular regarding its perceived distributional impact) can be formidable, and often insurmountable, particularly where the organisation of the public services does not allow for a sufficiently effective compensation for the poorer households.

Some countries have broadened their VAT base at standard rate or increased their reduced VAT rates since 2016. Norway raised its reduced VAT rate (on hotel accommodation, passenger transport, public broadcasting, admission to sporting events, museums, cinemas and amusement parks) from 10% to 12%, following an increase from 8% to 10% in 2016. France has increased the VAT rate applied to social housing from 5.5% to 10%. Belgium has reduced the scope for the application of the reduced rate on renovation of dwellings. Ireland raised its VAT rate to the standard rate on sunbeds. In Greece, the reduced VAT rate applicable on some islands will be removed on 31 December 2018.

On the other hand, a number of OECD countries have lowered their VAT rates on a number of items for equity reasons. Latvia introduced a new 5% reduced VAT rate for certain fruit, berries and vegetables. In Greece, the VAT rate on retirement homes was lowered to 13%. Italy lowered the VAT rate to 4% for the construction of certain categories of residential housing; and for food served in schools, canteens and soup kitchens. Hungary reduced its VAT rate on restaurant services from 27% to 18% in 2017, and reduced it further to 5% in 2018. Hungary also lowered the reduced VAT rate for Internet access from 18% to 5%.

In addition, the scope of reduced VAT rates was broadened in a number of countries, often to support specific sectors of the economy. In Greece and the Netherlands, the application of the reduced VAT rate of respectively 13% and 6% was extended to intermediate farm inputs. Hungary broadened the scope of its 5% reduced rate to milk, eggs and poultry in 2017 and to pork and fish on 1 January 2018. In Switzerland and Iceland, e-books are now subject to the reduced VAT rates of respectively 2.5% and 11%. Sweden now applies its 6% reduced rate to "the exhibition of natural areas", to promote tourism. In Italy, urban development construction is now subject to the reduced VAT rate of 10%.

The EU amended its VAT Directive in 2018 to give EU member states the right to tax e-books at reduced rate.

Given the political difficulty to significantly reduce the scope of reduced rates (and exemptions) and the limited scope for increasing standard VAT rates, which are already at a relatively high level in many cases, countries are increasingly looking at other measures to raise additional VAT revenue and improve the efficiency of their VAT systems (OECD, 2018[2]). These measures mainly include the collection of VAT on the supplies of goods and services from online sales (see Chapter 1) and measures designed to improve compliance and combat fraud (see Section 2.8).

2.3. Exemptions

VAT regimes in the OECD make extensive use of exemptions, in addition to reduced rates (see Annex Table 2.A.3). In this context, exemption means that the supplier does not charge the VAT on its outputs and, as a consequence, has no right to recover the VAT on its related inputs. In some jurisdictions, exemption is referred to as "input taxation" to indicate that the supply is not free of VAT but that there is a "hidden VAT" in the price of the exempt supply - i.e. the VAT burden incurred on the inputs is embedded in the price of the exempt outputs. Exemption is thus not the same thing as absence of taxation.

Although it is a significant departure from the basic concept of VAT, all OECD countries apply a number of exemptions. A wide variety of motivations exist for the application of VAT exemptions. These include the difficulty to determine the tax base (e.g. financial and insurance services) or the desire to exclude activities from the VAT base that are considered as public service or as serving a purpose of general and/or social interest (education, health, postal services, charities). A number of other exemptions have their roots in tradition, such as letting of immovable property and the supply of land and buildings. Certain sectors that are exempt from VAT may be subject to other specific taxes (e.g. property, insurance, financial services).

Exemptions beyond these core items are also numerous and cover a wide diversity of sectors such as culture, legal aid, passenger transport, public cemeteries, waste and recyclable material, water supply, precious metals and agriculture (see Annex Table 2.A.3).

The standard advice in VAT design is to have a short list of exemptions, limited to basic health, education and perhaps financial services. By not allowing the deduction of input tax, VAT exemptions create an important exception to the neutrality of VAT (see Chapter 1). The following paragraphs provide an overview of the main, often adverse consequences of exemptions.

VAT exemptions introduce a cascading effect when applied in a B2B context. The business making an exempt supply can be expected to pass on the uncreditable input tax by including it in the price of this supply. This "hidden tax" will subsequently not be deductible/recoverable by the recipient business. If the outputs of this recipient business are not also exempt, this hidden VAT will presumably be part of the price for the supplies on which it will charge output VAT. The result is a hidden tax at a variable rate depending on the number of production stages that are subject to the tax. This distorts businesses' production decisions and choices of organisational form. The size of this cascading effect depends on where the exemption is applied in the supply chain. If the exemption is applied at the stage of the final sale, there is no cascading effect and the consequence is simply a loss of tax revenue since the value added at the final stage escapes tax. If the exemption occurs at some intermediate stage, the consequence of the cascading effect may be an increase of net revenues in a non-transparent manner.

Exemptions create incentives for reducing tax liability by vertical integration ("self-supply") and disincentives for outsourcing as firms have an incentive to produce their inputs internally rather than to purchase externally and incur irrecoverable VAT. This may lead to economic inefficiencies from the distortion of the structure of the supply chain. It can also initiate a dynamic whereby exemptions feed on each other resulting in "exemption creep": once a sector receives an exemption, it has an incentive to lobby for exemptions for those from whom it buys its inputs in order to avoid paying hidden VAT on its inputs.

Exemptions generally lead to the under-taxation of supplies to consumers, who face a tax burden equal to the tax on inputs used by the businesses without its value-added, and an over-taxation of businesses who are unable to deduct the "hidden" tax embedded in their inputs. It also leads to the taxation of investments rather than consumption, which is in contradiction with the main purpose of the tax.

In the international context, exemptions compromise the destination principle for taxation of internationally traded goods and services (see Chapter 1). When an exporter uses exempt inputs, it is not possible to remove the irrecoverable VAT resulting from the exemption applied at an earlier stage in the production chain. The export thus becomes effectively "input taxed". On the other hand, businesses that use exempt inputs have an incentive to import from countries where these inputs are zero rated for export instead of purchasing them from exempt domestic providers. It has been suggested that managing exemptions also imposes increased administrative and compliance costs. As is the case for differentiated rate structures, it may often be difficult for businesses and tax administrations to distinguish between exempt and taxable supplies, in particular in complex areas such as financial services. Businesses that make both taxable and exempt supplies are often faced with complex allocation rules to determine the share which is attributable to taxed outputs and for which it is thus entitled to an input tax credit. However, there is little evidence on the quantitative extent to which exemptions increase administration and compliance costs (Bird and Gendron, 2007[3]).

For further reading on the theoretical and practical justification of exemptions, see (de la Feria,(n.d.)[4]); and on the potential of broadening the tax base by reducing the scope of exemptions as an alternative to increasing VAT rates, see (European Commission, 2011[5]).

2.4. Restrictions to the right to deduct VAT on specific inputs

Although the burden of the tax should not fall on businesses, the right to deduct the VAT on inputs is limited to the extent that those inputs are used for producing taxable outputs. The right to input-VAT deduction is legitimately denied in cases where inputs are used to make onward supplies that are not taxable, i.e. exempt without credit (e.g. health care, financial services – see Section 2.3 above) or outside the scope of VAT (e.g. supplies for no consideration). Input-VAT deduction is also denied when purchases are not (wholly) used for the furtherance of taxable business activity, for example, when they are used for the private needs of the business owner or its employees (i.e. final consumption). All these limitations to the right to deduct input VAT result from the application of the basic principles of VAT design.

In addition to the rules described above, most OECD countries have legislation in place that provides for restrictions to input-VAT deduction on a number of goods and services because of their nature rather than because of their use by businesses. This is often with a view to ensuring the (input-)taxation of their deemed final consumption (see Annex Table 2.A.4).

Restrictions to the deduction of input VAT on business entertainment costs are the most widespread, although the items included in that category may vary widely. These restrictions may include VAT incurred on restaurant meals; on (alcoholic) beverages; reception costs; hotel accommodation; attendance at sporting or cultural events; and on gifts and transport services. Only three OECD countries (Israel, Japan, and Switzerland) have not implemented any such limitations to the right of deduction. In addition, the deduction of input VAT on the purchase and/or the use of cars is often subject to limitations.

The restriction to input-VAT deduction may often be limited to a portion of the VAT incurred. This can for instance be the case for the VAT incurred on the use of cars by the employees of a business, which can be limited to a fixed percentage. Some countries restrict the deduction of input VAT on cars to 50%, even if the car is fully used for business purposes.

The rationale behind those limitations is generally threefold. First, it aims at avoiding the administrative burden associated with the need to control the actual use of goods and services that may easily be used for dual business/private purposes due to their very nature. Second, it is a way of reducing the risks of fraud. Third, such commodities often contain an element of "consumption" - for example restaurant meals. This third justification may be considered inconsistent with the main features of the VAT system. Indeed, businesses (or their employees) never actually "consume" goods and services within the meaning of the VAT when they are used in the furtherance of a taxable activity.

2.5. Registration and collection thresholds

All taxes impose compliance costs on businesses and administrative costs on tax authorities, but VAT is often considered as particularly burdensome for small and medium size businesses (SMEs) to comply with (European Commission, 2013[6]) (Evans et al., 2018[7]). Many countries have therefore introduced simplified regimes for SMEs to ease their compliance burden. These regimes can be grouped into three main categories: those that provide for an exemption from the VAT regime (exemption thresholds); those that facilitate the calculation of the VAT liability; and those that simplify accounting, filing and/or payment obligations (OECD, 2015[8]).

Most OECD countries (except Chile, Mexico, Spain, and Turkey) apply exemption thresholds below which small businesses are not required to charge and collect the tax on their outputs and their input VAT is not deductible. The consequences of such exemptions are equivalent to treating small businesses as non-taxable businesses. There are two kinds of exemption thresholds: registration thresholds that relieve suppliers from both the requirement to register for VAT and to collect the tax; and collection thresholds for which taxpayers, even those below the threshold, are required to register for VAT, but are relieved from collecting the tax until they exceed the threshold. Different types of activities (e.g. supply of services vs supply of goods) or sectors (e.g. the non-profit sector) may be subject to different thresholds or even be excluded from their application (e.g. the construction sector). In most cases registration thresholds do not apply to foreign businesses and in some cases collection thresholds apply only to individuals or to businesses for which commercial accounting is not compulsory.

Annex Table 2.A.5 provides an overview of applicable collection and registration thresholds in OECD countries. In principle, the calculation of thresholds is based on annual turnover. In the Netherlands, the basis for calculation is the net annual VAT due. In Japan, businesses (companies and individuals) are not required to register and account for VAT during the first two years of establishment if they remain below a capital-based threshold; a threshold based on an annual taxable turnover applies after the first two years (with some exceptions, based on levels of turnover). Even in countries where the threshold is based on an annual turnover, its application may be subject to additional rules and conditions. The levels of these thresholds vary significantly across OECD countries and may be split into three broad groups below.

Nineteen countries have a relatively high threshold (more than USD 30 000): Australia, Austria, Belgium, Czech Republic, Estonia, France, Hungary, Ireland, Italy, Japan, Latvia, Lithuania, Luxembourg, New Zealand, Poland, Slovak Republic, Slovenia, Switzerland and the United Kingdom. Of these France, Italy, Japan, Poland, Slovak Republic and the United Kingdom have a particularly higher threshold (above USD 90 000).

Nine countries have a relatively low threshold (between USD 5000 and 30 000): Canada, Denmark, Finland, Germany, Greece, Iceland, Israel, Korea, and Portugal.

Three countries have a low threshold (less than USD 5000): Netherlands, Norway and Sweden.

Since 2016, six countries have raised their threshold: Estonia, Hungary, Iceland, Luxembourg, Poland, and the United Kingdom while only one has reduced its threshold (Latvia). Sweden has reintroduced its threshold of SEK 30 000. France has experimentally introduced (for 5 years) a higher threshold of EUR 100 000 in some overseas departments (Guadeloupe, Martinique, Réunion).

There are no definitive arguments on the need for, or the level of, thresholds. The main reasons for excluding small businesses (a notion that may vary considerably across countries) are that the costs of tax administration are disproportionate to the VAT revenues raised and, similarly, the VAT compliance costs can be disproportionate for many small businesses compared to their turnover. It is also assumed that smaller businesses may be less compliant. A relatively high threshold may give an advantage to small businesses, distorting competition with larger companies. A relatively low threshold act as a disincentive for businesses to grow or as an incentive to avoid VAT by splitting activities artificially. It can also frustrate policy efforts to formalise the economy. However, the latter may be at least partly addressed by applying a simpler alternative tax to businesses below the VAT threshold and thus bring them into the "formal" economy. The level of the threshold is often the result of a trade-off between minimising compliance and administration costs, and the need to protect revenue and avoid competitive distortion.

Most OECD countries that have a registration or collection threshold give the option to businesses below the threshold to register and account voluntarily for VAT. The exceptions are Israel, Korea and the Netherlands. Voluntary registration is often intended to provide an option for small businesses to avoid the disadvantages of non-registration - but they increase tax administration costs and impose compliance costs on entities that elect to be in the system. This also increases the risk of VAT fraud by "fly-by-night" traders, who register and claim VAT refunds before disappearing again... Countries therefore often impose a minimum period of time during which taxpayers that have registered voluntarily must remain registered. This period varies from one year (Australia, Canada, Czech Republic, Hungary, Japan, Slovak Republic and Switzerland) to two years (Denmark, France, Greece, and Norway) or in some cases, three years (Sweden) or five years (Austria, Germany, and Slovenia).

One challenge of VAT thresholds is to minimise incentives for small businesses to underreport turnover so as to remain below the exemption threshold, and/or to incentivise small businesses to grow their business. The adoption of a flexible threshold is one option. Under such a regime, small businesses that exceed the regular VAT threshold are not obliged to register immediately but are allowed to continue to benefit from the exemption as long as they do not exceed the threshold by a significant percentage. For example in France, businesses that exceed the regular thresholds of EUR 82 200 (for goods) and EUR 33 200 (for most services) may continue to benefit from the exemption if their turnover does not exceed EUR 91 000 and EUR 35 200 respectively for more than a year. The Netherlands operate a flexible collection threshold based on the net annual VAT due: no VAT is due as long as its annual amount remains below EUR 1 345; when the net annual VAT due is between EUR 1 345 and EUR 1 883 the taxpayer receives a gradual tax reduction, which facilitates smooth transition to a taxpaying position.

Other ways exist to reduce compliance costs for SMEs while avoiding the disadvantages of the exemption. One way used in many countries is to apply simplified presumptive schemes to facilitate the calculation of the VAT liability. For example, certain small businesses may be allowed to apply a single flat rate to turnover for determining the amount of VAT to be remitted to tax authorities instead of requiring a detailed VAT calculation of input and output VATs. An alternative simplification scheme for calculating VAT liability relies on simplified input tax credit calculations. A more detailed description of such regime is given in an OECD study on SME taxation (OECD, 2015[8]).

2.6. Usage of margin schemes

Most countries allow or utilise specific methods for determining the VAT liability in special circumstances. The purpose of these methods is usually to simplify VAT administration and compliance and/or to address specific circumstances. Typical examples are the margin schemes, which are often used when the deduction of input tax according to the normal rules is considered too difficult or impossible – see for instance the resale of second-hand goods bought from private individuals, and the activities of travel agencies. Under a margin scheme, the tax base is calculated on the difference between the price paid by the taxpayer and the price of resale rather than on the full selling price. The reseller is not allowed to deduct the input VAT embedded in the buying price of the items that are resold under the margin scheme. Annex Table 2.A.6shows that all the EU countries employ a margin scheme for travel agencies, second-hand goods, works of art, collector's items and antiques since they share the same legislative root. Beyond the EU, five other OECD countries employ margin schemes, i.e. Australia (on new residential property, gambling and second hand goods); Chile (second-hand real property); Israel (on coins and postal stamps, furniture, dwellings, used vehicles and foreign currency exchange); Norway (on second hand goods, works of art, collectors' items and antiques) and Turkey (on travel agencies).

2.7. Measuring performance of VAT: the VAT Revenue Ratio

VAT performance can be measured through different methods, depending on the dimension of the performance to be measured. It has traditionally been measured by the "efficiency ratio", defined as the ratio of VAT revenues to GDP divided by the standard rate (expressed as a percentage). Although the efficiency ratio has been widely used as a diagnostic tool in evaluating VATs, it does not distinguish a product-type VAT from a consumption-type VAT. This difficulty is addressed by taking final consumption as a reference for the potential tax base rather than production (Ebrill et al., 2001[9]). If measured by the ratio of revenue from the tax to the product of the standard VAT rate and aggregate consumption, a benchmark VAT levied at a uniform rate on all consumption would have "C-Efficiency" of 100% provided that all the tax due is collected by the tax administration.

The estimates of the VAT Revenue Ratio (VRR) for OECD countries presented in this section builds on the "C-Efficiency ratio" principles. It provides an indicator that combines the effect of loss of revenues as a consequence of exemptions and reduced rates, fraud, evasion and tax planning. Although the VRR has to be interpreted with care and erosion of the tax base may be caused by a variety of factors, it may support policymakers in assessing the revenue raising performance of their VAT system and in identifying opportunities to raise additional revenues by improving VAT performance.

2.7.1. What does the VRR measure?

The aim of the VRR is to provide a comparative measure of a country's ability to effectively secure the potential tax base for VAT. The VRR measures the difference between the VAT revenue actually collected and what would theoretically be raised if VAT was applied at the standard rate to the entire potential tax base in a "pure" VAT regime and all revenue was collected:

$$\mathrm{VRR} = \frac{\mathrm{VR}}{\mathrm{B\,.\,r}}$$

Where: VR = actual VAT revenues; B = potential tax base and r = standard VAT rate

The 'standard' rate refers to the default rate applicable to the tax base, unless otherwise advised by legislation. Legislation can (and many countries do) provide that lower (or higher) rates are applicable to a defined list of products. Reduced VAT rates are still widely used in OECD countries, mainly for equity or social objectives (basic essentials, health, education, etc.). No OECD countries apply higher VAT rates (see Annex Table 2.A.1).

2.7.2. Assessing the tax base

The main methodological difficulty in the calculation of the VRR lies in the assessment of the potential tax base, since no standard assessment of the potential VAT base for all OECD countries is available. The potential VAT base includes all supplies of goods, services and intangibles made for consideration (or deemed to be made for consideration) by businesses or any other entity acting as a business (e.g. individuals, government entities providing supplies for direct consideration, etc.) to final consumers. In principle, the tax base ultimately corresponds to the expenditure made by final consumers to obtain goods, services and intangibles. In practice, however, many VAT systems impose VAT burden not only on final household consumption, but also on various entities that are involved in non-business activities or in VAT exempt activities (Chapter 1 and this chapter). In such situations, VAT can be viewed as treating such entities as if they were end consumers, or as "input taxing" the supplies made by such entities on the presumption that the burden of the VAT imposed will be passed on in the prices of the outputs of those non-business activities. The tax ultimately collected by the government in these situations is the tax on these inputs.

In the absence of a standard assessment of the potential VAT base for all OECD countries, the closest statistic for that base is final consumption expenditure as measured in the national accounts, VAT is indeed, ultimately a tax on final consumption. Final consumption expenditure in national accounts is calculated according to a standard international norm, the System of National Accounts (SNA 2008 - except for Turkey, Chile and Japan that still use SNA 1993) under Item P3 Final consumption expenditure.

2.7.3. The formula used to estimate the VRR of OECD countries

In the VRR calculation formula as presented above, the potential tax base (B) is based on the Final consumption expenditure under Item P3 in the national accounts. However, the SNA measures consumption expenditures at market prices, i.e. including VAT. This VAT element must be deducted from the amount under P3 for the VRR calculation, because the theoretical basis for taxation should not include the tax itself.

As a result, the VRR estimates presented in Table 3.A3.1 have been calculated as follows:

$$\mathrm{VRR} = \frac{\mathrm{VR}}{(\mathrm{FCE} - \mathrm{VR}).\,\mathrm{r}}$$

Where: VR = actual VAT revenues; FCE = Final Consumption Expenditure (Item P3 in National Accounts); and r = standard VAT rate.

2.7.4. The VRR estimates for OECD countries

Across the OECD, the unweighted average VRR of 0.56 has remained relatively stable since 2010 (0.55), after a decline during the financial and economic crisis in 2008 (from 0.57 to 0.54). This means that, on average, 44% of the theoretical potential VAT revenue is not collected. The VRR estimates vary considerably among OECD countries, as is shown in Annex Table 2.A.7. In 2016 the estimates ranged from 0.33 in Mexico and 0.38 in Italy to 0.92 in Luxembourg and 0.95 in New Zealand. The majority of countries (29 of 35) have a VRR below 0.65 and almost half (11 of 35) have a ratio below 0.50. This suggests that a considerable part of the theoretical potential VAT revenue remains uncollected in many OECD countries. The VRR rose in 20 countries compared to 2014, but this was offset by a fall in four countries, including Luxemburg with a significant drop of the VRR in 2016 at 0.92 compared to 1.25 in 2014, reflecting the 2015 reform in the EU (see below).

This VRR notably reflects the fact that preferential treatments, such as reduced rates and exemptions, are still widely used in OECD countries (see Annex Table 2.A.2 and Annex Table 2.A.3). This is confirmed by tax expenditures data, which reflect the cost of tax concessions (OECD, 2010[10]).

It appears that there is no direct correlation between the level of the standard VAT rate and the VRR. Countries with very different VAT rates may have comparable VRRs. Australia and Ireland, for example, both have a VRR of 0.50 while their standard VAT rates are respectively 10% and 23%. Although about two thirds of countries (22 of 35) have a VRR between 0.45 and 0.65, they have standard VAT rates, which vary widely, from 5% (Canada) to 25% (Denmark, Norway, and Sweden). Denmark, Norway and Sweden combine a high standard VAT rate (25%) with a VRR above the OECD average (respectively 0.60, 0.57 and 0.60) while Mexico and Turkey combine lower standard VAT rates (respectively 16% and 18%) with a VRR estimate considerably below the OECD average (respectively 0.33 and 0.40). Japan combines a low VAT rate (8%) and absence of reduced rates with a relatively high VRR (0.71).

Figure 2.3. VAT Revenue Ratio

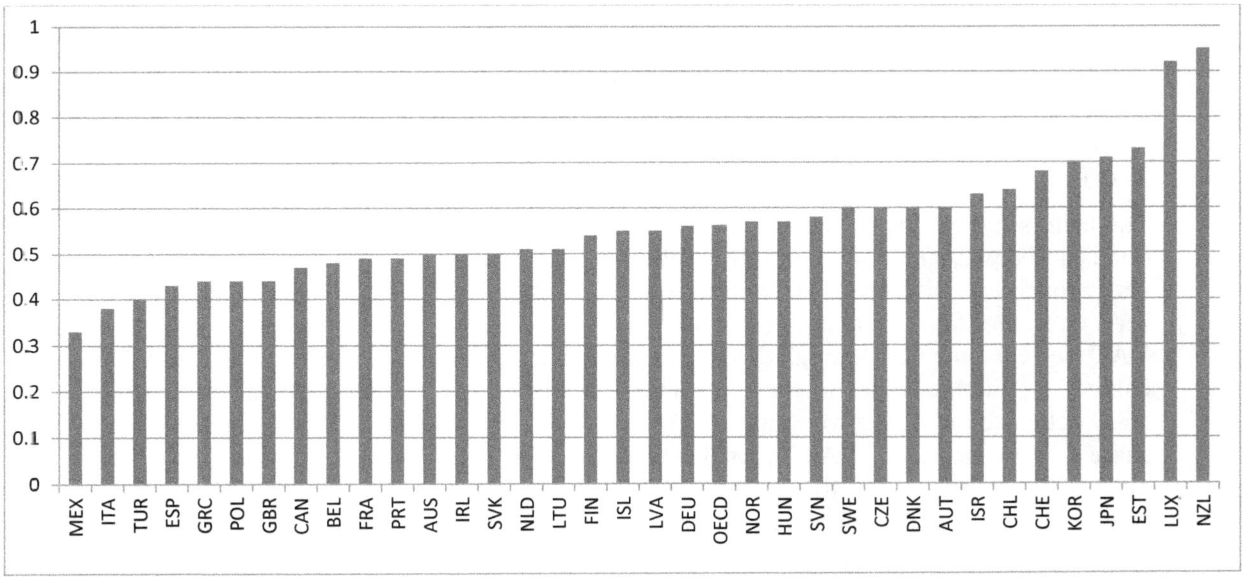

Note: OECD: OECD unweighted average.
Source: Author's calculations.

StatLink https://doi.org/10.1787/888933890179

The respective weight of the different factors that affect the VRR may vary widely across countries depending on the circumstances. The two countries with the highest VRR, New Zealand and Luxembourg, are both far above the OECD average (with respectively 0.95 and 0.92 compared to an average of 0.56) and even significantly above the country that immediately follows them (Estonia with a VRR of 0.73). However, the reasons behind these high ratios are very different.

The VRR for Luxembourg has constantly increased between 1996 (0.55) and 2014 (1.23). This increase is correlated with deep changes in the EU marketplace, in particular the liberalisation of financial services and the boom of e-commerce. It is reasonable to assume that these market factors and the specific VAT treatment of these markets have had a strong upward effect on Luxembourg's VRR. It may be assumed that Luxembourg's position as an international financial centre has resulted in additional VAT revenue for the country. According to EU VAT rules, the supply of financial services is generally exempt from VAT in Luxembourg without the right to deduct the input tax, including when supplied to customers in other EU member states. This means that the non-deductible VAT incurred by financial service providers in Luxembourg increases Luxembourg's VAT revenues while a large share of the corresponding final consumption occurs in other EU member states, as a result of the increased cross-border trade in financial services. Luxembourg had also become an international centre for e-commerce, notably as a consequence of the VAT treatment of this activity under EU VAT legislation until 1st January 2015. According to this legislation, e-commerce supplies to final consumers in other EU member states were taxed in the member state where the supplier was established. The low standard VAT rate in Luxembourg, the lowest of the EU (15 % until 2014), acted as an incentive to e-suppliers to establish in Luxembourg; and this generated additional and continuously increasing revenue for the country as the internet economy continued to grow. This changed as of 1 January 2015. Since that date, intra-EU e-commerce sales to final consumers are no longer subject to VAT in the member state where the supplier is established (which was often Luxemburg). These sales are now subject to VAT in the member state of these consumers' residence and at the rate applicable in that member state. This change of intra-EU place of taxation rules is now reflected in the VRR estimates for Luxembourg (declining from 1.25 in 2014 to 0.92 in 2016).

The factors underlying the constant very high VRR since the implementation of the VAT (GST) in New Zealand are very different. First, unlike Luxembourg, New Zealand has a very broad base with limited exemptions (see Annex Table 2.A.3) and a limited use of a zero rate (see Annex Table 2.A.2). Second, New Zealand taxes public services under VAT (see Chapter 1). Although this does not generate actual additional revenue (the VAT charged by public bodies to the government is covered by budgetary transfers and the VAT collected on local government activities is included in local taxes), this increases the share of revenues from VAT in total tax revenues, which has an upward effect on the VRR. On the other hand, the potential VAT base as measured by the national accounts (see section above) does not include the value added by the government. The combination of these factors may explain why the VRR for New Zealand is so high and even sometimes above 1.

At the opposite end, Mexico has the lowest VRR (0.33) amongst OECD countries. This is likely to be due to a combination of factors such as the scope of VAT exemptions, the extensive application of a domestic zero rate and a low compliance level.

2.7.5. Factors that may influence the VRR

In theory, the closer the VAT system of a country is to a "pure" VAT, the closer its VRR is to 1. A lower value reflects such factors as the effects of reduced rates, exemptions or a failure to collect all tax due. A VRR above 1 is possible in theory where almost all the tax base is covered by the standard rate and a number of exemptions without right to deduction apply so that the cascading effect of the exemption provides additional revenue for the government that exceeds the cost of the exemption. A VRR close to 1 is taken as an indicator of a VAT bearing uniformly on a broad base with effective tax collection. In practice, the VRR rarely equals 1 and a number of complex factors, alone or in combination, may influence the results positively or negatively. These include:

- The application of lower VAT rates to a number of goods and services and the level of such lower rates that reduce the tax revenue and have a negative impact on the VRR.
- The level of the registration and/or collection threshold under which small businesses do not account for VAT. These thresholds reduce the amount of VAT collected, although it could be argued that the adverse revenue consequences of such thresholds are likely to be limited since the businesses under the thresholds will generally not be able to deduct any input VAT and their value added can be expected to be modest.
- The scope of the exemptions. Depending on the features of the exemptions and market structures, exemptions may influence the VRR upwards or downwards. Exemptions may reduce the tax revenue (when exemption applies to goods and services directly supplied to final consumer e.g. healthcare) or may increase revenue when the exemption occurs early in a supply chain (e.g. financial services made to businesses) and the revenue arising from the cascading effect exceeds the potential tax arising from taxation at standard rates with deduction of input tax. The application of a VAT exemption for financial services may often have a considerable impact on the VRR, given the economic importance of this sector in many countries.
- The VAT treatment of public sector activities. Final consumption by government is the second largest final use in national accounts after household consumption. From a VAT perspective, governments' activities are exempt or outside the scope of VAT in most countries, New Zealand being the notable exception treating all governments activities as taxable. As a consequence, public bodies cannot deduct the input VAT paid on their taxable expenditure, again with the exception of New Zealand that provides a full right to deduct input tax for government activities. A number of countries have created mechanisms for balancing the adverse effects of the exemption, such as targeted VAT refunds, full or partial right to deduct input VAT, budgetary compensations or extended taxation of government activities. The different options chosen by governments may have varied impacts on the VRR. Compensations outside of the VAT system (e.g. a simple budgetary compensation) have no direct effect on the VRR. The government activities remain input taxed, generating the corresponding VAT revenue, before and after the compensation measures. A measure that provides the right to input-VAT deduction to government bodies will normally reduce VAT revenue if the outputs remain exempt, and hence influence the VRR downwards. Applying VAT to government activities like New Zealand does, on the other hand, will increase the amount of VAT collected and influence the VRR upwards, as it results in the taxation of the total output rather than just the inputs.
- Place of taxation rules for international trade may diverge from the destination principle and may not always allow the full taxation of the potential tax base in

the destination country. Depending on the position of the country (net exporter or net importer) and its VAT regime (taxation at origin or destination) the VRR can be influenced upwards or downwards. Inconsistent place of taxation rules may also lead to double taxation of cross-border trade.

- The capacity of the tax administration to manage the VAT system efficiently and the degree of compliance by taxpayers influences the VRR as low compliance has a negative impact on actual VAT revenue. Taxpayers' insolvencies and bankruptcies can also influence the VRR downwards.
- The failure of a tax administration to operate an appropriate VAT refund process (with timely refunds of excess input-VAT credits to domestic businesses and/or refunds to non-resident businesses), which is contrary to the fundamental principle of VAT-neutrality, may influence the VRR upwards (for "wrong" reasons).
- The evolution of consumption patterns may also affect the tax revenue. The VRR can for instance decline, all other things equal, when the share of consumption of necessities that are taxed at the lower rate increases, e.g. as a result of an economic crisis.
- Finally, also the possible impact of the differences between the measurement of final consumption expenditure in the national accounts and countries' potential VAT base should be taken into account when interpreting the VRR.

For further technical discussion on the factors influencing the calculation of the VRR see (OECD, 2016[11]).

2.7.6. Assessing the relative impact of the various factors that may impact the VRR

The level of the VRR rarely depends on one factor in isolation but rather on the interaction between them. For example, a high standard rate may create an incentive for evasion while multiple lower rates may lead to revenue loss due to misclassifications. Exemption of certain sectors of activity may create distortions and incentives for avoidance, which require additional administrative capacities that cannot be used for the efficient collection of VAT. Inefficient tax administration, burdensome administrative requirements and complex VAT mechanisms may reduce taxpayer compliance levels.

These potentially influencing factors can be divided in two main categories:

- those resulting from policy decisions, mainly affecting the tax base or the coverage of the standard rate (i.e. reduced VAT rates and exemptions), and
- those related to the efficiency of the tax collection and compliance levels ("compliance gap").

The VRR is a combination of the result of policy decisions and the "compliance gap". Methods may be developed to produce breakdowns of the composition of the VRR. One method may consist in using the tax expenditure (i.e. the revenue cost of departure from the application of the standard rate to the 'entire' tax base) for calculating the policy efficiency ratio. The remaining difference between 1 and the actual VRR would provide the compliance efficiency ratio by deduction. However, given the number of other factors that may influence the VRR, such figures should be used with caution.

Another method would be to calculate the "tax gap" i.e. the difference between tax collected and the tax that should be collected if all consumers and businesses fully complied with the law. This method is employed for the VAT in the EU (Institute for Advanced Studies, 2015[12]) (CASE, 2018[13]), where the VAT Gap is defined as the difference between the amount of VAT actually collected and the theoretical tax liability according to tax law (VAT Total Tax Liability VTTL). The VAT Gap is estimated using a "top-down" approach that applies respective VAT rates to the relevant components of consumption (including final consumption of households; final consumption of government and non-profit institutions, intermediate consumption for partially exempt businesses; expenditure on housing, country-specific, adjustments, etc.). Australia uses a similar method (Australian Taxation Office, 2018[14]).

2.8. Combatting VAT avoidance and evasion

2.8.1. VAT revenue losses remain significant

Reducing the revenue losses from VAT non-compliance remains a key challenge and a priority for countries around the world. An increasing number of tax administrations carry out research to estimate the VAT compliance gap, i.e. the revenue loss due to avoidance, evasion and fraud. In the European Union, the VAT gap in the 28 member states for 2016 (CASE, 2018[13])is estimated at EUR 147.1 billion. In relative terms, the VAT Gap share of the VAT total tax liability (VTTL) dropped to 12.3 percent from 13.2 percent in 2015. The smallest gaps were observed in Sweden (1.24%), Luxembourg (3.80%) and Finland (6.92%), and the largest gaps were registered in Romania (37.89%), Lithuania (35.94%) and Malta (35.32%). The United Kingdom estimated its VAT gap at GBP 13.3 billion in 2017-18, i.e. 9.6% of the estimated net VTTL (Carroll, Delgado and Booth, 2018[15]). A number of other OECD countries provide public estimates of their VAT gap. In Australia the GST gap is estimated at AUD 5.3 billion or 7.9% of VTTL (Australian Taxation Office, 2018[14])); in Canada, the multi- year average GST/HST gap for 2000- 2014 is estimated at 5.6% VTTL (Canada Revenue Agency,(n.d.)[16]) and in Chile (Servicio de Impuestos Internos, 2017[17])where the VAT gap is estimated at 16.6% VTTL.

Losses of VAT revenue from non-compliance can result from a number of factors. In addition to "traditional" VAT avoidance (i.e. arrangements intended to reduce the tax liability that could be strictly legal but in contradiction with the intent of the law) and evasion (illegal arrangements where liability to tax is ignored or hidden) there has been a continuous, significant and worrying trend of increasing criminal attacks on the VAT system. This organised and criminal VAT fraud has been shown to have connections with other criminal activities such as terrorism and money laundering in a number of cases.

The most common type of organised VAT fraud is the "missing trader" or "carousel" fraud. It arises when a business makes a purchase without paying VAT (typically a transaction for which tax self-assessment applies), then collects VAT on an onward supply and disappears without remitting the VAT collected. Originally, the fraud involved primarily high-value goods that can easily be moved across borders, such as computer chips and cell phones - but it expanded to services that can be bought and sold like goods. Organised VAT fraud in CO_2 emission trading, for instance, caused billions of Euros of VAT revenue losses in a range of countries. Energy markets have also become vulnerable to organised VAT fraud. European energy regulators, energy trading firms and gas and electricity operators notably warned EU authorities about the serious impact of VAT carrousel fraud on the functioning of European gas and electricity markets (Europex – Association of European Energy Exchanges, 2018[18]). They reported signs of "a major penetration of the gas and electricity markets by VAT fraudsters". Research also showed that certain accounting software products contained hidden tools (zappers) for the manipulation of VAT receipts (OECD, 2013[19]).

The digitalization of the economy creates new challenges for VAT regimes in addressing fraud and non-compliance, notably in light of the exponential growth of cross-border e-commerce (OECD, 2015[20]).

Tax authorities are developing, and implementing, a growing variety of responses to the increasingly complex challenge of protecting important VAT revenues against VAT fraud and non-compliance. The following sections look in slightly more detail at three categories of responses that can increasingly be observed among OECD countries: changes in VAT collection mechanisms; reinforcement in taxpayer's reporting obligations and data analysis; and international administrative cooperation and exchange of information.

2.8.2. Changes in the VAT collection methods: domestic reverse charge and split payment.

One way of counteracting missing trader fraud is the implementation of a domestic reverse charge mechanism for collecting the VAT on domestic B2B supplies of certain goods and services susceptible to fraud, such as mobile phones, integrated circuit devices, gas and electricity, telecom services, game consoles, tablet PCs and laptops, cereals and industrial crops and raw and semi-finished metals. EU member states can apply a domestic reverse charge mechanism to a determined list of supplies, on an optional and temporary basis. EU member states have also been allowed since 2013 to apply a domestic reverse charge to any kind of supply in case of sudden and massive VAT fraud.

Such a reverse charge mechanism shifts the liability to pay the VAT from the supplier to the customer. Business customers with a normal right to input VAT deduction report the VAT due on these purchases as deductible input tax in their VAT returns, and no net tax will be payable on these transactions. This reverse charge mechanism removes the possibility for taxpayers to disappear with the VAT collected from their customers without remitting it to the tax authorities (as no VAT changes hands) and to claim a credit for unpaid input VAT. It is recognised, however, that the implementation of a domestic reverse-charge mechanism needs to be considered with care. One concern is that it would transform the VAT effectively into a sales tax if applied too extensively, with the concentration of revenue risks in the stage of the final sale or in a limited number of points in the value chain, and with the inherent weaknesses of such a system.

Annex Table 2.A.12 shows that the use of domestic reverse charge as a means to combat fraud is widely used in the 23 OECD countries that are EU member states. Each of these countries uses this mechanism to some extent, in particular for the supply of CO_2 emission certificates (all except Latvia and Lithuania); scrap materials and waste (all except Belgium, Luxembourg and the United Kingdom); and construction work (all except Estonia, Luxembourg, Poland and the United Kingdom). The domestic reverse charge also applies to the supply of gold (14 countries on 23); electronic devices such as laptops, chips, cell phones etc. (11 countries on 23) and the supply of gas and electricity to taxable dealers (7 countries on 23). Also a number of other OECD countries use a domestic reverse mechanism albeit to a much lesser extent, i.e. Australia (supplies of new residential premises); Canada (supplies of real property by non-residents and some supplies between provinces); Chile (supplies of rice, construction works, waste and certain plants and animals); Israel (metal debris); Mexico (waste, some supplies made by individuals); New Zealand (supplies of land incorrectly zero rated); Norway (supply of CO2 emission allowances and investment gold) and Turkey (some supplies made by non-taxable persons). Such a mechanism has not been implemented in Iceland, Japan and Switzerland.

Another means of reducing the vulnerability of VAT regimes to fraud and non-compliance is through the implementation of a so-called split payment (or withholding tax) mechanism. Under such a mechanism, the supplier charges the VAT on its domestic supplies to the customer according to normal rules, but the VAT paid by the customer (or part of it) is remitted directly to the tax authorities rather than to the supplier. This is typically organised through the intervention of financial and/or payment intermediaries (bank, credit card company, online payment service provider…), which split the gross amount paid by the customer into a net amount and a VAT amount and remit the latter to the tax authorities. In practice, such a system has a similar effect as a domestic reverse charge mechanism in that it removes the possibility for a supplier to collect the VAT without remitting it to the tax authorities.

Table 1.A.12 shows that this system can be used in the Czech Republic as a condition for customers to avoid the joint and several liability with suppliers (when the bank account used for the payment is not certified by the tax authorities); in Italy for the supplies of goods and services made to public authorities; in Korea for the supply of gold, copper and iron; and in Poland when the customer opts for the payment of the VAT on the supplier's "VAT account". Turkey requires certain customers to withhold a percentage of the VAT charged to them by suppliers and remit it directly to the tax authorities in certain sectors, such as construction, scrap metal, glass, plastic and paper, advisory, supervisory and audit services maintenance and repair services for machinery, equipment and other fixed assets.

2.8.3. Collecting transaction data from the taxpayer

Most OECD countries have reinforced taxpayer's reporting obligations over the last two decades. After a generalisation of mandatory e-filing of VAT returns (OECD, 2015[21]), many OECD countries have introduced or consider introducing a requirement for taxpayers to provide transaction data to tax authorities, sometimes in real time. These measures typically require detailed information to be provided in an electronic format at individual taxable transaction level. This information can include invoicing information and accounting data or any other information that allows tax authorities to monitor supplies made and/or received by individual taxpayers.

Annex Table 2.A.11 shows that almost all OECD countries have implemented transaction information reporting obligations since 2000, except Canada, Estonia, Finland and Turkey. Amongst these countries, thirteen impose a specific format for such reporting (Chile, France, Israel, Korea, Lithuania, Luxembourg, Mexico, Netherlands, Norway, Poland Portugal, Slovak Republic, Slovenia and Spain). Nine of them use (a variation of) the Standard Audit File for Tax (SAF-T) format developed by the OECD Forum on Tax Administration (OECD, 2005[22]). This involves the use of accounting software to create an electronic file (the SAF-T) containing tax-relevant accounting data. The SAF-T format enables the transfer of these data from the taxpayer to the tax authorities in a standardised electronic format. About half of the countries requiring electronic transaction reporting (14 out of 31) require the systematic transmission of such information to the tax administration (Chile, Czech Republic, Greece, Hungary, Israel, Italy, Korea, Lithuania, Mexico, Poland, Portugal, Slovak Republic, and Spain) and five of these require this transmission to happen in (near) real time (Chile, Hungary, Italy, Korea and Spain).

Countries are also increasingly concerned with the monitoring of transactions in cash in the business-to-consumer (B2C) environment and approximately one third of OECD countries (13 on 35) have implemented requirements for taxpayers to use electronic cash registers (Austria, Belgium, France, Greece, Israel, Korea, Latvia, Norway, Poland, Slovak Republic, Slovenia, Sweden and Switzerland).

2.8.4. International administrative cooperation

There is also a growing recognition that effective strategies to tackle VAT fraud and evasion require strongly enhanced international administrative co-operation. Governments increasingly recognise that information exchange and administrative co-operation play a significant role in combatting international VAT fraud and ensuring effective tax collection, not least in the context of the digitalisation of the economy (OECD, 2015[20]); (Court Auditors, 2015[23]). This need was also recognised in the 2018 OECD Report on Tax Challenges Arising from Digitalisation (OECD, 2018[24]) and the OECD is developing work in this context.

A number of instruments already exist that provide the legal foundation for the international administrative co-operation in the area of VAT. These include the Multilateral Convention on Mutual Administrative Assistance in Tax Matters (OECD/Council of Europe, 2011[25]), the bilateral treaties implementing the current Articles 26 and 27 of the OECD and UN Model Tax Conventions, and Tax Information Exchange Agreements (TIEAs) based on the OECD Model. Regional agreements also provide legal base for such co-operation. These include EU Regulation No 904/2010, the Nordic Mutual Assistance Convention on Mutual Administrative Assistance in Tax Matters, the CIAT Model Agreement on the Exchange of Tax Information, and the African Tax Administration Forum Agreement on Mutual Assistance in Tax Matters.

Amongst these instruments, the Multilateral Convention on Mutual Administrative Assistance in Tax Matters (the Convention) is considered the most promising. The Convention was developed jointly by the Council of Europe and the OECD. It was opened for signature by the member states of both organisations in 1988. It was then aligned with the internationally agreed standard on transparency and exchange of information and opened to all countries in 2011. It provides for all possible forms of administrative co-operation between the Parties in the assessment and collection of taxes, in particular with a view to combating tax avoidance and evasion. The Convention has a very wide scope and covers all forms of compulsory payments to general governments (i.e. the central government and its political subdivisions) including VAT (although the obligations set forth in the Convention are subject to any reservations by the Parties). As of November 2018, 126 jurisdictions participate in the Convention.

In the EU, co-operation among member states is supported by Eurofisc, the EU's network of anti-fraud experts. The EU adopted a proposal to reinforce administrative cooperation within the EU in 2018. It sets out to improve the exchange and analysis of information shared by the member states' tax administrations and with law enforcement bodies, and to strengthen the Eurofisc network of national tax officials for the exchange of information on VAT fraud. The EU also signed a bilateral exchange of information agreement on VAT with Norway in February 2018.

References

Australian Taxation Office (2018), *Measuring the gap _ Australian Taxation Office*, https://www.ato.gov.au/About-ATO/Research-and-statistics/In-detail/Tax-gap/Goods-and-services-tax-gap/?page=2. [14]

Bird, R. and P. Gendron (2007), *The VAT in Developing and Transitional Countries*, Cambridge University Press, Cambridge, http://dx.doi.org/10.1017/cbo9780511619366. [3]

Canada Revenue Agency((n.d.)), *Estimating and Analyzing the Tax Gap Related to the Goods and Services Tax/Harmonized Sales Tax - Canada.ca*, https://www.canada.ca/en/revenue-agency/corporate/about-canada-revenue-agency-cra/tax-canada-a-conceptual-study/estimating-analyzing.html. [16]

Carroll, W., T. Delgado and K. Booth (2018), *Preliminary estimate of the VAT gap for 2017-18 An Official Statistics release*, https://www.gov.uk/government/uploads/system/uploads/attachment_data/file/715744/HMRC_. [15]

CASE (2018), *Study and Reports on the VAT Gap in the EU-28 Member States: 2018 Final Report*, European Commission, http://www.ihs.ac.at. [13]

Court Auditors, E. (2015), *Tackling intra-Community VAT fraud: More action needed*, http://dx.doi.org/10.2865/623638. [23]

de la Feria, R. ((n.d.)), "EU VAT rate structure: towards unilateral convergence?", in *La réorientation européenne de la TVA à la suite du renoncement au régime définitif*, Presses de l'Université Toulouse 1 Capitole, http://dx.doi.org/10.4000/books.putc.1430. [4]

Ebrill, L. et al. (2001), *The Modern VAT*, http://www.imf.org. [9]

European Commission (2013), *Results of the public consultation on the TOP10 most burdensome legislative acts for SMEs*. [6]

European Commission (2011), *European Commission (2011) Green paper on the future of VAT COM(2010)695 final*. [5]

Europex – Association of European Energy Exchanges (2018), *Europex Common energy sector statement on VAT fraud*, https://eur-lex.europa.eu/legal-content/EN/TXT/?uri=celex%3A32013L0043. [18]

Evans, C. et al. (2018), "The Development and Testing of a Diagnostic Tool for Assessing VAT Compliance Costs Draft Report of Pilot Study Findings [ATAX version]", https://www.business.unsw.edu.au/About-Site/Schools-Site/Taxation-Business-Law-Site/Documents/ime-Highfield,-Walpole-Evans-VAT-Diagnostic-Tool-paper.pdf. [7]

Institute for Advanced Studies (2015), *Study and Reports on the VAT Gap in the EU-28 Member States: 2018 Final Report*, https://ec.europa.eu/taxation_customs/sites/taxation/files/2018_vat_gap_report_en.pdf. [12]

OECD (2018), *Tax Challenges Arising from Digitalisation – Interim Report 2018: Inclusive Framework on BEPS*, OECD/G20 Base Erosion and Profit Shifting Project, OECD Publishing, Paris, https://dx.doi.org/10.1787/9789264293083-en. [24]

OECD (2018), *Tax Policy Reforms 2018: OECD and Selected Partner Economies*, OECD Publishing, Paris, https://dx.doi.org/10.1787/9789264304468-en. [2]

OECD (2016), *Consumption Tax Trends 2016: VAT/GST and excise rates, trends and policy issues*, OECD Publishing, Paris, https://dx.doi.org/10.1787/ctt-2016-en. [11]

OECD (2015), *Addressing the Tax Challenges of the Digital Economy, Action 1 - 2015 Final Report*, OECD/G20 Base Erosion and Profit Shifting Project, OECD Publishing, Paris, https://dx.doi.org/10.1787/9789264241046-en. [20]

OECD (2015), *Tax Administration 2015: Comparative Information on OECD and Other Advanced and Emerging Economies*, OECD Publishing, Paris, https://dx.doi.org/10.1787/tax_admin-2015-en. [21]

OECD (2015), *Taxation of SMEs in OECD and G20 Countries*, OECD Tax Policy Studies, No. 23, OECD Publishing, Paris, https://dx.doi.org/10.1787/9789264243507-en. [8]

OECD (2013), *Electronic Sales Suppression: A threat to tax revenues - OECD*, http://www.oecd.org/ctp/crime/electronic-sales-suppression-a-threat-to-tax-revenues.htm. [19]

OECD (2010), *Choosing a Broad Base - Low Rate Approach to Taxation*, OECD Tax Policy Studies, No. 19, OECD Publishing, Paris, https://dx.doi.org/10.1787/9789264091320-en. [10]

OECD (2005), "Guidance on Tax Compliance for Business and Accounting Software", https://www.oecd.org/tax/forum-on-tax-administration/publications-and-products/hnwi/34910263.pdf. [22]

OECD/Council of Europe (2011), *The Multilateral Convention on Mutual Administrative Assistance in Tax Matters: Amended by the 2010 Protocol*, OECD Publishing, Paris, https://dx.doi.org/10.1787/9789264115606-en. [25]

OECD/KIPF (2014), *The Distributional Effects of Consumption Taxes in OECD Countries*, OECD Tax Policy Studies, No. 22, OECD Publishing, Paris, https://dx.doi.org/10.1787/9789264224520-en. [1]

Servicio de Impuestos Internos (2017), *Subdirección de Gestión Estratégica y Estudios Tributarios SII Serie de Evasión de IVA 2003-2015 Base MIP 2008*, http://www.sii.cl/estadisticas/evasion_iva_rt.pdf. [17]

Zhang, H. (2018), *The Development and Testing of a Diagnostic Tool for Assessing VAT Compliance Costs Draft Report of Pilot Study Findings [ATAX version]*. [26]

Annex 2.A. Data on VAT rates and structures

Annex Table 2.A.1. VAT rates[1]

	Implemented	1975	1995	2005	2007	2008	2009	2010	2011	2012	2013	2014	2015	2016	2017	2018	Reduced rates[2]	Specific regional rates
Australia	2000	-	-	10	10	10	10	10	10	10	10	10	10	10	10	10	0	-
Austria*	1973	16	20	20	20	20	20	20	20	20	20	20	20	20	20	20	10.0/13.0	19
Belgium	1971	18	20.5	21	21	21	21	21	21	21	21	21	21	21	21	21	0.0/6.0/12.0	-
Canada*	1991	-	7	7	6	5	5	5	5	5	5	5	5	5	5	5	0	13.0/15.0
Chile	1975	20	18	19	19	19	19	19	19	19	19	19	19	19	19	19	-	-
Czech Republic	1993	-	22	19	19	19	19	20	20	20	21	21	21	21	21	21	10.0/15.0	-
Denmark	1967	15	25	25	25	25	25	25	25	25	25	25	25	25	25	25	0	-
Estonia	1991	-	18	18	18	18	18	20	20	20	20	20	20	20	20	20	0.0/9.0	-
Finland	1994	-	22	22	22	22	22	22	23	23	24	24	24	24	24	24	0.0/10.0/14.0	-
France*	1968	20	20.6	19.6	19.6	19.6	19.6	19.6	19.6	19.6	19.6	20	20	20	20	20	2.1/5.5/10.0	0.9/2.1/10.0/13.0 & 1.05/1.75/2.1/8.5
Germany	1968	11	15	16	19	19	19	19	19	19	19	19	19	19	19	19	7	-
Greece*	1987	-	18	18	19	19	19	19	23	23	23	23	23	23	24	24	6.0/13.0	4.0/ 9.0/17.0
Hungary	1988	-	25	25	20	20	20	25	25	27	27	27	27	27	27	27	5.0/18.0	-
Iceland	1990	-	24.5	24.5	24.5	24.5	24.5	25.5	25.5	25.5	25.5	25.5	24	24	24	24	0.0/11.0	-
Ireland	1972	19.5	21	21	21	21	21.5	21	21	23	23	23	23	23	23	23	0.0/4.8/9.0/13.5	-
Israel*	1976	-	17	17	15.5	15.5	15.5	16	16	16	17	18	18	17	17	17	0	0
Italy	1973	12	19	20	20	20	20	20	20	21	21	22	22	22	22	22	4.0/5.0/10.0	-
Japan	1989	-	3	5	5	5	5	5	5	5	5	5	8	8	8	8	-	-
Korea	1977	-	10	10	10	10	10	10	10	10	10	10	10	10	10	10	0	-
Latvia	1995	-	-	18	18	18	21	21	22	22	21	21	21	21	21	21	5.0/12.0	-
Lithuania	1994	-	18	18	18	18	19	21	21	21	21	21	21	21	21	21	5.0/9.0	-
Luxembourg	1970	10	15	15	15	15	15	15	15	15	15	15	17	17	17	17	3.0/8.0/14.0	-
Mexico	1980	-	10	15	15	15	15	16	16	16	16	16	16	16	16	16	0	-
Netherlands	1969	16	17.5	19	19	19	19	19	19	19	21	21	21	21	21	21	6	-
New Zealand	1986	-	12.5	12.5	12.5	12.5	12.5	12.5	15	15	15	15	15	15	15	15	0	-
Norway	1970	20	23	25	25	25	25	25	25	25	25	25	25	25	25	25	0.0/12.0/15.0	-
Poland	1993	-	22	22	22	22	22	22	23	23	23	23	23	23	23	23	5.0/8.0	-
Portugal*	1986	-	17	19	21	21	20	20	23	23	23	23	23	23	23	23	6.0/13.0	4.0/9.0/18.0 & 5.0/12.0/22.0

Slovak Republic	1993	-	25	19	19	19	19	19	20	20	20	20	20	20	20	20	10	-
Slovenia	1999	-	-	20	20	20	20	20	20	20	20	22	22	22	22	22	9.5	-
Spain*	1986	-	16	16	16	16	16	16	18	18	21	21	21	21	21	21	4.0/10.0	0.0/2.75/3.0/7.0/9.5/13.5/ 20.0 & 0.5/10.0
Sweden	1969	17.7	25	25	25	25	25	25	25	25	25	25	25	25	25	25	0.0/6.0/12.0	-
Switzerland	1995	-	6.5	7.6	7.6	7.6	7.6	7.6	8	8	8	8	8	8	8	7.7	0.0/2.5/3.7	-
Turkey	1985	-	15	18	18	18	18	18	18	18	18	18	18	18	18	18	1.0/8.0	-
United Kingdom	1973	8	17.5	17.5	17.5	17.5	15	17.5	20	20	20	20	20	20	20	20	0.0/5.0	-
Unweighted average		15.6	17.7	17.8	17.8	17.7	17.8	18.2	18.7	18.9	19.1	19.2	19.3	19.3	19.3	19.3		

* See country notes.

1. Yearly data: the rates shown in the table are rates applicable on 1 January of each year. Reduced rates and specific rates applicable in specific regions are those applicable as at 1 January 2018.

2. Reduced rates include zero-rates applicable to domestic supplies (i.e. an exemption with right to deduct input tax). They do not include zero-rated exports or other supplies subject to similar treatment such as international transport or supplies to embassies, international organisations and diplomatic missions.

Source: national delegates - position as at 1 January 2018.

StatLink https://doi.org/10.1787/888933890084

Country notes to Annex Table 2.A.1

Austria. A standard rate of 19% applies in Jungholz and Mittelberg.

Canada. The following provinces have harmonised their provincial sales taxes with the federal Goods and Services Tax and therefore levy a rate of GST/HST of: New Brunswick, Newfoundland and Labrador, Nova Scotia, Prince Edward Island: 15%; and Ontario: 13%. Québec applies GST at a rate of 5% and Québec Sales Tax at a rate of 9.975% (applied on the same tax base as the GST). Other Canadian provinces, with the exception of Alberta, Yukon, Northwest Territories and Nunavut apply a provincial sales tax to certain goods and services in addition to the Federal GST.

France. Rates of 0.9%; 2.1%; 10.0%; 13.0% and 20.0% apply in Corsica; rates of 1.05%; 1.75%; 2.1% and 8.5% apply to overseas departments (DOM) excluding French Guyana and Mayotte.

Greece. Specific regional rates of 4.0%; 9.0% and 17.0% apply in the islands of Leros, Lesbos, Kos, Samos and Chios until 31 December 2018.

Israel. The rate of 0% applies when an Eilat resident dealer buys goods from Eilat non-residents. Supplies made by an Eilat resident supplier (to be consumed in Eilat) are exempt from VAT. The statistical data for Israel are supplied by and under the responsibility of the relevant Israeli authorities. The use of such data by the OECD is without prejudice to the status of the Golan Heights, East Jerusalem and Israeli settlements in the West Bank under the terms of international law.

Portugal. In the Islands of Azores, the standard VAT rate is 18% and the reduced rates are 4% and 9%. In the Islands of Madeira the standard rate is 22% and reduced rates are 5% and 12%.

Spain. Rates of 0.0%, 2.75%; 3.0%; 7.0%, 9.50%; 13.50%, 20% apply in the Canary Islands. Rates of 0.5% and 10% apply in Ceuta and Melilla.

Annex Table 2.A.2. Application of reduced VAT rates

Country	Reduced VAT rates, including domestic zero rate[1]
Australia	0%: most food and beverages for human consumption (excl. prepared food); most health and medical supplies; some education courses and students accommodation; some child care services; some religious services; some activities of charitable institutions; water (except supplied in, or transferred to, a container less than 100L); sewerage and drainage; sales of businesses as going concerns; precious metals (first supply after refinement); grants of freehold and similar interests by governments; farm land; cars for use by disabled people subject to a (general) threshold of AUD 57 466; supplies of accommodation and meals to residents of retirement villages by certain operators; certain government services; some telecommunication supplies made under arrangements for global roaming in Australia; international mail.
Austria	10%: food; water supply; pharmaceuticals; passenger transport (except domestic flights); books; newspapers and periodicals; pay television; some supplies of artists, writers and composers; forestry; restaurants (except beverages); collection of domestic waste and street cleaning; sewage. 13%: hotel accommodation, supply of wine by producing farmers; agricultural supplies; admission to cultural, sporting events and cinemas; domestic flights.
Belgium	0%: cars for disabled persons; certain newspapers and periodicals, certain recovered materials and by products 6%: food; some beverages; water supply; pharmaceuticals; feminine hygiene products and external defibrillators; equipment for the disabled; passenger transport; books; newspapers and periodicals; culture; sport; works of art, collectors' items and antiques; works of art delivered by their authors/creators; agriculture; hotel accommodation and camping sites; renovation of dwellings over 10 years old; private homes and establishments for disabled; subsidised social housing; some labour intensive services (small repair services); reconstruction subsequent to demolition works leading to the construction of new private housing (under strict conditions and specific limitations as to the amount); funeral services; cut flowers and plants. 12%: restaurants (except beverages); certain energy products (coal, coke; lignite); certain social housing.
Canada	0%: prescription medicine, basic groceries; certain financial services provided by financial institutions (usually to non-residents); certain agricultural and fishing products; certain medical devices; international bridge or tunnel authorities (on certain purchases only); precious metals; sales of 25 cents or less made through mechanical coin-operated devices.
Chile	–
Czech Republic	10%: essential child nutrition; gluten-free products; certain pharmaceutical products; certain printed books. 15%: food; pharmaceutical products and printed books (when not subject to the lower rate of 10%) some beverages; water supply; medical services (if not exempt); equipment and repair for the disabled; passenger transport; art; cultural services; newspapers and periodicals; construction of private dwellings and social housing; renovation and repair of private dwellings; collection and treatment of waste and waste water; hotel accommodation; health care and domestic care services; cleaning in households; funeral services; sport activities; agricultural products; cut flowers and plants; heating.
Denmark	0%: newspapers and periodicals. 5%: first time sale of products of artistic work valued over DKK 300 000 (the standard rate of 25% applies to 20% of the tax base resulting in an effective rate of 5%).
Estonia	0%: certain commercial aircraft and sea-going vessels and certain supplies of goods and services related to them; international transport of passengers. 9%: pharmaceuticals; medical equipment or devices for disabled; books; newspapers and periodicals; hotel accommodation.
Finland	0%: printing services for certain membership publications; certain vessels. 10%: pharmaceuticals; passenger transport; books, subscribed newspapers and periodicals; hotel accommodation; admission to cultural, entertainment and sporting events and cinema performances; use of sports facilities; works of art supplied by their creators or imported; copyrights to literary and artistic works; TV licence fees. 14%: food; non-alcoholic drinks; animal food; restaurants (except alcoholic beverages).

France	2.1%: newspapers and periodicals; pharmaceuticals. 5.5%: most food products and beverages (except alcoholic beverages); water supply; equipment for the disabled; books; admission to cultural services; work on dwellings over 2 years old under certain conditions; domestic care services; subscription fees to natural gas and electricity networks; district heating; supplies of works of art by their creators; women's sanitary products. 10%: passenger transport; social housing; admission to amusement parks; pay TV; domestic care services; restaurant services and catering (except alcoholic beverages); hotel accommodation; farm products; gardens, plants and flowers; treatment of waste; sewage; passenger transport; author's rights.
Germany	7%: food; water supply; equipment for the disabled; medical services (if not exempt); books and newspapers; plants; flowers; certain cultural events; museums; zoos; circuses; charitable work (if not exempt); author's rights; local public passenger transport within a municipality or if the distance covered is not more than 50 km; hotel accommodation; cut flowers and plants; works of art supplied by their creator or successors in title and importation of collector's items.
Greece	6%: pharmaceutical drugs and vaccines for human medicine; books; children's picture books; newspapers, journals and periodicals; admission to the theatre (theatrical plays). 13%: water, basic food goods (meat and abattoir by-products; meat preparations; fish, squid, octopus and cuttlefish excluding livers, eggs and semen; milk and dairy products; birds' eggs; natural honey; vegetables, plants, some types of roots and tubers; animal food falling within CN code 230990, oil cake, seeds for sowing; fruit and nuts; cereal; flour and flour products; olive oil; preparations for infant use, put up for retail sale; pasta not baked or stuffed or otherwise processed; bread; excluding the undermentioned subject to the standard rate: most types of processed food, beverages, alcoholic products, fruit and vegetable juices, aerated waters); farm supplies that are usually intended to be used as intermediate inputs by farmers and farm industries; live plants and their roots, cuttings and slips; pharmaceutical products (besides those subject to 6%); medical equipment and other appliances for the disabled persons; intrauterine contraceptives; catheters; feeding syringes; «talking» sphygmomanometers; needles for insulin pens and dialysis needles; water supply; electricity; natural gas; district heating; hotel and similar accommodation; home care services; retirement home services that are subject to VAT.
Hungary	5%: pharmaceuticals for humans; certain equipment for the blind; books, newspapers and sheet music; live pigs and carcasses of pig; certain live cattle, sheep, lamb, goat, and their meat in bulk; meat of domestic pig; meat and edible offal of poultry; fresh eggs; fresh milk; edible offal and inner parts of domestic swine; live fish (excluding ornamental fish) and the body/parts/fillet of fish for human consumption; district heating; services supplied by performing artists; internet access services; restaurant meals and supply of non-alcoholic beverages prepared on site. 18%: milk and dairy products; products containing cereals, flour, starch or milk; provision of accommodation; certain open-air concerts.
Iceland	0%: shipbuilding and maintenance of ships and aircraft; services to foreign fishing vessels related to landing and sale of fish in Iceland; direct payments to farmers. 11%: food and beverages; passenger transport (if not exempted); services of travel agencies, travel organizers and touring associations; travel guidance; books including music books; audio recordings of books. CD's and similar media with text as well as electronic version of such books; magazines, newspapers and countryside- and district newspapers with text as well as electronic version of such papers and magazines; periodicals with text as well as electronic version of such periodicals; subscriptions to radio and TV; rental of hotels, guestrooms and other guest services; hot water, electricity and fuel oil used for the heating of houses and swimming pools; admission tolls to land transportation projects; CD disks, records, magnetic tapes and other similar means of music recordings, other than visual records. Electronic version of music other than visual; condoms; diapers for children; admission fees to bathhouses, bathings, saunas and spas (if not exempted).
Ireland	0%: books; children's clothing and footwear; oral medicine; certain medical equipment; food products; seeds; fertilisers; certain aircraft and sea-going vessels. 4.8%: livestock and horses for food or agricultural production. 9%: newspapers and certain periodicals; admission to cinemas/certain musical performances and provision of sporting facilities; recreational and sport services; certain nursery and garden centre; holiday accommodation; restaurant/hotel meals; agricultural services. 13.5%: waste disposal; energy for heating and light; fuel for certain purposes; gas; electricity; building services; immovable goods; repair services; tour guide services; photographic prints; works of art; short-term car and boat hire; driving instruction; veterinary services; plants and flowers; medical services (if not exempt).

Israel[2]	0%: hotel accommodation for foreign tourists and another hotel services (serving food and beverage, laundry, pool, gym, etc.); sale of, to a foreign tourist, tickets for an international conference in which more than 50 foreign tourists are in attendance; rental of a private motor vehicle to a tourist to drive himself; transportation of tourists in a private motor vehicle, a bus or an airplane; hospitalization of a foreign tourist; sale of fruits and vegetables; sale of dealer's/dealers' assets to a company in exchange for the company's stock only, provided that the dealer/dealers owns 90%, or more, of the voting power immediately after the assets transfer; sale of all of the company's assets to its shareholders in a liquidation process, in which, the assets are divided amongst the said shareholders in proportion to the shares respectively held by them; supplies of goods to who would be exempted from sales tax due to entry to Israel (supplies of certain goods to new immigrants and to students returning from study abroad); sale of a real estate by a non-profit organization or by a financial institution to a non-profit organization or to a financial institution as part of restructuring; renting exhibition space by non-resident; services given by an Israeli production company to a non-resident for film production in Israel; services given to a non-resident in respect of human clinical trials; an Eilat resident dealer buys goods from an Eilat non-resident.
Italy	4%: certain food; medications and health products/services and equipment for the disabled; supply of services for certain residential housing constructions; books; newspapers; weekly magazines; supply of food by schools, canteens and *soup kitchens*. 5%: aromatic herbs, social and health service for the elderly, drug addicts, migrants, prisoners, handicapped, AIDS patients, transport services on urban waterways (see, river, lake or lagoon). 10%: certain food and beverage, water supply; pharmaceutical products (for humans and animals); medical services (if not exempt); passenger transport; combustible gas for cooking; mineral oil; electricity; gas; urban waste; purification stations; livestock meat and fish; renewable-source energy; works of art; admission to shows and cultural events; letting of immovable property by building enterprises; renovation and maintenance work for residential housing; restaurants; construction of urban development; hotel and similar accommodation services.
Japan	–
Korea	0%: supply of certain machinery and materials for agriculture; fishery; livestock and forestry; supply of mineral oil used for certain purposes in agriculture, fishery and forestry; certain equipment for the disabled.
Latvia	12%: medicinal products; medical devices; food for infants; pharmaceutical products; inland passenger transport services; books, newspapers and periodicals; hotel accommodation; district heating, transport of passengers. 5%: Certain supplies of fresh fruits, berries and vegetables.
Lithuania	9%: heating power used for heating residential premises, hot water (including cold water used for preparing hot water and to heating power used for preparation of hot water) supplied to residential premises; books, non-periodical information and periodical publications; inland passenger transport; accommodation services. 5%: certain medicines and medical aid equipment (including prescription drugs); technical aids for disabled persons and repairs of such aids.
Luxembourg	3%: food for human and animal consumption; water supply; pharmaceutical products; certain medical equipment; certain aids and other appliances normally intended to alleviate or treat disability; passenger transport; accommodation; books, newspapers and periodicals, but excluding material with predominantly adult content; admission to cultural and sporting events; use of sporting facilities; restaurant services but excluding alcoholic beverages; author's rights; goods and services of a kind normally intended for use in agricultural production; services supplied in connection with waste collection and treatment; children's clothing and footwear; housing used by the owner, for his own use, as principal dwelling; substantial works on housing used as principal dwelling and (i) constructed more than 20 years prior to the start of the works (ii) newly acquired, the works to be completed in the five years following the acquisition; funeral services; reception of radio and television broadcasting services but excluding exclusively adult content services. 8%: certain labour intensive services; works of art delivered by their authors/creators or by their heirs or imported; gas; electricity; firewood; district heating; flowers and ornamental plants. 14%: certain wines; certain fuels; washing and cleaning products; printed advertising; heat and air conditioning; certain financial services.
Mexico	0%: sale of non-industrialised animals (except dogs, cats and small species used as home pets) and vegetables (except rubber); patent medicines; milk; bottled water; juices, nectar and concentrated fruits and vegetables; ice; food (except sale of processed food in restaurants and food establishments, chewing gum, caviar, smoked salmon, foie gras, pet food and soft drinks); agricultural equipment; machinery and fishing boats; wholesale of gold; gold bullion (with a content of at least 80% of gold) and jewellery; some agricultural and fishing services; magazines, books and newspapers printed by the taxpayer himself; domestic water supply; hotel services provided to foreign tourists participating in congresses, conventions and trade shows; use of convention centres by event organisers who are residents abroad; call centre services for telephone calls originated abroad, as long as the services are contracted and paid a foreign resident without a permanent establishment in Mexico.
Netherlands	6%: food; catering; goods and services for the disabled; medicine; accommodation; books; lending of books; newspapers; magazines; passenger transport (except passenger transport by air); water supply; entrance fees for sports events; amusement; parks; museums; cinemas; zoos and circuses; cut flowers and plants; restaurant and hotel meals; aids for the visually disabled; use of sports

	accommodation; art and antiques; hotel and holiday accommodation; certain labour intensive services like some specific services for the maintenance and isolation of dwellings; cleaning of dwellings and hairdressing.
New Zealand	0%: supply of taxable activity (business) as a going concern; supply of fine metal (gold, silver or platinum) from a refiner in fine metal to a dealer in fine metal; supply by local authorities of the local authorities petroleum tax; supply of financial services to registered GST businesses. Supply of land by and to a GST registered person when the recipient intends to use it to make taxable supplies and it is not intended to be used as a principal place of residence (this zero-rating between GST-registered persons is equivalent to the domestic reverse charge). Long-term stay in a commercial dwelling; certain services provided as part of the right to occupancy (taxed at the standard rate on 60% of the value of the supply).
Norway	0%: books; newspapers; certain periodicals and publications; electronic news services; electricity and energy supplied from alternative energy sources for household use in the counties of Finnmark, Troms and Nordland; the purchase and leasing/hiring of electric motor vehicles and batteries; second-hand vehicles covered by re-registration tax; supply of certain ships, aircrafts and drilling platforms and hiring out such vessels; services that are directly related to the construction of embassy buildings (to final consumer); goods and services to specific international military forces and command units; supply of taxable activity (business) as a going concern; supply of human organs, blood; supply by funeral directors of services relating to the transportation of deceased persons. 12%: accommodation, passenger transport and transport of vehicles by ferries or other vessels in connection with the domestic road network; public broadcasting; admission to sporting events, museums, cinemas and amusement parks. 15%: food and non-alcoholic beverages.
Poland	5%: certain food; certain beverages; certain books and periodicals; 8%: certain food; treatment, distribution and trade services of water through water mains; pharmaceutical products; certain goods for disabled; veterinary services; passenger transport; certain newspapers; services (other than electronic services) enabling the reception of television and radio programmes with the exclusion of VOD; admission to cultural and sporting events; author's rights; construction, repairs, modernisation, thermo-modernization and reconstruction of social housing; hotel accommodation; restaurant services except beverages; cemetery services; collection and treatment of waste; some labour intensive services; certain live animals and certain products of animal origin; animal feeding stuffs; certain agricultural means of production; certain agriculture services; children's car seats.
Portugal	6%: essential food; water supply; pharmaceutical products; devices for the disabled; medical services (if not exempt); books, newspapers and periodicals; passenger transport; hotels and similar services; social housing; some goods used in agriculture; certain agriculture products and certain agriculture services. 13%: some other food; still wine; diesel fuel for agriculture; machinery mainly used in agricultural production; admission to cultural events.
Slovak Republic	10%: certain food; radioactive elements and isotopes and compounds for health service; pharmaceutical products; diagnostic or laboratory reagents; certain medical and sanitarian means; printed books, brochures, leaflets and similar printed matter; music; orthopaedic appliances; contact and spectacle lenses; certain means for blind and partly blind persons, hard-of-hearing persons and hard health-disabled persons.
Slovenia	9.5%: foodstuff (for human and animal consumption); preparation of food; water supply; medicine, devices for the disabled; passenger transport; books on all physical means of support, newspapers and periodicals; admission to cultural and sporting events; author's rights; import and supply of certain works of art, collectors' items or antiques; social housing; renovation and maintenance work of residential housing not provided as part of a social policy; livestock and certain supplies in connection with agricultural production; hotel accommodation; restaurant (except beverages); use of sporting facilities; supplies by undertakers and cremation services; public hygiene services; window-cleaning and cleaning in private households; minor repairing of bicycles, shoes and leather goods; domestic care services; hairdressing; cut flowers and plants.
Spain	4%: food (for human and animal consumption); social accommodation; medicines and other medical devices (e.g. lenses); books, newspapers and periodicals; supply of new buildings for private and social housing. 10%: water supply; supplies to the disabled; passengers transport; minor work on private housing; cleaning; restaurants and catering; certain cultural and entertainment services; hotels; public amenities; agriculture and forestry products used as food; goods used in agricultural and forestry undertakings, including flowers and plants; waste treatment; cleaning of public sewage; burial services; cleaning and maintenance services.
Sweden	0%: commercial aircraft and ships and certain services related to these; aircraft fuel; prescribed medicine; printing of certain membership publications. 6%: passenger transport; books, newspapers and magazines; culture (theatre, cinema, etc.); author's rights; zoos; commercial sports events; commercial museums, exhibition of natural areas.

	12%: food and restaurants services; accommodation; works of art owned by the originator; import of antiques, collector's items and works of art; repair of bikes, shoes and other leather goods and household linen.
Switzerland	0%: Supply of services by travel agents and organisers of events, if they make use of supplies of goods and services by third parties that are provided abroad; certain supplies of goods and services to international airlines; state minted gold coins, fine gold for investment purposes and gold destined for refining or recovery. 2.5%: tap water; food; cattle; poultry; fish; grains; seeds; planting roots and bulbs; living plants; cuttings; scions and cut flowers and branches; animal feed; silage acids; scatterings for animals; fertilisers; pesticides; mulch; medication; books, newspapers and magazines, including in electronic format; non-commercial services of radio and television companies, certain supplies in connection with agricultural production. The 2.5% rate also applies to certain cultural services supplied directly to the public, considerations demanded for sporting events, cultural services and the supply of works by their creators when the suppliers have opted for taxation (otherwise those supplies are exempt without right of deduction). 3.7%, accommodation services.
Turkey	0%: supply of ships, aircraft, and rail transportation vehicles; supply of services related to the manufacture, repair, maintenance of such vehicles; supply of services to ships and aircraft at harbours or airports; supply of goods and services for the exploration, management and refining of gold, silver, platinum, and oil; supply of machinery and equipment to persons who have an investment incentive document; goods and construction works for the construction, restoration and enlargement of seaports and airports; some goods and services related to national security; international roaming services supplied in Turkey according to the reciprocity principle; supply of goods that are listed in the second list of excise duty tax law to the prime ministry central organisation; the first supply of product certificate that are drawn up according to agricultural product license warehousing law via commodity exchange market; exemption for delivery of equipment produced for the disabled; deliveries and services made to Turkey Red Crescent Society; fertilizer and feed deliveries; resident or workplace deliveries to non-residents in Turkey; deliveries of goods and services made in the scope of construction of organized industrial zones and small industrial sites; deliveries and services made to donators in the scope of facilities that are donated to general and special budget public administrations, special provincial administrations, municipalities and villages by these donators; health services provided to foreigners; new machinery and equipment deliveries to those that perform R & D, innovation and design activities. 1%: some agricultural products; second-hand cars; newspapers and periodicals; e-books and e-newspapers; funeral services; supply of residential housing under 150 m2 in cities other than metropolitan ones and in metropolitan cities if land value per m^2 lower than TRY 500; lease of specified machinery and equipment; seeds. 8%: basic food; books; blood and blood component; cinema; theatre; opera and ballet tickets; private educational service; vaccines; some medical products and services; ambulance services; medicine; medical equipment; textile and confection products and custom manufacturing of them; accommodation services; meal services at non-luxury restaurants (excluding alcoholic beverages); services provided by orphanage and nursing homes; some constructional and agricultural machines; clothing; stationery goods; waste water services; supply of residential housing under 150 m^2 in metropolitan cities and with land value per m^2 is between TRY 500 and TRY 999.
United Kingdom	0%: food; certain services and goods supplied to charities; children's clothing; passenger transport; books; newspapers; domestic sewage and water; prescribed drugs; medicine; certain aids and services for disabled people; new housing, including the construction of new houses; residential and some charitable buildings. 5%: fuel and power for domestic and charity use; certain energy saving materials supplied together with fitting services to recipient of benefits; certain grant-funded installations of heating equipment; children car seats; certain pharmaceutical products.

* See country notes.

[1]. For the purpose of this table, reduced rates also include "domestic zero rates" (0%) i.e. instances where VAT is not charged by the supplier on domestic supplies while related input VAT is deductible. In some countries, these supplies are called "exempt with right of deduction" and in others "GST free". They do not include zero-rate applied to exports, supplies of goods or services used or consumed abroad or other supplies subject to similar treatment such as international transport or supplies to embassies, international organisations and diplomatic missions.

[2]. Israel: The statistical data for Israel are supplied by and under the responsibility of the relevant Israeli authorities. The use of such data by the OECD is without prejudice to the status of the Golan Heights, East Jerusalem and Israeli settlements in the West Bank under the terms of international law.

Source: National delegate; position as at 1 January 2018.

Annex Table 2.A.3. VAT Exemptions[1]

Country	Exemptions	Taxation of "common exemptions" in the country[2]
Australia	Financial services; residential rent and residential premises (other than new residential premises); certain supplies of precious metals; school canteens operated by non-profit bodies (optional); certain fund raising events conducted by charitable institutions.	Domestic postal services; sporting services; cultural services excluding religious services (zero rate); insurance and reinsurance excluding health insurance (zero rate); gambling (including lottery tickets and betting); supplies of land and buildings (except certain supplies of farm land and supplies of going concerns– zero rate and existing residential premises – exempt).
Austria	Common exemptions[2]	Letting (private housing)
Belgium	Common exemptions[2]	-
Canada	Common exemptions[2]; legal aid; public transit; ferry, road and bridge tolls; child and personal care services; certain regulatory/administrative supplies by a government or a municipality.	Most betting, lotteries and gambling; supply and leasing of commercial land and buildings; sales of newly constructed or substantially renovated housing; domestic postal services; most cultural and sporting services e.g. adult programmes; services provided by other than public sector bodies; most admissions to a place of amusement (e.g. museums, films, professional performances and sporting events, etc.); human blood and certain biologicals (zero rate).
Chile	Used motor vehicles; goods provided by the employer to dependant employees; domestic raw materials used in the production, processing or manufacture of goods for export; some imports by the Ministry of Defence, the Army and other related organisms; some imports by the Cuerpos de Bomberos and the Junta Nacional de Cuerpos de Bomberos; some imports by Casa de Moneda de Chile S.A. and other persons provided that the import is made in the context of operations with the Central Bank of Chile; capital goods imported and assigned to projects involving investments of USD 5 000 000 or more; income received from tickets to shows and meetings; international freight, passenger transport; premiums and disbursements of reinsurance contracts; commissions earned by the Regional and Metropolitan Housing and Urbanisation Services and Social Security Institutions on mortgages; non-taxable income; income subject to additional income tax; income such as wages, salaries, pensions, income obtained by independent workers and directors fees if taxed with income tax; insertions and notices to be published and disseminated under the right of reply; certain insurance premiums; financial interests; commissions coming from guarantees issued by financial institutions; letting and lease with a purchase option of immovable property; remunerations linked to exports; income obtained from services rendered to persons domiciled or resident abroad and qualified as exportable services by Customs; income of hotels relating to services rendered to foreign tourists; fees paid for managing retirement savings earned by specific authorized institutions; income obtained by independent professionals, where the physical effort is more relevant than the capital or materials used; construction contracts and finance lease of a house financed with a housing subsidy granted by the Ministry of Housing and Urban Development; broadcasting and television enterprises excluding income from advertisement; news agencies; educational services; health services; health contributions paid to Private Health Insurance Companies; manufacturing of currency by Casa de Moneda de Chile; postal services rendered by Servicio de Correos y Telégrafos de Chile; interests, premiums, commissions or other forms of remunerations paid by	Income from artistic shows or plays not sponsored by the Ministry of Culture, Arts and Heritage; income from certain circus and sports events if certain requirements are not met.

	Polla Chilena de Beneficencia and Lotería de Concepción to individual or legal entities for business services; other minor exemptions.	
Czech Republic	Common exemptions[2]; public television and radio.	Certain cultural services (e.g. admission to theatres, cinemas, concerts, etc. subject to reduced rates); sporting services provided by others than by non-profit making organisations; supply of construction land; supply of new building and building land (subject for the option to taxation).
Denmark	Hospital and medical care; dental care; social service; education; non-commercial activities of some non-profit making organisations; non-profit sport activities etc.; cultural services (some exceptions); literary and composing activities; creative artist; letting of immovable property; supply of immovable property; insurance and reinsurance; financial services; lotteries and gambling; postal service; stamps; transport of persons; funeral service; certain fund-raising events; charitable work	Cultural services as radio, television broadcasting, cinema, theatre, concerts etc.; short term letting of immovable property; option to tax commercial letting; supply of new building and building land; some commercial postal service
Estonia	Common exemptions[2]	Immovable property, except dwellings (optional); financial services (optional); cultural services
Finland	Common exemptions[2]; services of performers; copyright to literary and artistic works (excluding payments to or from an organisation representing the copyright holders); certain transactions by blind people; public cemetery services; self-picked natural berries.	Cultural services; letting of commercial buildings in certain cases (optional)
France	Common exemptions[2]; construction, improvement, repair and maintenance work on monuments, cemeteries and graves commemorating war victims undertaken for public authorities and non-profit bodies; commodity futures transactions carried out on a regulated market; services rendered by resource consortia to their members composed of natural or legal persons that are VAT exempt or not subject to VAT.	Letting of immovable property (full taxation for letting of developed immovable property and land for professional use; option to tax for letting of undeveloped immovable property for professional use in certain circumstances and letting of land and buildings for agricultural use); transport services for sick/injured persons in vehicles not specially equipped for this purpose and/or carried out by persons who do not have administrative certification; recreational and sporting services; cinemas, concerts and theatres.
Germany	Common exemptions[2]	
Greece	Common exemptions[2]; national radio and TV broadcasting activities other than those of commercial nature; remunerative contributions imposed by Organizations of Territorial Improvements to their members for the supply of irrigating water and relative supplies directly connected thereto; services provided by dental technicians and the supply of dental prosthetics by dentists and dental technicians; supply of breast milk; supply of goods of an enterprise, in whole or in part, to an existing legal person or one being set up against a consideration, or as a gift or as contribution, provided that the goods were used until then exclusively in an exempt from (or out of scope of) VAT activity (or supply of goods to special scheme farmers) and the supplier was not granted or exercised input tax deduction.	Postal services not rendered by the Greek Post Office (ELTA.); charitable work when provided by organisations without state recognition; hospital and medical care supplied by profit organisations or by non-profit private organisations under distortion of competition; sporting, cultural, religion related or philosophy related etc. services supplied by profit organisations or subject to distortion of competition; supply of new buildings; letting of immovable property for professional use (optional taxation).
Hungary	Common exemptions[2]; public radio and TV broadcasting (except for commercial activities).	Building land, supply of new buildings (taxation of further supplies and letting of immovable property is optional); certain cultural services (e.g. admission to theatres, cinemas, concerts), certain sporting services (e.g. swimming pool services, entrance tickets to sporting events).
Iceland	Common exemptions[2]; sports, admission fees to athletic events and health facilities; public transportation, organized transportation of disabled, elderlies and school children, taxi services; authors, composers, burials and church-related services; medical and social services; cultural services; operation of schools and educational institutions; rental of real properties and parking spaces; lotteries and betting pools, charities.	

Ireland	Common exemptions[2] ; passenger transport; national broadcasting; supply of water by public authorities; admissions to sporting events; funeral undertaking.	Letting of commercial immovable property (subject to the option for taxation by the landlord); supply of undeveloped land and buildings that are not new; recreational and sporting services.
Israel[3]	Rentals for residential purposes for a period of not more than 25 years; the sale of a part of a building which was approved as a rental building; transactions of an exempt dealer, other than transactions that are sales of real estate; the sale of an asset, on which input tax in respect of its acquisition or importation could not be deducted lawfully at the time of its acquisition or importation; deposits in a financial institution or giving a loan to a financial institution; goods whose import is tax exempt in certain cases; supplies made by an Eilat resident supplier(to be consumed in Eilat); the sale of residential dwelling to Real Estate Investment Trust (REIT) by a person who is not a dealer and the sale of that dwelling by the REIT.	Non-commercial activities of non-profit making organisations; financial services (specific regime).
Italy	Common exemptions[2]; taxi; funeral services.	Supply and letting of land; supplies of buildings are taxed in the first five years when sold by building enterprises within five years from their construction or after five years if the latter has opted for non-exemption. This scheme applies in the case of commercial buildings, while for residential housing taxation only applies when let by building enterprises which have opted for non-exemption. Rates are 4% for non-luxury owner-occupied dwelling, 10% for other non-luxury houses and 22% for luxury housing. Certain social assistance services provided by public bodies and non-profit organisations; welfare services to employees.
Japan	Common exemptions[2]; social welfare services; sale of certain kinds of equipment for the disabled people; administrative services; alienation of securities, textbooks, tuition fees.	Postal services; supply of buildings; cultural and sporting services provided by others than non-profit organisations; letting of immovable property by business.
Korea	Common exemptions[2]; certain public transport; supply of water and certain coal; mineral oil used for certain purposes in agriculture and fishery; funeral undertaking; certain personal services similar to labour; books, newspapers and magazines; broadcasting services; supply of farm, marine and forest products.	Rental and supply of commercial buildings; commercial cultural services; gambling in licensed clubs.
Latvia	Common exemptions[2]; royalty received by the author.	Supply of used immovable property (only a registered taxable person has the right to apply tax on the supply thereof).
Lithuania	Common exemptions[2]; public television and radio, sale of postal and fiscal stamps, social welfare services and goods related to it, services supplied to members.	Supply of building land and new (24 months) buildings, short-term (up to 2 months) letting of residential premises, letting of parking spaces and similar, supply of land and used buildings when option to tax is exercised.
Luxembourg	Common exemptions[2].	-
Mexico	Common exemptions[2]; gold and silver coins; shares; foreign currency; retailing of gold bullion with a content of at least 99 % gold; authors' rights; urban, suburban and metropolitan public transport of passengers by land (including by train); sale of used movable property (with exception of those sold by companies); professional medical services.	Postal services; insurance services (except life and agricultural insurance); transport of sick/injured persons; private hospital and medical care, sports services; financial services for consumer and personal credits; certain kinds of public spectacles like movie tickets; supplies of land and buildings (except housing) and certain fund raising events.
Netherlands	Common exemptions[2]; burials; cremations; public broadcasting; sports clubs; the services of composers, writers and journalists.	Cultural services (mostly lower rate); letting of immovable property other than houses (only at combined request by letter and hirer); supply of immovable property (only at the combined request of supplier and purchaser); the use of sports accommodation; recreational and sporting services; admission to cinemas, concerts and theatres; sporting events; museums and zoological gardens.
New Zealand	Financial services; supply of residential accommodation in a dwelling; fine metal; supply by a non-profit body	Postal services; human blood, tissues and organs; hospital and medical care; transport of

	of donated goods and services.	sick/injured persons; dental care; charitable work; certain fund raising events; education; non-commercial activities of non-profit making organisations (other than unconditional gifts); cultural services; sporting services; insurance and reinsurance (other than life insurance and reinsurance); letting of immovable property (other than residential accommodation); betting, lotteries and gambling; supply of land and buildings (other than land and buildings which have been used for the provision of residential accommodation for five years or more).
Norway	Common exemptions[2]; certain alternative treatments/fringe medicine; burials; stamps and coins for collection purposes; management services by a housing association to an affiliated housing cooperative; services in the form of membership of a board, supervisory board, committee, council or similar if the consideration is included in the employer's National Insurance contributions; services in the form of offsetting emission allowances	Postal services; infrastructural services within the passenger transport sector; admission to sporting events, museums, cinemas and amusement parks; letting of commercial buildings (optional).
Poland	Common exemptions[2]; public radio and television.	Rental or tenancy of the dwelling buildings used for commercial purposes; supply of building land or land for development and buildings.
Portugal	Common exemptions[2], burials and cremations, copyright to the literature and works of art.	-
Slovak Republic	Common exemptions[2]; public television and radio; services supplied to members; sale of postal and fiscal stamps.	Supply of a construction, including the supply of building land, on which the structure is constructed, provided that the supply is made within five years after the first approval of the building or a part thereof based on which the building or a part thereof was approved for use or within five years from the day when the building or a part thereof was put in use for the first time; option to tax supply and letting of immovable property; training, educational, sporting and cultural services provided by others than by non-profit making organisations.
Slovenia	Common exemptions[2]; public television and radio.	Supply of new buildings; admission to cultural and sporting events; educational, sporting and cultural services provided by profit making organisations; option to tax letting of immovable property.
Spain	Common exemptions[2]; copyright to literature and works of art; services provided by associations, entities, groups (including "economic interest groupings) and other legal persons to their members when they are exclusively integrated by taxable persons carrying out economic activities exempted or not subject to VAT; certain social assistance services provided by public bodies or not-for-profit organisations.	Cultural and sporting services provided for taxable persons different from public bodies and non-profit making organisations; letting of commercial buildings; building land; supply of new buildings.
Sweden	Common exemptions[2]; public television and radio; public cemetery services; social services; creative artists.	Most cultural services; letting of commercial buildings in certain cases (optional).
Switzerland	Common exemptions[2]; cultural services and the supply of cultural works by their creators, such as authors, composers, film makers, painters, sculptors and services supplied by publishers and collecting societies in order to circulate these works; the supply of used movable goods, which were used exclusively for the provision of supplies exempt from the tax without credit; the sale of agricultural, forestry and market garden products cultivated in their own business by farmers, foresters or gardeners, the sale of cattle by cattle dealers, and the sale of milk by milk collection points to milk processing plants; publicity services, which charitable organisations provide for the benefit of third parties or third parties for the benefit of charitable organisations; the exercise of arbitration functions. supplies between organisational units within the same public authority, between private or public law companies owned wholly by public authorities and the public authorities that own them or their organisational units, between institutions or foundations that were founded	The dispensing of artificial limbs and orthopaedic equipment; renting of exhibition stands and individual rooms in exhibition and congress buildings.

	exclusively by public authorities and the public authorities that founded them or their organisational units; the provision of staff by public authorities to other public authorities; supplies between education and research institutions that are involved in education and research cooperation, provided those supplies are made as part of the cooperation, irrespective of whether the education and research cooperation is liable to value added tax.	
Turkey	Importation of goods for cultural and educational purposes or for social purposes; restoration project related to cultural object; delivery of goods and provision of services to military factories, shipyards and factory plants; exempted taxpayers according to Income Tax Law; mergers and transfer according to Corporate Tax Law; transactions on leasing of real properties not included in economic enterprises; banking and insurance transaction; transactions of the Mint House and the Stamp Printing House; supply of precious mine and waste; supply of water used in agriculture; services supplied in free trade area; transportation of foreign oil and gas by pipelines; supply of land and workplace for organised industrial zone; supply of goods within the scope of financial restructuring; the transactions of Savings Deposit Insurance Fund; news service provided to General Directorate of Press and Information; renting work place in customs area; delivery and leasing of immovable property by the Treasury ; transfers and deliveries resulting from the sales of shares and real properties that have been included for at least two years in the assets of institutions; transfer of movable and immovable assets and intangible assets to the asset leasing company and the leasing of assets by asset leasing company; services provided by "Insurance Arbitration Commission" about settling disputes; roaming services received from abroad in the scope of international roaming agreements and reflection of these services to customers in Turkey.	Private education; private cultural services and sporting services; private hospital and medical care and dental care; human blood; transport of sick/injured persons(lower rate); postal services; sale of commercial buildings; letting; radio and television broadcasting; betting, lotteries and gambling; financial services that made by financial corporation; supply of land and buildings included in economic enterprises (standard rate); public hospital and medical care and dental care; public education; public cultural services and sporting services; tissues and organs; certain charitable work that is made by public organization or certificated institution; insurance and reinsurance; letting of immovable property not included in economic enterprises (exemption); non-commercial activities of non-profit making organisations; certain fund-raising events(non-taxable).
United Kingdom	Common exemptions[2]; burials and cremations; sports competitions; certain luxury hospital care; works of art.	Standard rated: freehold sales of new commercial buildings (standard rated for three years from completion date) and "option to tax" for other ordinarily exempted supplies of commercial buildings; gaming machines and certain gambling in licensed clubs Zero-rated: New housing, including construction of new houses; residential and some charity buildings.

1. Exemptions: for the purposes of this table, "exemption" refers to supplies for which VAT is not levied on the amount charged by the supplier while the latter is not allowed to deduct related input tax. In some countries, such supplies are called "input taxed supplies".

2. Common exemptions: in this table, "Common exemptions" refer to exemptions generally applied in most OECD countries i.e. postal services; transport of sick/injured persons; hospital and medical care; human blood, tissues and organs; dental care; charitable work; education; non-commercial activities of non-profit making organisations; sporting services; cultural services (except radio and television broadcasting); insurance and reinsurance; letting of immovable property; financial services; betting, lotteries and gambling; supply of land and buildings; certain fund-raising events

3. Israel: the statistical data for Israel are supplied by and under the responsibility of the relevant Israeli authorities. The use of such data by the OECD is without prejudice to the status of the Golan Heights, East Jerusalem and Israeli settlements in the West Bank under the terms of international law.

Source: National delegates; position as at 1 January 2018

Annex Table 2.A.4. Restrictions to the right to deduct VAT on specific inputs[1]

Country	Inputs on which the right to deduct VAT is denied or limited
Australia	**Entertainment:** recreational club leisure facility, entertainment, meal entertainment, family maintenance, relative's travel **Vehicles:** the amount of GST recoverable on the acquisition of a car is limited to that applicable to the car depreciation limit for the income year, currently AUD 57 466. **Others:** penalties, non-compulsory uniforms. GST is not recoverable on the expenses above to the extent they are not eligible for a deduction under the income tax law.
Austria	**Entertainment:** all entertainment expenses. **Vehicles:** vehicles, except used for commercial passenger transport, for leasing purposes or used at least 80% for driving schools.
Belgium	**Entertainment:** full input tax block for restaurant and hotel (with a number of strict exceptions), certain alcoholic beverages (with a number of strict exceptions) and reception and hospitality costs. **Vehicles:** Expenses relating to vehicles for transport of persons and/or goods by road. The right to deduct input tax may in principle not exceed 50% (with a number of strict exceptions). **Others:** supplies relating to special VAT scheme (e.g. margin scheme, special VAT scheme for tobacco).
Canada	**Entertainment**: deduction restrictions apply to memberships in dining, recreational or sporting facilities clubs; deduction for food, beverages, and entertainment expenses generally limited to 50% of the GST/HST payable. Food and beverage expenses for long-haul truck drivers are limited to 80%. **Vehicles:** deduction is limited on passenger vehicles acquired as capital property to the GST/HST payable on the capital cost value (CAD 30 000); deduction is limited on passenger vehicles leases to the GST/HST payable on CAD 800 monthly lease payments. **Others:** home office expenses restriction to the extent that the consumption or use of a property or service of such quality, nature, or cost is unreasonable given the person's commercial activity. **Local limitations**: large businesses (generally those with annual taxable supplies in excess of CAD 10 million) that acquire certain property or services (e.g. energy, telecommunications, road vehicles) for use in the province of Prince Edward Island are subject to input tax credit restrictions on the provincial portion of the HST. These restrictions are being phased out beginning in 2018.
Chile	**Vehicles:** automobiles, station wagons and similar vehicles as well their lubricants, spare parts, repairs or maintenance unless the regular business activity of the taxpayer is the sale, rental or lease of automobiles or unless the Commissioner of the Internal Revenue Service consider the relevant expenses as deductible for income tax purposes. **Fuels**: products or components that have any form of subsidy for end consumers. Supermarkets: expenses made in supermarkets and similar businesses when they exceed 5 Monthly Tax Units (CLP 235 095 - USD 382) and information specified in the law is not given to the tax authority.
Czech Republic	**Entertainment:** representation expenditures as defined in the income tax law for which there is no tax allowance according to the income tax law (except small gifts).
Denmark	**Entertainment:** expenses of entertainment, restaurant and presents. Vehicles: supply of vans with a weight of 3000kg or less used for both taxable and non-taxable purpose; cars with room for less than 10 persons; leased cars. **Others:** employee telephones paid by employer; board of employees and owner of the company; other objects in favour of the employees.
Estonia	**Entertainment**: goods or services relating to the reception of guests or the provision of meals or accommodation for employees. This restriction does not apply to accommodation services received during a business trip. **Vehicles**: the right of deduction is limited to 50% on purchase, import, lease or hire of passenger cars not wholly used for business purposes and on the related expenditures, except for cars purchased for resale, hire or lease, for cars used for the transportation of passengers (e.g. taxis) and for cars used for driving lessons.
Finland	**Entertainment:** representation and entertainment expenses. **Vehicles,** boats and aircraft: used for sporting and leisure purposes, cars, motorcycles and caravans. However, any means of transport which are to be resold, rented out or used in professional passenger transport or in driving lessons as well as passenger cars used only for taxable transactions are deductible. **Others:** travelling costs of personnel between home and workplace; goods and services related to dwellings or buildings provided for the recreation of personnel.

France	**Vehicles**: vehicles or equipment, whatever their nature, designed to carry persons or mixed-use, except those for resale as new; leased, having in addition to the driver's seat more than eight seats used by companies to bring their staff on the workplace, assigned exclusively to the driving instruction, all type of road vehicles exclusively for the operation of ski lifts and ski areas, vehicles acquired by companies of public passenger transport and assigned exclusively to the realisation of such transport. Components, parts and accessories of vehicles and machines previously referred. **Others:** goods and services used by taxable persons for more than 90% for a non-business purpose; gifts above a certain value; goods or services linked to the free supply of housing to officers or employees of a company, except when it's for the security staff on construction sites or in company premises; goods or services used for advertising alcoholic beverages; supply of passenger transport and services ancillary to such transport, except those produced either on behalf of an enterprise of public passenger transport, or under a permanent contract of transport by companies to bring their staff on the workplace; most fuels not subsequently delivered or sold as is or as other petroleum products. **Partial restrictions**: The right of deduction is limited to 50% for gas oil and other hydrocarbons in gaseous state and kerosene used as fuel, when such products are used for vehicles and equipment mentioned above. The right of deduction is limited to 20%. The right of deduction is limited to 80% for gas oils and bio ethanol E85 used as fuel for vehicles and equipment mentioned above, except those used for testing for the purposes of making engines of motorised equipment and insofar as they are not subsequently delivered or sold as is or as other petroleum products.
Germany	**Entertainment:** representation expenditures as defined in the income tax law for which there is no tax allowance according to the income tax law (e.g. gifts except small gifts, restaurant, catering, entertainment expenditure except appropriate ones, expenditures on hunting and fishing, sailing yacht or motor yachts and expenditures of similar nature).
Greece	**Entertainment:** receptions, recreation and hospitality in general; accommodation, food, drinks, transport and recreation for the personnel or representatives of the business. **Means of transport:** motor passenger vehicles of "private use" of up to 9 seats; motorcycles and mopeds, vessels and aircrafts of "private use" intended for recreation or sports, and the related supplies of fuel, repair, maintenance, rental/leasing and circulation in general. The restriction does not apply to the aforementioned means of transport when they are intended for sale, rental/leasing or transport of persons for a fare. **Others:** manufactured tobacco products, spirituous or alcoholic beverages intended to be used in non-taxable activities.
Hungary	**Entertainment**: services of restaurants and other public catering services; entertainment services; food and beverages. Vehicles: passenger cars (except hearses), motorcycles above 125 cubic centimetres; yachts and vessels. **Others**: supplies of motor fuels, other fuels, other goods used in connection with the operation or maintenance of passenger cars; residential properties, goods and services used for the construction or remodelling of residential properties; taxi services, parking services, highway toll services; 30% of input tax regarding fixed phone, mobile phone and VOIP service; 50% of input tax regarding the services used for the operation or maintenance of passenger cars.
Iceland	**Entertainment**: all expenses related to catering and food for the taxable person. Vehicles: supply, running and rental of passenger cars; delivery trucks, trucks and off-road vehicles with a weight of 5.000 kg or less, unless used for specially regulated taxable purpose. **Others**: all expenses related to residential property for the owner and the employees of the taxable person. All expenses which come instead of salaries to the owner and the employees of the taxable person. All expenses related to summer houses and similar entertainment for the owner and the employees of the taxable person; presents.
Ireland	**Entertainment:** food, drink, accommodation (except for qualifying conferences), personal services, entertainment. **Vehicles:** purchase or hire of passenger vehicles (20% of the cost is allowed where the car meets certain conditions regarding business use and emission levels). **Others**: petrol (unless part of stock in trade).
Israel[2]	None
Italy	**Entertainment**: entertainment expenses, food and beverages. **Vehicles**: means of transport and services of transport (motor vehicles, aircraft and yachts) – for means of transport 60% of the input VAT is not deductible; passenger transport. **Others**: luxury goods and connected services, buildings.
Japan	None
Korea	**Entertainment**: entertainment expenses and similar expenditures. **Vehicles**: purchase and maintenance of non-business small automobiles

Latvia	**Entertainment**: 60 % shall not be deductible from the tax as input tax from the tax amount to be paid into the State budget for the goods acquired and services received for the representation needs. **Vehicles:** 50 % shall not be deductible from the tax as input tax from the tax amount to be paid into the State budget for an acquired, leased or imported passenger car the number of seats of which, not including the driver's seat, does not exceed eight seats, as well as the costs related to the maintenance of such car, including expenses for repair of the car and purchase of fuel. Fully non-deductible is the tax amount to be paid into the State budget for buying, renting and importing passenger car the number of seats of which, not including the driver's seat, does not exceed eight seats and value higher than EUR 50 000 (exclusive of VAT), as well as the costs related to the maintenance of such car, including expenses for repair of the car and purchase of fuel.
Lithuania	**Entertainment**: representation and entertainment expenditures as defined in the income tax law for which there is no tax allowance according to the income tax law. **Vehicles**: passenger cars (up to 8 passengers excluding driver), except in cases where the cars are supplied, leased, used for taxi services or where the cars are classified as special purpose vehicles
Luxembourg	**Entertainment**: not strictly business expenditures such as luxuries, entertainment or amusements.
Mexico	No restrictions list. The law establishes that deductions must come from goods and services that are "strictly indispensable" for the principal activity. The expenses deductible for VAT purposes must be deductible in terms of the Income Tax Law. The Income Tax Law has list of "Authorized deductions" for each type of regime.
Netherlands	**Entertainment**: restaurant services. Also certain representation and gift expenditures.
New Zealand	**Entertainment**: entertainment expenses are in effect only 50% deductible. Businesses may claim a full deduction when the goods and services are acquired and must annually calculate and repay the deemed 50% private portion.
Norway	**Entertainment**: catering and hiring of locations related to catering; entertainment expenses; the construction, maintenance, renting or operation of real property for accommodation or welfare needs. **Vehicles**: procurement, operation or maintenance of passenger vehicles. **Others**: works of art or antiques; accommodation of- and remuneration in kind to the owner, management, employees or pensioners of an enterprise; business gifts, goods and services for distribution for advertising purposes; cash payments above NOK 10 000 (USD 1040).
Poland	**Entertainment**: restaurant services and accommodation. **Vehicles**: limitation to 50% of the right to deduct VAT on the purchase, intra- Community acquisition, import, hire or lease of motor vehicles as well as VAT charged on expenditure related to those vehicles, where the vehicle is not entirely used for business purposes. **Others**: limitation to 50% of the right to deduct VAT on the purchase of motor fuels, fuel oil &and natural gas used by aforementioned vehicles.
Portugal	**Entertainment**: transport, accommodation or meals (except connected with conferences, seminars, fairs or exhibitions, which, under certain conditions, are deductible in 25% or 50%). Luxury and entertainment expenses. **Vehicles**: acquisition or hiring of light vehicles deemed to be used for non-business purposes, as well as pleasure boats, helicopters, aircrafts and motorcycles (except if intended for sale or constitute the core of the business activity). **Others**: fuel used in motor vehicles (other than gas oil, liquefied petroleum gas, natural gas and bio fuels, which are deductible at 50%; or fully deductible if used in certain heavy vehicles or tractors).
Slovak Republic	**Entertainment**: goods and services for the purposes of treat and entertainment **Others**: suspense items (Suspense items means expenses paid on behalf and for the account of the purchaser or the customer, which the supplier charges to the purchaser or the customer.
Slovenia	**Entertainment**: entertainment expenses (where entertainment expenses shall include only the costs of entertainment and amusement during business or social contacts); meals (including drinks) and accommodation expenses, except expenses incurred by taxable person in connection with these supplies in the ordinary course of his business. **Vehicles**: yachts and boats intended for sport and recreation; aircrafts other than those used for transport of passengers and goods, leasing, renting and resale. Passenger cars and motorcycles other than: vehicles used for transport of passengers and goods, leasing, renting and resale, vehicles used in driving schools for the provision of the driver's training program in accordance with the regulations in force and combined vehicles for carrying out an activity of a public line and special line transport, and special vehicles adapted exclusively for the transport of deceased people. **Others**: fuels, lubricants, spare parts and services which are closely linked to vehicles above.
Spain	**Entertainment:** access to shows and services of a recreational character; travel, accommodation and catering services, unless they are deductible as a cost in income taxes. **Others**: jewellery, gold and platinum objects, pearls, precious stones; food, drinks and tobacco; goods or services used as gifts to clients, employees or third parties;
Sweden	**Entertainment:** representation expenditures as defined in the income tax law for which there is no tax allowance according to the income tax law (costs of a maximum of a taxable amount of SEK 300 per person and occasion regarding restaurant services). **Vehicles:** cars with a weight of 3500 kg or less used for both taxable and non-taxable purposes unless the purpose is for taxi, car renting, car sales or driving school. Limitation to 50 % of the right to deduct VAT on the purchase of fuel used by those vehicles.

	Others: Expenses connected to a permanent residence.
Switzerland	None
Turkey	**Cars**: purchases of cars except when used by car renting companies **Others**: Missing and stolen stocks (excluding those lost due to fire in places of compelling reason declared by Ministry of Finance).
United Kingdom	**Entertainment**: business entertainment; in general terms the free provision of any hospitality to business contacts is not recoverable. The exception is where the entertainment is provided to non-UK customers. However, it is likely that if recovery is granted it would be off-set by a private use charge that would effectively cancel out any credit obtained. **Vehicles**: motor cars in general, except motor cars that are stock in trade (car dealers etc.); tools of the trade (driving schools etc.) or exclusively used for business purposes with no availability for private use (leasing companies etc.); lease of a motor car (right to deduction is limited to 50%).

1. Restrictions to the right to deduct VAT on specific inputs: the table includes limitations of the right to deduct input VAT on specific goods, services and intangibles because of their nature, generally with a view to achieving the (input) taxation of their deemed final consumption. The table does not include input tax blockings related to the exemption of outputs (e.g. limited right of deduction for inputs used to provide financial and insurance services, medical care, education, etc. listed in Annex Table 2.A.3 on VAT exemptions) or to VAT inputs that are not connected with the business taxable activity.

2. Israel: the statistical data for Israel are supplied by and under the responsibility of the relevant Israeli authorities. The use of such data by the OECD is without prejudice to the status of the Golan Heights, East Jerusalem and Israeli settlements in the West Bank under the terms of international law.

Source: National delegates; position as at 1 January 2018.

Annex Table 2.A.5. Annual turnover concessions for VAT registration and collection

	National currency	Registration/collections thresholds[1]					Voluntary registration or collection[2]	Minimum registration period[3]	Limitations or specific rules for application of the thresholds[5]
		Registration or collection threshold	General threshold		Other thresholds				
			Nat. Curr.	USD[4]	Nat. Curr.	USD[4]			
Australia*	AUD	R	75 000	50 951	150 000	101 902	Yes	1 year	See note
Austria[6]	EUR	R	30 000	37 457			Yes	5 years	
Belgium[6]*	EUR	C	25 000	31 109			Yes	None	See note
Canada*	CAD	R	30 000	23 976	50 000	39960	Yes	1 year	See note
Chile*	CLP	None	None						See note
Czech Republic[6]	CZK	R	1 000 000	76 297			Yes	1 year	
Denmark[6]*	DKK	R	50 000	6 908	170 000 300 000	23 486 41 446	Yes	2 years	See note
Estonia[6]	EUR	R	40 000	72 612			Yes	None	
Finland[6]*	EUR	R	10 000	11 062	30 000	33 187	Yes	None	See note
France[6]*	EUR	R	82 800	103 913	33 200 42 900	41 666 53 839	Yes	2 years	See note
Germany[6]*	EUR	C	17 500	22 436	50 000	64 161	Yes	5 years	See note
Greece[6]*	EUR	C	10 000	16 711			Yes	1 year	See note
Hungary[6]	HUF	C	8 000 000	57 602			Yes	1 year	
Iceland	ISK	R	2 000 000	14 202			Yes	None	
Ireland[6]*	EUR	R	75 000	92 218	37 500	46 109	Yes	None	
Israel*	ILS	C	99 003	26 132			No	None	See note
Italy[6]*	EUR	C	65 000	90 381	50 000	69 524	Yes	None	See note
Japan*	JPY	R	10 000 000	100 408			Yes	1 year	See note
Korea	KRW	C	24 000 000	27 364			No	None	
Latvia[6]	EUR	R	40 000	79 774			Yes	None	
Lithuania[6]*	EUR	R	45 000	97 563			Yes	None	See note
Luxembourg[6]*	EUR	C	30 000	33 690			Yes	None	See note
Mexico	MXN	None	None						
Netherlands[6]*	EUR	C	1 345	1 650	1 883	2 296	No	None	See note
New Zealand	NZD	R	60 000	40 813			Yes	None	
Norway*	NOK	R	50 000	4 917	3 000 000 140 000	295 002 13 767	Yes	2 years	See note
Poland[6]	PLN	R	200 000	111 215			Yes	None	See note
Portugal[6]*	EUR	C	10 000	16 886	12 500	21 108	Yes	None	See note
Slovak Republic[6]	EUR	R	49 790	100 753			Yes	1 year	
Slovenia[6]	EUR	R	50 000	83 257			Yes	5 years	
Spain[6]	EUR	None	None						
Sweden[6]	SEK	R	30 000	3 297			Yes	3 years	See note
Switzerland*	CHF	R	100 000	81 953	150 000	122 930	Yes	1 year	See note
Turkey	TRY	None	None						
United Kingdom[6]	GBP	R	85 000	119 167			Yes	None	

* See country notes

1. Registration/collection thresholds identified in this table are general concessions that relieve domestic suppliers from the requirement to register for and/or to collect VAT until such time as they exceed the threshold. Except where specifically identified, registration thresholds also relieve suppliers from the requirement to charge and collect VAT on supplies made within a particular jurisdiction. Relief from collection and/or registration may be available to specific industries or types of traders (for example non-resident suppliers) under more detailed rules, or a specific industry or type of trader may be subject to more stringent registration and collection requirements. The "R" indicates countries where a registration threshold applies, i.e. where suppliers having a turnover below the threshold are not required to register for VAT and are relieved from any VAT obligation. The "C" indicates countries where a collection threshold applies, i.e. where all suppliers are required to register for VAT but are not required to charge and collect VAT until they exceed the collection threshold. Thresholds shown in this table apply to businesses established in the relevant country. In most countries, the registration threshold does not apply to foreign businesses, i.e. businesses having no seat, place of business, fixed establishment, domicile or habitual residence within the country.
2. "Yes" means a supplier is allowed to voluntarily register and collect VAT where its total annual turnover is less than the registration threshold.
3. Minimum registration/collection periods apply to general concessions. This period is the minimum term during which the concession is applied to taxpayers that have opted for it.
4. Exchange rates for conversion into USD are Purchase Parity Rates (PPPs) for GDP.
5. Restrictions or conditions to the application of the tax relief for businesses below the threshold
6. Limitations for member states of the European Union. Directive 2006/112/EC excludes from the application of the threshold the supply of new buildings or building land, certain supplies of new means of transport and disposals of the assets of the enterprise. The threshold does not apply to non-resident businesses and to supplies taxable under the EU Mini One Stop Shop (MOSS).
Source: National delegates; position as at 1 January 2018.

StatLink https://doi.org/10.1787/888933890103

Country notes to Annex Table 2.A.5

Australia. For taxi drivers, including chauffeur driven limousines and hire cars, there is no registration threshold; they must register and account for GST on any supplies made. The applicable registration threshold to not-for-profit organisations is AUD 150 000.

Belgium. The registration threshold for Belgium does not apply to several sectors: real estate; hotels and restaurants; sale of used and waste materials. A number of specific supplies are also excluded from the application of the threshold: several supplies of new real estate, supplies of certain products subject to excise duties and undeclared and illicit activities.

Canada. The registration threshold does not apply to certain selected listed financial institutions, non-residents who enter Canada to make taxable supplies of admissions to a place of amusement, a seminar, an activity or an event, and persons who carry on a taxi or limousine business (which include a commercial ride-sharing business). These persons are required to register for and collect GST/HST. An alternative threshold applies to charities and public institutions. A charity or public institution is not required to register if either its revenue from worldwide taxable supplies is CAD 50 000 or less in a calendar quarter and over the last four consecutive calendar quarters, or its gross revenue in either of its two preceding fiscal years is CAD 250 000 or less.

Chile. All taxpayers are required to register and obtain a taxpayers' identification number that not only serves for VAT purposes but for all types of taxes. However, small businesses, craftsman and small service providers can be subject to a special regime according to which they account for output VAT a monthly fixed amount based on the average level of income for the last 12 months, which cannot exceed 20 Monthly Tax Units (CLP 940 380 - USD 1 530). This simplified tax regime does not apply to legal entities but only to individuals. This system must be adopted for at least for 12 months after which the taxpayer can return back to the ordinary regime.

Czech Republic. A taxable person that is not established in the Czech Republic should register immediately once he starts to provide any taxable supply within the territory of the country, except for supplies being subject to the reverse charge mechanism or to the mini one-stop shop (MOSS).

Denmark. A higher threshold of DKK 170 000 (EUR 22 840) applies to the blind, and a threshold of DKK 300 000 (EUR 40 300) applies to the first sale of works of art by their creator or his successors in title. For the purposes of the latter exemption, the threshold of DKK 300 000 must not have been exceeded in the current or preceding year.

Finland. Where a business has exceeded the registration threshold of EUR 10 000, it must register and is subject to VAT, but a graduated relief is available until they reach a second threshold of EUR 30 000.

France. The VAT relief applies to businesses whose annual turnover does not exceed EUR 82 800 or when their turnover does has not exceeded EUR 91 000 the preceding calendar year (when the turnover has not exceeded EUR 82 800 the penultimate year). For supplies of services (except hotel accommodation and food and drink in restaurants), the annual turnover must not exceed EUR 33 200 or EUR 35 200 the preceding calendar year (when the turnover has not exceeded EUR 33 200 the penultimate year). For lawyers (in the furtherance of their regulated business), writers and artists, the turnover must not exceed EUR 42 900 (the threshold is EUR 17 500 for their supplies outside the normal framework of their affairs). Experimentally, for a period of five years, a specific threshold of EUR 100000 has been implemented in Guadeloupe, Martinique and La Réunion.

Germany. Taxpayers are relieved from VAT obligations if their annual turnover does not exceed EUR 17 500 and their expected turnover for the current calendar year will not exceed EUR 50 000.

Greece. If the annual turnover is less than EUR 10 000, the business can voluntarily at the beginning of the following year enter the Special Scheme for small businesses under which no VAT is collected. Yet each new business has to register and collect VAT during the first administrative period regardless of its asset or equity size, legal status etc. In case the first administrative period is less than a year, the annual turnover is calculated on a proportional basis for the purposes of the application of the Special Scheme the next year. Each small business entering the Special Scheme has to remain in this scheme for two years. Farmers under the flat-rate scheme are not eligible to enter the Special Scheme for small businesses. From 1 January 2019 onwards, only taxable supplies will be taken into account for the threshold of EUR 10 000. New businesses will be able to enter the Special Scheme upon registration. Small businesses that have entered the Special Scheme will be obliged to enter the "normal" scheme and collect VAT from the moment they perform a taxable supply on account of which they exceed the threshold (and for the full value of that supply); minimum period of 2 years in the Special Scheme abolished.

Ireland. While the general turnover threshold for the supply of goods is EUR 75 000, persons supplying goods liable at the reduced or standard rates which they have manufactured or produced from zero-rated materials must register if their turnover is EUR 37 500 or more. While the general turnover threshold for the supply of services is EUR 37 500, for persons supplying both goods and services where 90% or more of the turnover is derived from supplies of goods (other than of the kind referred to in the previous sentence) then the threshold for Goods applies.

Israel. Self-employed persons with annual revenue below NIS 99 003 are considered "Exempt Dealers". Some professions are not allowed to be Exempt Dealers: agronomist, architect, technician, private investigator, rabbinical attorney, dental technician, organizational consultant, management consultant, scientific consultant, economist, engineer, surveyor, bookkeeper, translator, insurance agent, lawyer, accountant or appraiser, chemical or medical laboratory owner, artistes, various others in show business, doctor, psychologist, physiotherapist, veterinary surgeon, dentist, driving school owner, school owner, real estate agent or dealer. The statistical data for Israel are supplied by and under the responsibility of the relevant Israeli authorities. The use of such data by the OECD is without prejudice to the status of the Golan Heights, East Jerusalem and Israeli settlements in the West Bank under the terms of international law.

Italy. The micro-sized taxpayers' scheme ("Regime forfetario") applies to small businesses that have a turnover up to a certain threshold, comprised between EUR 25 000 or 50 000 (depending on the activity) and whose costs have not exceeded the threshold fixed by law. It notably involves the exemption from VAT (excluded taxpayers subject to reverse charge mechanism). The regime does not apply to persons who are members of partnerships, professional associations or SRLs (limited liability companies) and are subject to the "regime di trasparenza" for income tax; persons who carry out sale of buildings or land or intra-EU supplies of new cars and trucks. Are also excluded foreign businesses not established in Italy, except for those who are established in one of the EU Member States, or in a State party of the European Economic Area, and produce in Italy at least 75 percent of their total revenue.

Japan. Domestic and foreign businesses (both companies and individuals) whose taxable sales in Japan are less than 10 million yen, as well as new businesses of up to 2 years (except for the subsidiary of a certain large corporation) are exempt from JCT return. Exempted businesses can opt to be liable for Consumption Tax, in which case they shall remain liable for at least two years.

Luxembourg. Taxpayers established in Luxembourg are entitled to opt for the special scheme; the exemption only applies to goods and services supplied in Luxembourg. Taxpayers can opt out of the special scheme but have then to apply the normal VAT rules for at least five years.

Netherlands. The VAT relief threshold applies to individuals or associated groups of individuals (e.g. partnerships) but excluding corporate businesses. The threshold is not determined with reference to the turnover but on the net annual VAT due: where the total amount of VAT (output tax less input tax) due for a calendar year on supplies of goods and services does not exceed EUR 1 345, the taxpayer is exempt from VAT (but still has to register as a VAT taxpayer). If the annual VAT due is more than EUR 1 345 but less than EUR 1 883, the taxpayer gets a partial VAT rebate.

Norway. The higher threshold of NOK 3 000 000 applies for admission to sporting events. The higher threshold of NOK 140 000 applies to charitable institutions and organisations.

Poland. The registration threshold does not apply to taxpayers supplying (a) certain types of silver, gold, platinum, knives, cutlery, jewelry, non-hazardous metal waste, museum collections and coins; (b) goods subject to excise duty with a number of exceptions; (c) certain buildings, structures and their parts; (d) building land; (e) new means of transport. The threshold does also not apply to taxpayers supplying (a) legal services; (b) consulting and expert services with certain exceptions; (c) jeweler services and taxpayers not established in Poland.

Portugal. The collection threshold does not apply to commercial legal entities. For small retailers that fulfil some specific conditions the collection threshold is EUR 12 500.

Sweden. The threshold does not apply to taxable persons not established in Sweden, taxable persons voluntarily registered for VAT for rental of immovable property, trade with investment gold and artists.

Switzerland. The thresholds refer to the worldwide turnover. The higher threshold of CHF 150 000 applies to non-for-profit sport and cultural associations and to public interest institutions.

Annex Table 2.A.6. Usage of margin schemes

	Usage of margin schemes[1]
Australia	A margin scheme can be used on certain sales of new residential or commercial property. It is generally based on the difference between the tax inclusive sale price and the original purchase price. Special rules apply in certain cases, such as sales between associates or members of the same GST group. Gambling: GST applies to the gambling margin calculated based on the total amount wagered less total monetary prizes awarded. Second hand goods when second-hand dealers adopt a special 'global' accounting method. It applies when (1) second-hand goods are acquired from an unregistered supplier and are divided up for re-supply and (2) the dealer exercises the option to apply the global method over a specified category of second-hand good.
Austria	Travel agencies; second-hand goods, works of art, collector's items and antiques (EU Directive)
Belgium	Travel agencies; second-hand goods, works of art, collector's items and antiques (EU Directive)
Canada	-
Chile	Used real estate property in which no value added tax has been paid, made by a professional seller. The tax base is the difference between the sale and purchase prices. For these purposes, the acquisition value of the property must be readjusted in accordance with the variation percentage experienced by the consumer price index in the period between the month prior to the acquisition and the month prior to the sale date. However, in the determination of the referred tax base, the value of the land included in both operations must be deducted from the purchase price and the sale price. For these purposes, the seller may deduct from the sale price as the maximum value assigned to the land, the commercial value of it at the date of the operation. Once this deduction has been made, the seller must deduct from the purchase price of the property an amount equivalent to the percentage that represents the commercial value assigned to the land in the sale price.
Czech Republic	Travel agencies; second- hand goods; works of art; collector's items and antiques (EU Directive)
Denmark	Travel agencies; second-hand goods, works of art, collector's items and antiques (EU Directive)
Estonia	Travel agencies; second-hand goods, works of art, collector's items and antiques (EU Directive)
Finland	Travel agencies; second-hand goods, works of art, collector's items and antiques (EU Directive)
France	Travel agencies; second-hand goods, works of art, collector's items and antiques (EU Directive); real estate agents.
Germany	Travel agencies; second-hand goods, works of art, collector's items and antiques (EU Directive)
Greece	Travel agencies; second-hand goods, works of art, collector's items and antiques (EU Directive); sales by public auction (using the relevant option of the EU VAT Directive for member states)
Hungary	Travel agencies; second-hand goods; works of art, antiques, collectors' items (EU Directive)
Iceland	-
Ireland	Optional margin scheme for antiques, works of art and second hand goods (EU Directive). Mandatory margin scheme for auctioneers and travel agents.
Israel[2]	Sale of used furniture by a dealer whose business is the sale of such furniture; Sale of used vehicle, motorcycle or cross-country vehicle by a dealer whose business is a purchase and sale of used vehicles; Sale of dwellings by a real estate dealer who acquired it from a person who is not a non-profit organisation, a financial institution nor a dealer. Sale of coins and medals, which the seller has purchased such coins and medals from a non-licensed dealer (i.e. not VAT registered business). Sale of postage stamps and revenue stamps by a person whose business is the sale of such stamps (deemed to be a service). Sale of foreign currency, securities or other negotiable instruments, including the acquisition of aforesaid securities and instruments in order to collect their redemption or retirement price, by a dealer whose business is the sale of such assets or the sale of foreign currency, shall be deemed to be a brokerage service rendered by the dealer, between the dealer's supplier and the dealer's customer.
Italy	Travel agencies; second-hand goods, works of art, collector's items and antiques (EU Directive)
Japan	-
Korea	-
Latvia	Travel agencies; second-hand goods, works of art, collector's items and antiques (EU Directive)
Lithuania	Travel agencies; second-hand goods, works of art, collector's items and antiques (EU Directive)
Luxembourg	Travel agencies; second-hand goods, works of art, collector's items and antiques (EU Directive)
Mexico	Sale of used cars, previously acquired by a company from an individual
Netherlands	Travel agencies; second-hand goods, works of art, collector's items and antiques (EU Directive)
New Zealand	-
Norway	Voluntary margin scheme for second hand goods, works of art, collectors' items and antiques.

Poland	Travel agencies; second-hand goods; works of art; collector's items and antiques (EU Directive).
Portugal	Travel agencies; second-hand goods, works of art, collector's items and antiques (EU Directive) and fuel retailers.
Slovak Republic	Travel agencies; second-hand goods, works of art, collector's items and antiques (EU Directive)
Slovenia	Travel agencies; second-hand goods, works of art, collector's items and antiques (EU Directive)
Spain	Travel agencies; second-hand goods, works of art, collector's items and antiques (EU Directive)
Sweden	Travel agencies; second-hand goods, works of art, collector's items and antiques (EU Directive)
Switzerland	Collector's items such as works of art, antiques and suchlike.
Turkey	Travel agencies (commission taken from tour sold abroad is exempt; commission taken from tour sold in Turkey is subject to tax.) Deliveries of second hand motor vehicles or immovable properties (without making any fundamental changes in their nature) by taxpayers that are in second hand motor vehicles or immovable property business after purchasing them from non-VAT-Taxpayers (including purchases from taxpayers in the scope of exemption).
United Kingdom	Travel agencies; second-hand goods, works of art, collector's items and antiques (EU Directive)

1. Margin scheme: In this context, a margin scheme means a scheme where the tax base is calculated on the difference between the price paid by the taxpayer for an item and the resale price rather than on the full selling price. The reseller is not allowed to deduct the input VAT embedded in the buying price of the items resold under the margin scheme.

2. Israel: The statistical data for Israel are supplied by and under the responsibility of the relevant Israeli authorities. The use of such data by the OECD is without prejudice to the status of the Golan Heights, East Jerusalem and Israeli settlements in the West Bank under the terms of international law.

Source: national delegates; position as at 1 January 2018.

Annex Table 2.A.7. VAT Revenue Ratio (VRR)

Country	Standard VAT rate 2016	1976	1980	1984	1988	1992	1996	2000	2005	2006	2007	2008	2009	2010	2011	2012	2013	2014	2015	2016	Difference 2014 - 2016
Australia	10.0								0.56	0.54	0.54	0.49	0.51	0.49	0.47	0.47	0.49	0.48	0.50	0.50	0.01
Austria	20.0	0.66	0.65	0.64	0.62	0.61	0.60	0.61	0.58	0.57	0.58	0.59	0.58	0.58	0.58	0.59	0.58	0.58	0.59	0.60	0.01
Belgium	21.0	0.56	0.60	0.49	0.52	0.49	0.46	0.50	0.50	0.50	0.51	0.48	0.46	0.48	0.48	0.48	0.47	0.47	0.47	0.48	0.00
Canada	5.0					0.43	0.47	0.49	0.50	0.47	0.51	0.49	0.49	0.49	0.48	0.47	0.47	0.47	0.48	0.47	0.00
Chile	19.0					0.63	0.67	0.64	0.67	0.64	0.68	0.71	0.60	0.63	0.64	0.65	0.64	0.64	0.64	0.64	0.00
Czech Republic	21.0						0.42	0.42	0.56	0.52	0.54	0.56	0.55	0.53	0.55	0.57	0.57	0.58	0.59	0.60	0.02
Denmark	25.0	0.63	0.60	0.60	0.60	0.56	0.57	0.59	0.62	0.64	0.65	0.61	0.58	0.57	0.58	0.59	0.57	0.57	0.57	0.60	0.02
Estonia	20.0						0.73	0.72	0.70	0.81	0.80	0.67	0.73	0.67	0.67	0.69	0.66	0.70	0.73	0.73	0.03
Finland	24.0						0.54	0.61	0.60	0.61	0.60	0.58	0.56	0.55	0.56	0.56	0.55	0.54	0.53	0.54	0.00
France	20.0	0.65	0.69	0.62	0.62	0.53	0.53	0.51	0.52	0.52	0.51	0.50	0.47	0.48	0.48	0.48	0.48	0.48	0.49	0.49	0.00
Germany	19.0	0.55	0.56	0.51	0.49	0.61	0.60	0.60	0.54	0.56	0.54	0.55	0.55	0.54	0.55	0.55	0.54	0.55	0.56	0.56	0.01
Greece	23.0				0.46	0.47	0.43	0.49	0.47	0.46	0.48	0.46	0.39	0.44	0.37	0.37	0.36	0.37	0.38	0.44	0.07
Hungary	27.0					0.30	0.43	0.52	0.48	0.55	0.58	0.56	0.62	0.52	0.52	0.52	0.52	0.56	0.60	0.57	0.01
Iceland	24.0					0.63	0.54	0.59	0.62	0.64	0.59	0.52	0.45	0.43	0.44	0.45	0.45	0.46	0.52	0.55	0.09
Ireland	23.0	0.30	0.21	0.44	0.42	0.45	0.52	0.61	0.66	0.67	0.63	0.55	0.46	0.47	0.46	0.44	0.45	0.48	0.48	0.50	0.01
Israel	17.0						0.66	0.62	0.62	0.62	0.66	0.64	0.65	0.65	0.65	0.64	0.64	0.63	0.62	0.63	0.01
Italy	22.0	0.44	0.42	0.38	0.40	0.37	0.39	0.43	0.39	0.41	0.41	0.39	0.36	0.40	0.40	0.38	0.37	0.37	0.38	0.38	-0.01
Japan	8.0					0.68	0.71	0.68	0.70	0.70	0.68	0.66	0.66	0.68	0.68	0.68	0.69	0.69	0.73	0.71	0.02
Korea	10.0					0.64	0.58	0.59	0.64	0.63	0.63	0.63	0.65	0.67	0.67	0.69	0.67	0.69	0.64	0.70	0.00
Latvia	21.0							0.51	0.57	0.60	0.61	0.49	0.38	0.42	0.42	0.46	0.49	0.51	0.52	0.55	0.05
Lithuania	21.0						0.46	0.52	0.52	0.55	0.61	0.58	0.47	0.49	0.51	0.50	0.50	0.50	0.51	0.51	0.00
Luxembourg	17.0	0.59	0.61	0.64	0.66	0.45	0.55	0.69	0.86	0.83	0.95	0.95	0.96	0.99	1.06	1.11	1.17	1.25	0.96	0.92	-0.33
Mexico	16.0		0.33	0.27	0.25	0.30	0.21	0.25	0.29	0.32	0.32	0.33	0.30	0.32	0.31	0.31	0.28	0.32	0.32	0.33	0.01
Netherlands	21.0	0.47	0.51	0.49	0.54	0.55	0.54	0.57	0.55	0.57	0.58	0.56	0.52	0.54	0.52	0.52	0.47	0.47	0.49	0.51	0.05
New Zealand	15.0				0.89	0.96	0.98	0.97	1.01	1.02	0.95	0.96	0.96	1.09	0.92	0.93	0.93	0.95	0.96	0.95	0.00
Norway	25.0	0.66	0.66	0.63	0.69	0.58	0.60	0.67	0.57	0.61	0.63	0.57	0.54	0.56	0.56	0.57	0.57	0.56	0.56	0.57	0.00
Poland	23.0						0.42	0.42	0.47	0.51	0.53	0.50	0.45	0.47	0.47	0.43	0.42	0.44	0.44	0.44	0.01
Portugal	23.0				0.45	0.49	0.55	0.60	0.56	0.51	0.51	0.49	0.43	0.48	0.45	0.47	0.46	0.49	0.50	0.49	0.01

Slovak Republic	20.0						0.48	0.44	0.60	0.57	0.52	0.53	0.47	0.46	0.48	0.43	0.46	0.49	0.51	0.50	-0.01
Slovenia	22.0							0.67	0.66	0.68	0.69	0.68	0.59	0.59	0.59	0.58	0.60	0.59	0.59	0.58	0.02
Spain	21.0				0.57	0.60	0.44	0.52	0.56	0.56	0.53	0.43	0.31	0.45	0.39	0.40	0.39	0.41	0.43	0.43	0.03
Sweden	25.0	0.44	0.40	0.38	0.40	0.41	0.50	0.53	0.55	0.56	0.57	0.58	0.57	0.59	0.58	0.56	0.56	0.57	0.58	0.60	-0.02
Switzerland	8.0						0.67	0.73	0.72	0.74	0.73	0.74	0.70	0.72	0.71	0.71	0.71	0.70	0.69	0.68	0.00
Turkey	18.0				0.45	0.44	0.43	0.46	0.40	0.42	0.38	0.37	0.36	0.41	0.44	0.40	0.44	0.40	0.42	0.40	0.00
United Kingdom	20.0	0.42	0.41	0.44	0.48	0.43	0.43	0.44	0.43	0.44	0.44	0.42	0.42	0.43	0.43	0.43	0.43	0.43	0.44	0.44	0.01
Unweighted average	19.1	0.53	0.51	0.50	0.53	0.52	0.53	0.56	0.58	0.59	0.59	0.57	0.54	0.55	0.55	0.54	0.55	0.55	0.55	0.56	0.01

Note: **Calculation formula:** VRR = VAT Revenue/[(Consumption - VAT revenue) x standard VAT rate]. Consumption = Final Consumption Expenditure (Heading P3) in national accounts. VAT rates used are standard rates applicable as at 1 January of each year.

Time series: Since data beyond 2016 is not available for all countries at the time of publication, VRR is not calculated after this date.

Canada: VRR Calculation includes federal VAT only.

Canada, Japan and New Zealand: Annual final consumption expenditure in national accounts was adjusted to ensure matching between the fiscal year for the VAT revenue and the civil year for final consumption figures.

Israel: The statistical data for Israel are supplied by and under the responsibility of the relevant Israeli authorities. The use of such data by the OECD is without prejudice to the status of the Golan Heights, East Jerusalem and Israeli settlements in the West Bank under the terms of international law. Although VAT was implemented in Israel in 1976, the VRR is only calculated from 1996 onwards since tax revenue figures are not available before that year.

Japan: given the substantial VAT rate hike on 1 April 2014, an average VAT rate was used to calculate the VRR for 2014 i.e. (5X3+8X9)/12=7.25%

Source: OECD.

StatLink https://doi.org/10.1787/888933890122

Annex Table 2.A.8. Mechanisms for collecting VAT on cross-border supplies of services and intangibles1 from non-resident suppliers ("inbound supplies")

Country	Regime for the collection of VAT on inbound supplies of services and intangibles by foreign suppliers[2]	Proxies for determining place of taxation[3]	Threshold4
Australia	**VAT collection mechanism**: ***B2C supplies***: the foreign supplier is required to register. Simplified "pay-only" registration and reporting is available; Full standard registration is allowed. ***B2B supplies***: the customer is liable to account for GST under the reverse-charge mechanism only if the business customer cannot claim a full GST credit. **Criteria for distinguishing B2C from B2B supplies:** Australian Business Number (ABN) of the customer; and a statement that the business is registered for GST **Supplies covered by the B2C rule**[3]: Inbound supplies of services and intangibles (anything other than goods or real property), including services such as architectural or legal services. **Implementation:** as of 1 July 2017	B2C: Customer's location B2B: Customer's tax residency status	AUD 75 000 (USD 58 537) Same as for domestic suppliers
Austria	European Union scheme (see below)		
Belgium	European Union scheme (see below)		
Canada	**VAT collection mechanism:** ***B2C and B2B supplies***: the customer is liable to account for GST under the reverse charge mechanism. For B2B supplies, the reverse-charge mechanism applies only if the customer cannot claim a full GST credit. **Criteria for distinguishing B2C from B2B supplies:** no distinction is made **Supplies covered**[4]: supplies of services and intangible properties **Implementation:** as of 1 January 1991	B2C and B2B: recipient's usual residence or location	Not applicable
Chile	**VAT collection mechanism:** ***B2C and B2B supplies***: the customer is liable to account for VAT under the reverse-charge mechanism **Criteria for distinguishing B2C from B2B supplies**: no distinction made **Supplies covered**[3]: selected services of a non-professional, consultancy and technical nature **Implementation**: as of 1975		No threshold
Czech Republic	European Union scheme (see below)		
Denmark	European Union scheme (see below)		
Estonia	European Union scheme (see below)		
Finland	European Union scheme (see below)		
France	European Union scheme (see below)		
Germany	European Union scheme (see below)		

Greece	European Union scheme (see below)		
Hungary	European Union scheme (see below)		
Iceland	**VAT collection mechanism**: ***B2C supplies***: the foreign supplier is required to register under standard registration procedure; no simplification is available. ***B2B supplies***: exempt if the customer has a full right of deduction. If not, the same procedure as for B2C supplies applies. **Criteria for distinguishing B2C from B2B supplies**: VAT registration number of the customer **Supplies covered**[3]: electronically supplied services and non-digital services such as services of consultants, lawyers, accountants and other similar specialised services. **Implementation**: 1 November 2011	B2C: customer's usual residence B2B: customer's location (permanent place of business)	ISK 2 million (USD 14 200) Same as for domestic suppliers
Ireland	European Union scheme (see below)		
Israel[5]	**VAT collection mechanism:** ***B2C supplies***: self-assessment by customer. ***B2B supplies***: reverse-charge mechanism applies. **Supplies covered**[3]**:** Services, including digital services. **Criteria for distinguishing B2C from B2B supplies:** VAT registration number of the customer. **Implementation:** 1 November 2011	**B2C and B2B**: the residence of the customer is in Israel or the supply is connected to an asset in Israel.	N.A.
Italy	European Union scheme (see below).		
Japan	**VAT collection mechanism:** ***B2C supplies***: the non-resident service provider, which does not maintain a branch or an office in Japan, must appoint a tax agent to register under the standard registration procedure. ***B2B supplies:*** reverse charge mechanism applies A foreign business shall notify its Japanese customers that they (customers) shall account for VAT under the reverse charge mechanism. **Criteria for distinguishing B2C from B2B supplies:** the nature of the services provided. **Supplies covered by B2C rule**[3]**:** "Electronic services" as defined by law (e.g. online e-books, online game, music movies, cloud services, Internet shopping or auction site). **Implementation:** 1 October 2015	**B2C and B2B:** the place where the customer is located (i.e., address or domicile for private customers and head office or principal office for businesses).	JPY 10 million (USD 95.000) Same as for domestic suppliers
Korea	**VAT collection mechanism:** ***B2C supplies:*** the foreign supplier is required to register. Simplified electronic registration is available; ("pay only" registration). ***B2B supplies:*** out of the scope. **Criteria for distinguishing B2C from B2B supplies:** the nature of the services provided. **Supplies covered by the B2C rule**[3]**:** "Electronic services" as defined by law (e.g. applications, games, music, films, electronic documents, software, etc.). **Implementation:** 1 July 2015	**B2C**: customer location **B2B:** not applicable	No threshold
Latvia	European Union scheme (see below)		
Lithuania	European Union scheme (see below)		
Luxembourg	European Union scheme (see below)		

Mexico	**VAT collection mechanism:** ***B2C supplies*:** final consumers are required to report transactions for statistical purposes. ***B2B supplies*:** the customer should self-assess the VAT (reverse-charge mechanism). **Criteria for distinguishing B2C from B2B supplies:** No distinction is made **Supplies covered[4]:** All services **Implementation:** 1980	**B2C and B2B:** Services: consumption or physical presence of the customer; Intangibles: residence of the acquirer or place of use	No threshold
Netherlands	European Union scheme (see below)		
New Zealand	**VAT collection mechanism:** ***B2C supplies***: the foreign supplier is required to register. Simplified electronic registration is available; ("pay only" registration). ***B2B supplies***: out of scope but if the purchaser's taxable supplies are mostly supplies that are exempt from GST (e.g. financial services) or the services are partly used for personal consumption a reverse-charge mechanism applies. **Supplies covered by the B2C rule[3]:** Remote services, including digital services such as e-books, music, videos and software downloads and non-digital services such as general insurance, consulting, accounting and legal services. **Criteria for distinguishing B2C from B2B supplies:** New Zealand GST registration number or business number. The Commissioner of Inland Revenue can prescribe or agree to an alternative method taking into account the nature of the supply; the value of the supply; and the terms and conditions of the provision of services. **Implementation:** 1 October 2016	**B2C:** customer's tax residence **B2B:** Customer's tax residence	NZD 60 000 (USD 41 000) Same as for domestic suppliers
Norway	**VAT collection mechanism:** ***B2C supplies***: the supplier must register for VAT. A simplified "pay only" registration (without tax representative) is available under a fully electronic procedure. Standard registration procedure (with right to deduct input tax) is also available. ***B2B supplies***: the reverse charge mechanism applies. **Supplies covered by the B2C rule[3]:** Telecommunication, radio and television broadcasting and electronically supplied services (TBE services). **Criteria for distinguishing B2C from B2B supplies:** VAT registration number of the customer **Implementation**: 1 July 2011	B2C: Customer's usual residence B2B: Customer's location	NOK 50 000 (USD 5 000) Same as for domestic suppliers
Poland	European Union scheme (see below)		
Portugal	European Union scheme (see below)		
Slovak Republic	European Union scheme (see below)		
Slovenia	European Union scheme (see below)		
Spain	European Union scheme (see below)		
Sweden	European Union scheme (see below)		
Switzerland*	**VAT collection mechanism:** ***B2C supplies***: the foreign supplier must register for VAT under the standard registration procedure (no simplified procedure is available; the appointment of a tax agent is required). ***B2B supplies***: most of the inbound supplies of services and intangibles are taxed under the reverse charge mechanism, unless the foreign supplier is registered for VAT (e.g. to account for B2C supplies).	B2C: Customer's usual residence B2B: Customer's location	CHF 100 000 (USD 101 000) The threshold refers to the global turnover of the supplier

	Supplies covered by the B2C rule[3]: Information and communication technology (ICT) services. **Criteria for distinguishing B2C from B2B supplies:** VAT registration number of the customer. **Implementation**: 1 January 2010		
Turkey	**VAT collection mechanism:** ***B2C supplies***: the supplier must register for VAT. A simplified registration (without tax representative) is available under a fully electronic procedure. VAT deduction is available. ***B2B supplies***: reverse-charge mechanism applies. **Supplies covered by the B2C rule**[3]: electronic services **Criteria for distinguishing B2C from B2B supplies**: VAT registration number of the customer **Implementation**: 1 January 2018	B2C: Customer's usual residence B2B: Customer's location	No threshold
United Kingdom	European Union scheme (see below)		
European Union	**VAT collection mechanism:** **B2C supplies**: the non-EU supplier can opt to register for VAT under the "One Stop Shop" mechanism. Through that mechanism, a simplified "pay only" registration (without tax representative) is available under a fully electronic procedure. **B2B supplies:** the reverse charge mechanism applies. **Criteria for distinguishing B2C from B2B supplies:** VAT registration number of the customer. **Supplies covered by the B2C rule**[3]**:** telecommunication, electronic and broadcasting services. **Implementation**: 2003: non-EU suppliers; 2015: intra-EU suppliers.	B2C: Customer's usual residence B2B: Customer's location	No threshold

1. In the context of this table:
"services and intangibles" refer to any supply of service or intangible by a non-resident supplier (with no establishment whatsoever in the customer's country).
"pay only registration" refers to a VAT registration regime for non-resident suppliers that seeks only the collection of VAT on inbound supplies of services and intangibles from these suppliers, without granting the right for these suppliers to deduct any VAT incurred in the taxing jurisdiction (although a refund or other relief procedure may be available).

2. The supplies covered in this table are those covered by the International VAT/GST Guidelines 3.1 to 3.4 and Guideline 3.6. Are therefore not covered in this table, the on-the sport supplies (Guideline 3.5), and supplies of services and intangibles subject to specific place of taxation rules including supplies directly connected to a specific immovable property, which are covered by Guidelines 3.7 and 3.8.

3. Some jurisdictions may limit the application of the International VAT/GST Guidelines 3.1 to 3.4 and/or Guideline 3.6 to certain categories of service supplies. Other place of taxation or VAT collection methods may therefore apply to supplies that are not covered by this definition.

4. The threshold applies for the registration of foreign suppliers in the jurisdiction of taxation. The amount in local currency is converted into USD according to the OECD Purchasing Power Parity price for GDP (PPPs). PPPs are the rates of currency conversion that equalise the purchasing power of different countries by eliminating differences in price levels between countries. They show the specified number of monetary units needed in each country to buy the same representative basket of consumer goods and services, which costs USD 1 in the United States. The currency conversion rates used in Consumption Tax Trends are the PPP rates for GDP (see Annex B).

5. The statistical data for Israel are supplied by and under the responsibility of the relevant Israeli authorities. The use of such data by the OECD is without prejudice to the status of the Golan Heights, East Jerusalem and Israeli settlements in the West Bank under the terms of international law.

Source: national delegates; position as at 1 January 2018.

Annex Table 2.A.9. Availability of VAT relief or refund to foreign taxpayers[1]

Jurisdiction	Availability of VAT relief/refund mechanism for foreign businesses	Approach	Reciprocity requirement	Availability of VAT deduction as part of the simplified registration and compliance regime[2]
Australia	Yes	Refund available for those registered other than as Limited Registration Entities	No	No ("pay-only" registration)
Austria	Yes	Refund available through direct refund mechanism (without registration or tax representative) or direct VAT registration: • Businesses established in the EU: refunds made under the terms of EU Directive 2008/9/EC; • Businesses established outside the EU: refunds made under the terms of the EU 13th Directive.	No	No ("pay-only" registration)
Belgium	Yes	Refund available through direct refund mechanism (without registration or tax representative) or direct VAT registration: • Businesses established in the EU: refunds made under the terms of EU Directive 2008/9/EC; • Businesses established outside the EU: refunds made under the terms of the EU 13th Directive.	No	No ("pay-only" registration)
Canada	Yes	Relief through zero-rating where appropriate. If not available, the following forms of relief may be available (facts and circumstances test): No VAT to be charged to a foreign business on an otherwise taxable supply of goods in Canada provided the supplier to the foreign business receives a "drop shipment certificate" from a VAT registered person who is physically receiving the goods; Allows a foreign business to "flow through" VAT paid on the importation of goods into Canada or paid to a VAT registered person to its VAT registered customer or supplier, who will in turn recover that VAT through its VAT returns.	No	N/A
Chile	No	N/A	N/A	N/A
Czech Republic	Yes	Refund available through direct refund mechanism (without registration or tax representative) or direct VAT registration: • Businesses established in the EU: refunds made under the terms of EU Directive 2008/9/EC; • Businesses established outside the EU: refunds made under the terms of the EU 13th Directive.	Yes: refunds are available only to businesses established in the EU and in countries that refund VAT to Czech businesses	No ("pay-only" registration)

Denmark	Yes	Refund available through direct refund mechanism (without registration or tax representative) or direct VAT registration: • Businesses established in the EU: refunds made under the terms of EU Directive 2008/9/EC; • Businesses established outside the EU: refunds made under the terms of the EU 13th Directive.	No	No ("pay-only" registration)
Estonia	Yes	Refund available through direct refund mechanism (without registration or tax representative) or direct VAT registration: • Businesses established in the EU: refunds made under the terms of EU Directive 2008/9/EC; • Businesses established outside the EU: refunds made under the terms of the EU 13th Directive.	Yes: refunds are available only to businesses established in the EU and countries that refund VAT to Estonian businesses	No ("pay-only" registration)
Finland	Yes	Refund available through direct refund mechanism (without registration or tax representative) or direct VAT registration: • Businesses established in the EU: refunds made under the terms of EU Directive 2008/9/EC; • Businesses established outside the EU: refunds made under the terms of the EU 13th Directive.	No	No ("pay-only" registration)
France	Yes	Refund available through direct refund mechanism (without registration or tax representative) or direct VAT registration: • Businesses established in the EU: refunds made under the terms of EU Directive 2008/9/EC; • Businesses established outside the EU: refunds made under the terms of the EU 13th Directive.	No	No ("pay-only" registration)
Germany	Yes	Refund available through direct refund mechanism (without registration or tax representative) or direct VAT registration: • Businesses established in the EU: refunds made under the terms of EU Directive 2008/9/EC; • Businesses established outside the EU: refunds made under the terms of the EU 13th Directive.	Yes: refunds available only to businesses established in the EU, and in countries with which Germany has signed a reciprocity agreement	No ("pay-only" registration)
Greece	Yes	Refund available through direct refund mechanism (without registration or tax representative) or direct VAT registration: • Businesses established in the EU: refunds made under the terms of EU Directive 2008/9/EC (electronic-based system); • Businesses established outside the EU: refunds made under the terms of the EU 13th Directive (paper-based system).	Yes refunds available only to businesses established in the EU, Norway and Switzerland	No ("pay-only" registration)
Hungary	Yes	Refund available through direct refund mechanism (without registration or tax	Yes: refunds available only to business	No ("pay-only" registration).

		representative) or direct VAT registration: • Businesses established in the EU: refunds made under the terms of EU Directive 2008/9/EC; • Businesses established outside the EU: refunds made under the terms of the EU 13th Directive.	established in the EU, Liechtenstein, Switzerland and Norway	
Iceland	Yes	Refund available through direct refund mechanism (without registration or tax representative).	No	N/A
Ireland	Yes	Refund available through direct refund mechanism (without registration or tax representative) or direct VAT registration: • Businesses established in the EU: refunds made under the terms of EU Directive 2008/9/EC; • Businesses established outside the EU: refunds made under the terms of the EU 13th Directive.	No	No ("pay-only" registration).
Israel3	No	N/A	N/A	N/A
Italy	Yes	Refund available through direct refund mechanism (without registration or tax representative) or direct VAT registration: • Businesses established in the EU: refunds made under the terms of EU Directive 2008/9/EC; • Businesses established outside the EU: refunds made under the terms of the EU 13th Directive.	Yes: refunds available only to businesses established in the EU, Israel, Norway and Switzerland	No ("pay-only" registration)
Japan	Yes	A non-established business must appoint a resident tax representative and elect to be treated as a taxable business.	No	No
Korea	Yes	Refund available through direct refund mechanism (without registration or tax representative).	Yes: Refunds available only to businesses established in foreign countries on a reciprocal basis	Information not available
Latvia	Yes	Refund available through direct refund mechanism (without registration or tax representative) or direct VAT registration: • Businesses established in the EU: refunds made under the terms of EU Directive 2008/9/EC; • Businesses established outside the EU: refunds made under the terms of the EU 13th Directive.	Yes: refunds available only to businesses established in the EU and in countries that refund VAT to Latvian businesses.	No ("pay-only" registration)

Lithuania	Yes	Refund available through direct refund mechanism (without registration or tax representative) or direct VAT registration: • Businesses established in the EU: refunds made under the terms of EU Directive 2008/9/EC; • Businesses established outside the EU: refunds made under the terms of the EU 13th Directive.	Yes: refunds are available only to businesses established in the EU and in countries that refund VAT to Lithuanian businesses. Also refunds are available to businesses established in OECD member countries that do not have VAT or similar tax.	No ("pay-only" registration)[2]
Luxembourg	Yes	Refund available through direct refund mechanism (without registration or tax representative) or direct VAT registration: • Businesses established in the EU: refunds made under the terms of EU Directive 2008/9/EC; • Businesses established outside the EU: refunds made under the terms of the EU 13th Directive.	No	No ("pay-only" registration)
Mexico	No	N/A	N/A	N/A
Netherlands	Yes	Refund available through direct refund mechanism (without registration or tax representative) or direct VAT registration: • Businesses established in the EU: refunds made under the terms of EU Directive 2008/9/EC; • Businesses established outside the EU: refunds made under the terms of the EU 13th Directive.	No	No ("pay-only" registration)
New Zealand	Yes	Two approaches available in relation to international services: Zero-rate supplies to non-residents who are outside New Zealand at the time of performance; Zero-rate a range of other specific supplies. Since 1 April 2014, a non-established business that does not make taxable supplies in New Zealand may register for GST to recover GST incurred in New Zealand. The following rules will apply: (1) the non-established business must be registered for GST or VAT in its own country; (2) the GST refund resulting from the first GST return must be more than NZD 500; (3) the GST input tax credits only arise when the non-resident has paid for the expenditure; (4) The non-resident cannot form a New Zealand GST group with New Zealand resident entities unless the non-resident is registered for GST under the ordinary rules; (5) the non-resident must not be making supplies of services that are likely to be received by a person in New Zealand who is not registered for GST; (6) the tax authority will not be legally obliged to refund the GST until 90 days after the GST return has been lodged.	No	No ("pay-only" registration). However, foreign suppliers may elect to do a full registration allowing them to claim GST back on New Zealand-based costs.

Norway	Yes	Refund available through direct refund mechanism (without registration or tax representative).	No	No ("pay-only" registration)
Poland	Yes	Refund available through direct refund mechanism (without registration or tax representative) or direct VAT registration: • Businesses established in the EU: refunds made under the terms of EU Directive 2008/9/EC; • Businesses established outside the EU: refunds made under the terms of the EU 13th Directive.	Yes: refunds available only to businesses established in the EU and countries that refund VAT to Polish businesses	No ("pay-only" registration)
Portugal	Yes	Refund available through direct refund mechanism: • Businesses established in the EU: refunds made under the terms of EU Directive 2008/9/EC; • Businesses established outside the EU: refunds made under the terms of the EU 13th Directive through the appointment of a VAT representative in Portugal.	Yes: refunds available only to businesses established in the EU and countries that refund VAT to Portuguese businesses	No ("pay-only" registration).
Slovak Republic	Yes	Refund available through direct refund mechanism (without registration or tax representative) or direct VAT registration: • Businesses established in the EU: refunds made under the terms of EU Directive 2008/9/EC; • Businesses established outside the EU: refunds made under the terms of the EU 13th Directive.	Yes: refunds available only to businesses established in the EU and countries that refund VAT to Slovakian businesses	No ("pay-only" registration)
Slovenia	Yes	Refund available through direct refund mechanism (without registration or tax representative) or direct VAT registration: • Businesses established in the EU: refunds made under the terms of EU Directive 2008/9/EC; • Businesses established outside the EU: refunds made under the terms of the EU 13th Directive.	Yes: refunds available only to businesses established in the EU and countries that refund VAT to Slovenian businesses	No ("pay-only" registration)
Spain	Yes	Refund available through direct refund mechanism (without registration or tax representative) or direct VAT registration: • Businesses established in the EU: refunds made under the terms of EU Directive 2008/9/EC; • Businesses established outside the EU: refunds made under the terms of the EU 13th Directive.	Yes: refunds available only to businesses established in the EU, Canada, Israel, Japan, Monaco, Norway and Switzerland through an appointment of a VAT representative in Spain	No ("pay-only" registration)

Sweden	Yes	Refund available through direct refund mechanism (without registration or tax representative) or direct VAT registration: • Businesses established in the EU: refunds made under the terms of EU Directive 2008/9/EC; • Businesses established outside the EU: refunds made under the terms of the EU 13th Directive. Non-established businesses may claim Swedish VAT to the same extent as VAT-registered businesses (effective as of 1 January 2010).	No	No ("pay-only" registration)
Switzerland	Yes	Switzerland refunds VAT incurred by businesses that are neither established nor registered for VAT in Switzerland or Liechtenstein and that have not made any supplies in Switzerland or Liechtenstein (subject to supplies that are exempt from the tax, services whose place of supply is the place of the recipient or supplies of electricity in cables, gas via the natural gas distribution network and district heating to persons liable to the tax on Swiss territory).	Yes Refunds are made on the condition of reciprocity	N/A
Turkey	Yes	Refund available through direct refund mechanism (without registration or tax representative) for certain transactions.	Yes (partially dependent on reciprocity)	Yes
United Kingdom	Yes	Refund available through direct refund mechanism (without registration or tax representative) or direct VAT registration: Businesses established in the EU: refunds made under the terms of EU Directive 2008/9/EC; Businesses established outside the EU: refunds made under the terms of the EU 13th Directive.	No	No ("pay-only" registration)

1. The VAT relief or refund mechanisms presented in this table do not include the mechanisms associated with the exports of goods.

2. The absence of input VAT deduction availability for foreign suppliers as part of the simplified registration and compliance regime generally does not prevent such foreign suppliers from exercising the right to obtain a relief of this input VAT under the standard procedure. For example, in the EU foreign suppliers registered under the MOSS can still apply for VAT refunds under the terms of the EU 13th Directive.

3. The statistical data for Israel are supplied by and under the responsibility of the relevant Israeli authorities. The use of such data by the OECD is without prejudice to the status of the Golan Heights, East Jerusalem and Israeli settlements in the West Bank under the terms of international law.

Source: national delegations; position as at 1 January 2018.

Annex Table 2.A.10. VAT relief for imports of low-value goods[1]

Country	Currency	Threshold in Local currency[2]	Threshold in USD[3]
Australia*	AUD	1 000	679
Austria	EUR	22	27
Belgium	EUR	22	27
Canada	CAD	20	16
Chile	CLP	0	0
Czech Republic	EUR	22	43
Denmark	EUR	10	10
Estonia	EUR	22	40
Finland	EUR	22	24
France*	EUR	0	
Germany	EUR	22	28
Greece	EUR	22	37
Hungary	EUR	22	51
Iceland*	ISK	2 000	14
Ireland	EUR	22	27
Israel*	USD	75	75
Italy	EUR	22	31
Japan	JPY	10 000	100
Korea*	USD	150	150
Latvia	EUR	22	44
Lithuania	EUR	22	48
Luxembourg	EUR	22	25
Mexico*	USD	300/50	300/50
Netherlands	EUR	22	27
New Zealand*	NZD	400	272
Norway*	NOK	350	34
Poland*	EUR	22	52
Portugal	EUR	22	37
Slovak Republic	EUR	22	45
Slovenia	EUR	22	37
Spain	EUR	22	33
Sweden*	EUR	22	25
Switzerland*	CHF	65	53
Turkey	TRY	0	0
United Kingdom*	GBP	15	22

* See country notes

1. This table shows VAT collection thresholds for low value import items dispatched by a foreign supplier to a buyer in the given country. It does not cover other import scenarios such as imports of goods exchanged between private individuals or imports of goods in the personal luggage of travellers. Imports of excisable goods are generally excluded from the tax reliefs.

2. Amounts in local currency: for Member States of the European Union, the threshold is mentioned in Euro (EUR) even for those that do not have the Euro as national currency (i.e. Czech Republic, Denmark, Hungary, Poland and Sweden), with the exception of the United Kingdom. The threshold applied in EU countries is determined in EUR by common EU legislation (Directive 2009/132/EC). The amount in EUR is converted into USD as follows: it is first converted into local currency at market exchange rate (Eurostat average 2015) and then into USD at PPP exchange rate. For Israel, Korea and Mexico, the threshold is not provided in local currency in national legislation but in USD. Except stated otherwise in the country notes, the amount reflects the intrinsic value of the goods (excluding freight, insurance and other costs and taxes).

3. Amounts are converted into USD at Purchase Parity Rates (PPPs) for GDP (see Annex B).

Source: national delegates; position as at 1 January 2018.

StatLink https://doi.org/10.1787/888933891167

Country notes to Annex Table 2.A.10

Australia. The application of the GST will be extended to low value goods imported by consumers from 1 July 2018. Foreign suppliers that have an Australian turnover of AUD 75 000 or more of these goods (plus any other sales that are connected with Australia), will be required to register for collecting and remitting the GST for low value goods supplied to consumers in Australia, using a vendor registration model.

France. An exemption threshold of EUR 22 applies for imports of goods that are imported outside the conditions of the distance sales (mail order).

Iceland. The threshold applies only to the importation of goods via "express deliveries". An exemption threshold of ISK 1 500 applies to imports of goods by importers registered for VAT purposes in Iceland.

Israel. The threshold is given in USD in national legislation. The statistical data for Israel are supplied by and under the responsibility of the relevant Israeli authorities. The use of such data by the OECD is without prejudice to the status of the Golan Heights, East Jerusalem and Israeli settlements in the West Bank under the terms of international law.

Korea. The threshold is given in USD in national legislation. Postal parcels and express consignments are exempt if their value does not exceed USD 150 and the quantity is such that the customs authorities recognise the goods as for personal use.

Mexico. The threshold is given in USD in national legislation. The threshold is of USD 300 if the importation is made by the postal service and USD 50 if the importation is made by courier services.

New Zealand. The threshold is not based on the value of the goods but on the amount of tax. Customs duty and VAT are not levied if the amount of tax due is NZD 60 or less. For ease of comparison, the equivalent threshold under the standard GST rate without applicable customs duties is shown in the table above i.e. NZD 400 x 15% GST = NZD 60.

Norway. Freight and insurance costs are included in the value of the threshold.

Poland. The threshold does not apply to goods imported on mail order.

Sweden. The threshold does not apply to goods imported on mail order (including via digital platforms).

Switzerland. The threshold is not based on the value of the goods but on the amount of tax. VAT is not levied if the amount of tax due is CHF 5 or less per declaration. For ease of comparison, the equivalent threshold under the standard VAT rate is shown in the table above i.e. CHF 65 x 7.7% VAT = CHF 5. For goods taxed under the reduced rate of 2,5 % (e.g. books) the value of the threshold would be max. CHF 200 till the tax amount of 5 CHF is reached.

United Kingdom. There is no low value consignments relief on imports of goods into the UK from the Channel Islands purchased as part of a mail order/distance sale transaction.

Annex Table 2.A.11. Electronic transaction reporting obligations[1]

Country	Mandatory electronic transaction reporting	Reporting format	Reporting provision	Reporting timing	Implementation date
Australia*	Transaction data : yes	No specific format is required	On request (based on risk assessment)	-	1 January 2000
	Electronic cash register : no	-	-	-	-
Austria*	Transaction data : yes	No specific format is required (SAF-T[2] is allowed since 2009)	On request	-	1 January 2000
	Electronic cash register : yes	No specific format is required	Systematic (periodically) and on request	Annual	1 April 2017
Belgium*	Transaction data : no	-	-	-	-
	Electronic cash register : yes	No specific format is required	On request	-	1 July 2016
Canada	Transaction data : no	-	-	-	-
	Electronic cash register : no	-	-	-	-
Chile*	Transaction data : yes	XML format determined by the tax authority	Systematic (real time direct automated access)	At the time the invoice is emitted (real time invoice reporting)	1 January 2003
	Electronic cash register : no (optional)	Subject to approval by the tax authorities.		Monthly	1 January 2014
Czech Republic	Transaction data : yes	Control Statement	Systematic (periodically)	At the same time as VAT return is lodged	1 January 2016
	Electronic cash register : no	-	-	-	-
Denmark*	Transaction data : yes	No specific format is required	On request	-	1 March 2015
	Electronic cash register : no	-	-		
Estonia	Transaction data : no	-	-	-	-
	Electronic cash register : no	-	-	-	-
Finland	Transaction data : no	-	-	-	-
	Electronic cash register : no	-	-	-	
France	Transaction data : yes	SAF-T[2]	On request		1 January 2014
	Electronic cash register : yes	No specific format is required			
Germany	Transaction data : yes				
	Electronic cash register : no				
Greece*	Transaction data : yes	No specific format is required	Systematic (periodically)	Annual	1 January 2014
	Electronic cash register : yes	No specific format is required			1990
Hungary*	Transaction data : yes		Systematic (real time)	At the time the invoice is emitted (real time invoice	1 July 2018

	Electronic cash register : no			reporting)	
Iceland	Transaction data : no	-	-	-	-
	Electronic cash register : no				
Ireland	Transaction data : yes	No specific format is required	On request	-	-
	Electronic cash register : no	-	-		
Israel*	Transaction data : yes	PCN874	Systematic (periodically)	Monthly	1 January 2010
	Electronic cash register : yes	No specific format is required	Systematic (periodically)	Monthly	1 January 2010
Italy*	Transaction data : yes	XML format	Systematic (real time)	At the same time the invoice is emitted (real time invoice reporting)	1 January 2019
	Electronic cash register : no				
Japan	Transaction data : no	-	-	-	-
	Electronic cash register : no				
Korea*	Transaction data : yes	Electronic Tax Invoicing format	Systematic (near real time)	One day after the invoice is emitted	1 January 2011
	Electronic cash register : Yes	No specific format is required	Systematic (daily)	Daily	1 January 2005
Latvia*	Transaction data : yes	No specific format is required	On request	-	26 October 2011
	Electronic cash register : yes	No specific format is required	On request	-	1 July 2017
Lithuania	Transaction data : yes	SAF-T²	Systematic	Monthly	1 October 2016
	Electronic cash register : no	Certified software	On request		
Luxembourg*	Transaction data : yes	SAF-T²	On request		1 January 2011
	Electronic cash register : no				
Mexico*	Transaction data : yes	SAF-T²	Systematic (automated, periodic and on request) -	At the same time the invoice is emitted (real time invoice reporting)	1 January 2015
	Electronic cash register : no	-			
Netherlands	Transaction data : yes	SAFT²	On request	-	1 January 2000
	Electronic cash register : no	-	_	-	
New Zealand	Transaction data : yes	No specific format is required	On request	-	
	Electronic cash register : no	-	-	-	
Norway*	Transaction data : yes	SAF-T²	On request (not yet implemented)		1 January 2020
	Electronic cash register : yes	Legal requirements	On request (not yet implemented)		1 January 2019
Poland	Transaction data : yes	SAF-T²	Systematic and on request	Monthly -	1 July 2016

	Electronic cash register : yes	Certified software	On request		1 January 2009
Portugal	Transaction data : yes	SAF-T[2]	Systematic and on request		1 January 2008
	Electronic cash register : no				
Slovak Republic	Transaction data : yes	Specific software is required	Systematic	At the same time as VAT return	1 January 2014
	Electronic cash register : yes	Certified software	Systematic	In real time	1 January 2012
Slovenia	Transaction data : yes	SAF-T[2]	On request	-	1 January 2018
	Electronic cash register : yes	Certified software	Systematic	In real time	2 January 2016
Spain*	Transaction data : yes	XML	Systematic (near real time)	Within four days of issuance of the invoice (near real time)	1 July 2017
	Electronic cash register : no	-	-		
Sweden*	Transaction data : yes	No specific format is required	On request	-	1985
	Electronic cash register : yes	Certified software	On request	-	
Switzerland*	Transaction data : yes	No specific format is required	On request	-	-
	Electronic cash register : no				
Turkey	Transaction data : no	-	-	-	-
	Electronic cash register : no				
United Kingdom	Transaction data : yes	Functional compatible software	Mandatory, quarterly VAT return data only – no transaction reporting		1 April 2019
	Electronic cash register : no				

* See country notes.

1. For the purpose of this table, electronic transaction reporting means the transmission by registered businesses of detailed information under electronic format concerning individual taxable transactions, including accounting information, invoicing information or any other information allowing tax authorities to obtain information on each taxable supply made or received by a taxpayer. This does *not* include the electronic provision of bulk data such as total sales/turnover or deductible amounts e.g. in periodic returns or statements.

2. SAF-T stands for Standard Audit File for Tax, a mechanism that was developed by the OECD Forum on Tax Administration. It involves the use of accounting software to create an electronic file (the SAF-T) containing accounting data. The SAF-T enables the transfer of data from the taxpayer to the tax authorities in a standardised, electronic format. (Guidance for Developers of Business and Accounting Software Concerning Tax Audit Requirements available here http://www.oecd.org/tax/administration/guidancenote-guidancefordevelopersofbusinessandaccountingsoftwareconcerningtaxauditrequirements.htm). In most cases, a local version of the SAF-T is created to respond to local needs.

Source: National delegations; position as at 1 January 2018.

Country notes to Annex Table 2.A.11

Australia. ***Electronic transaction information*** may be required from the taxpayer only when a risk assessment of activities reveals a need for further information. This may be simple a copy of invoices (possibly in pdf format), other substantiating document, or an electronic spreadsheet of transactions. It would be rare for the Australian Tax Administration to access the actual electronic records within the business system.

Austria. ***Electronic transaction information:*** from 2000, there is an obligation to provide transaction data on data carriers at the request of tax authorities (in the course of an audit). From 2009 data transmission under the SAF-T format is allowed. ***Electronic cash registers:*** the use of electronic cash registers is mandatory for taxpayers with a net annual turnover of EUR 15 000 or more, provided that the cash turnover exceeds EUR 7 500 per year. The applicable annual turnover is of EUR 30 000 for businesses in the following areas: outdoor sales; sales of alpine – mountain ski and refuge hunts; sales inspecific kinds of wine taverns ("Buschenschank"); sales in canteens of non-profit organisations. General exemption from the cash register obligation applies to non-profit organisations, charitable and ecclesiastic bodies; self-service automates with single sales of less than EUR 20.

Belgium. ***Electronic cash registers:*** the obligation to issue cash receipts delivered by a cash registered system (CRS) is imposed on taxpayers supplying meals or catering services on a regular basis when their annual turnover, excluding VAT, related to the restaurant and catering services, exclusive of the supply of drinks, exceeds EUR 25 000. If the threshold is exceeded, CRS cash receipts must be issued for all their supplies relating to the provision of meals and drinks (supplied during the meal or not), including all sales of food and drinks.

Chile. The obligation to use electronic invoicing and to provide B2B transaction information electronically to tax authorities started in 2003. In 2017, this obligation was extended to the provision of other accounting data to an electronic record kept by the tax authority. Transaction data must be transmitted to tax authorities in real time. Invoicing data must be cleared by tax authorities to be considered as a valid accounting document (incl. for the right to deduct input VAT). This obligation is imposed on all taxpayers. Cash registers can be used by any VAT taxpayer. Prior authorization of the tax authority is required when its vouchers replaces non-electronic VAT receipts. In this case, the tax authority requires the model of the cash register to be certified according to certain criteria. Authorization is issued on a per-case basis, upon request of the taxpayer.

Denmark. It is planned to introduce legislation in 2025 to require taxpayers to use electronic cash registers when they belong to a category considered at risk.

France. Since 1 January 2014, taxpayers keeping electronic accounts must provide them in the form of digital files upon request by tax administration for control purposes (these files should meet specific standards). In addition, from 1 January 2018, VAT registered taxpayers making sales to final consumers, which record payments using electronic cash registers must use certified software meeting several technical conditions (inalterability, security, preservation) for tax control purposes. However, the use of electronic cash registers is not mandatory.

Greece. Issuance of retail receipts through electronic cash registers ("tax machines") is mandatory, except for those listed by the tax administration regulation (e.g. solicitors, accountants, farmers, etc.). Transactions covered by issued and received tax records have to be reported annually. In particular for B2B and B2G transactions the aggregated amount of issued and received invoices per tax registration number of client/supplier should be reported and for B2C transactions the total amount of issued and received retail receipts should be reported. Furthermore, apart from the above-mentioned obligation, businesses-petrol stations have to report on-line each purchase/sale regarding fuel (petrol, oil).

Hungary. Invoicing information for invoices emitted by an invoicing programme (for invoices from HUF 100 000) must be transmitted to the tax authorities at the same time the invoice is emitted by the taxpayer (real time reporting).

Israel. ***Transaction data transmission:*** taxpayers ("licenced dealers") whose turnover exceeds ILS 2 500 000 or that are obliged to implement the double-entry bookkeeping system; or those whose turnover exceed ILS 1 500 000 and are required by law to prepare balance sheets and to appoint an auditor must transmit invoicing information every month (i.e. by the 23rd of the following month) to the tax administration under the prescribed format (PCN874). ***Certified electronic cash registers:*** the obligation to use certified electronic cash registers is imposed on/available to certain taxpayers depending on their activity and turnover. For example, all retailers must use certified electronic cash registers (no threshold applies but under ILS 350 000 annual turnover, the retailer can choose to use sales book instead). Wholesalers with turnover up to ILS 10 100 000 can use certified electronic cash registers as an option for cash transaction up to ILS 710 instead of invoices. Transportation service providers can use certified electronic cash registers (no threshold). For other services, electronic cash registers can be used (no threshold); if a transaction is recorded with a receipt, the receipt replaces the electronic cash registers. The statistical data for Israel are supplied by and under the responsibility of the relevant Israeli authorities. The use of such data by the OECD is without prejudice to the status of the Golan Heights, East Jerusalem and Israeli settlements in the West Bank under the terms of international law.

Italy. From 1 January 2019, all VAT-registered businesses established in Italy will be subject to a real-time reporting of all the invoices they emit. This measure is supported by the obligation to issue electronic invoices (*FatturaPA*). Invoices should be submitted to the Italian Revenue Agency's e-invoicing platform, *Sistema di Interscambio* (SdI). Invoices will need to be approved by the SdI to be considered legally valid. The measure has already been applied to Business to Government bodies (B2G) supplies and to supplies of automotive petrol and diesel since 1 July 2018.

Korea. ***Transaction data transmission***: all business operators and individual businesses whose total value of supplies of goods and services for the immediately preceding taxable year is at least KRW 300 million are required to issue electronic invoices under a prescribed format for all B2B supplies. The tax administration must have a direct automated access to invoicing information (only) 1 day after the invoice is emitted through the Electronic Tax Invoicing System. The invoicing information must be available to the tax administration for clearance before it can be considered as a valid accounting document, including as a supporting evidence for deduction of input VAT. ***Electronic cash receipts:*** individual businesses who supply goods or services mainly to final consumers must issue electronic cash receipts and transaction data must be transmitted daily to the tax authority.

Latvia. ***Transaction data transmission***: if a taxpayer maintains accounting registers in electronic form, it must, at the request of the tax administration, provide access to any information related to its economic activities, stored in electronic form. The accounting computer programme shall ensure the recording of accounting data in such formats: *MS Excel, dBase/FoxPro, Text Report files, Flat files, Excel, Access, PDF, Adobe PDF, XML or ODBC data sources.* ***Electronic cash receipts:*** in street trading venues, taxpayers shall use a cash register stipulated by law if the combined value of its supplies of goods and services does reach EUR 150 000 within the period of previous 12 months. For passenger transport activities, taxpayers shall use cash-register systems stipulated by law if the combined value of transactions performed in a particular structural unit or passenger transport vehicle exceeds EUR 1 500 000 during the period of previous 12 months. The use a cash register stipulated by law is mandatory for taxpayers registered with the Value Added Tax Payers Register of the State Revenue Service, petrol stations and taxi.

Luxembourg. The ***transaction information transmission*** obligation was implemented for the fiscal year 2011. The requirement to make transaction information available to the tax administration under the SAF-T format is not imposed on taxpayers who: are not liable to the *plan comptable normalisé* (standardised chart account); or benefit from the simplified regime; or whose turnover is below EUR 112 000; or having no reasonable volume of booking transactions (under +/- 500).

Mexico. Electronic invoicing is mandatory since 1 January 2014. The transmission of transaction data to the tax authority is mandatory since 1 January 2015. Invoicing information must transmitted to tax authorities at the time the invoice is emitted (real time transmission). This obligation applies to all taxpayers and covers the domestic supplies of goods and services for both B2B and B2C transactions. Periodic transmission of transaction information is also imposed to all taxpayers (federative entities, municipalities, trade unions and entities of the parastatal public administration; and taxpayers subject to the regime of leasing, professional services and fiscal incorporation are relieved from that obligation).

Norway. ***Transaction data transmission:*** the Norwegian Bookkeeping Regulation includes a requirement to disclose accounting data in the SAF-T format. The obligation does only apply to companies who have their bookkeeping available electronically. The new rules will apply from financial reporting periods starting 1 January 2020 or later. Until then, the use of the SAF-T format is voluntary. Businesses with an annual turnover of less than NOK 5 million are exempt from the requirement. However, if these businesses do have bookkeeping information available electronically, the requirement will apply. The companies subject to bookkeeping obligations are only obliged to submit accounting information in SAF-T format on request by the tax authorities. ***Cash registers:*** from 1 January 2017, cash register systems that are placed on the Norwegian market must meet the requirements laid down in the Norwegian Cash Register Systems Act with regulations. The suppliers have to declare the systems to be in compliance with the new rules. Companies subject to a bookkeeping obligation have to start using new cash register systems from 1 January 2019.

Poland. ***Transaction data provision:*** taxable persons must provide transaction data to the tax authorities under the SAF-T format on a monthly basis. Taxable persons carrying out only supplies exempt from VAT or those benefiting from the VAT exemption for the small enterprises whose annual turnover does not exceed PLN 200 000 (the registration threshold), are exempt from this obligation. The tax authority can also obtain electronic transaction information on request only from taxpayers who keep accounting books using computer programs. This obligation also applies to stock movement, invoicing and bank statement programs. The submission of transaction data under SAF-T format is imposed on large businesses since 1 July 2016; on SMEs since 1 January 2017 and on all taxable persons on 1 January 2018. ***Electronic cash registers:*** taxable persons whose annual turnover on B2C supplies, exclusive of VAT, does not in the current tax year exceed PLN 20 000 and did not do so in the course of the preceding tax year are exempt from the obligation to use certified electronic cash registers (the exemption does not apply to certain categories of goods /services). Are also exempt certain categories of supplies e.g. when an invoice is emitted and/or the payment is made by bank transfer.

Portugal. ***Transaction data provision:*** all VAT taxable persons must periodically provide transaction data to the tax authorities under a SAF-T format in the same time as VAT returns. Taxpayers with a permanent establishment in Portugal providing supplies subject to VAT must also systematically transmit invoicing data to the tax administration under a SAF-T format 20 days after the end of each month either by electronic transmission of data or by filing it directly in the Tax Authority Web portal. The tax administration can also request the transmission of accounting data in SAF-T format to all taxpayers. Taxpayers subject to Personal Income Tax (IRS) or Corporate Income Tax (IRC), with a turnover lower than or equal to EUR 100.000 during the previous taxation period (small taxpayers), issuing invoices according to specific legislation are required to use, exclusively, computer invoicing programs previously certified by the Tax and Customs Authority (AT). ***Common Simplified Report*** (IES) – since 2006, Portugal simplified the companies accounting and financial reporting information to different government bodies by merging it in one single common declaration to be shared by different authorities, such as the National Bank or National Statistics Institute. This declaration, became wider in order to fulfil the needs of all bodies. Considering that for the accounting records SAF-T could provide most of the information needed, it was decided to drop around half of the forms/fields of this declaration replacing them by a previous submission of the accounting records SAF-T file. This will allow the tax administration produce, for instance, the Balance Sheet and the Profit and Loss Account of each company and pre-file some of the fields remaining on the newer lighter version of the Common Simplified Report declaration (as of October 2018). ***Electronic cash registers:*** the use of certified ECR it's not mandatory but given the obligation to issue an invoice for any transaction and the obligation for small taxpayers to use certified accounting programs, most taxpayers use electronic cash registers certified invoicing software.

Slovak Republic. ***Transaction data provision:*** as of 1 January 2014, taxable persons registered for VAT purposes in the Slovak Republic are obliged to submit a special VAT Control Statement, together with their VAT returns to the Financial Administration (FA). VAT listings are submitted separately and are not dependant on the VAT return. Some crosschecking between VAT listings and VAT returns are built into the analytical system. ***Electronic cash registers:*** the use of certified cash registers is mandatory for all suppliers that receives payments in cash or by other payment methods replacing cash at the point of sale and those providing sole services listed in the law. Data from these electronic cash registers must be transmitted to the tax authorities in real time.

Spain. ***Transaction data provision:*** as of 1 July 2017, certain taxpayers (i.e. those registered in the monthly VAT refund register; those whose annual turnover exceed EUR 6 million and company groups for VAT purposes) are required to provide the tax administration with invoicing data in XML format within four calendar days after the invoice is issued or received (Immediate Supply of Information – SII). Information on investment goods should also be provided within the submission deadline of the last settlement period of the year.

Sweden. The use of certified electronic cash registers is mandatory for taxpayers above the annual turnover threshold of SEK 182 000. It is not imposed on certain taxpayers such as taxi drivers and sales from vending machines. Taxpayers can apply for an exemption of the obligation to use certified electronic cash registers.

Switzerland. ***Electronic cash registers:*** data on individual transactions must be transmitted to the tax administration on request or during an audit.

United Kingdom. From April 2019, under the Making Tax Digital initiative, VAT registered businesses with taxable turnover above the VAT registration threshold will need to keep digital records and submit VAT Returns to HMRC using functional compatible software.

Annex Table 2.A.12. Application of domestic reverse charge and split payment mechanisms

	Domestic reverse charge system[1]	Domestic split payment mechanism[2]
Australia	Supplies of new residential premises	-
Austria	Supply of laptops, tablets, PCs, game consoles, mobile phones and integrated circuit devices if the amount of the invoice is at least EUR 5,000; Supply of gas and electric energy to taxable dealers; Supply of gas and electric energy certificates; Supply of CO_2 emission allowances; Supply of certain metals and of taxable investment gold; Supply of scrap and industrial and non-industrial waste and recyclable waste; Construction services if the recipient is acting as general contractor or if he usually is rendering construction services; Supplies of staff engaged in the construction sector; Supply of goods provided as security by a VAT taxable person to another person in execution of that security; Supply of goods following the cession of the reservation of ownership to an assignee and the exercising of this right by the assignee; Supply of immovable property sold by the judgment debtor in a compulsory sale procedure to another person.	-
Belgium	Some supplies of investment gold and of gold products of a purity of at least 325 thousands; Supply of work on immovable property under several conditions; Supplies of staff engaged in the construction sector; Supply of CO_2 emissions allowances.	-
Canada	Certain purchasers of real property are required to self-assess (e.g. when the supplier is a non-resident; or when the purchaser is registered for GST/HST and, if he is an individual, the property is not a residential complex); Effective June 27, 2018, it is proposed that self-assessment would generally be required with respect to supplies of carbon emission allowances; In certain circumstances, persons may be required to self-assess the provincial part of the HST when certain property or services are moved from one province to another.	-
Chile	Supplies of rice, construction works, waste, marine species, livestock, legumes, wood, wild products, wheat and berries. The customer (who must be a VAT taxpayer) acts as a withholding agent.	-
Czech Republic	Supply of taxable investment gold and gold material of purity equal to or greater than 333 thousandths; Supply of designated categories of scrap and waste; Supply of CO^2 emission allowances; Supply of construction and assembly services provided between taxable persons registered for Czech VAT; Supply of mobile phones, integrated circuit devices, notebooks, tablets and videogame consoles; Supply of certain metals and basic products from metals; Supply of cereals and industrial crops, including oil seeds and sugar beet; Supply of immovable property under the option for taxation; Supply of gas and electric energy to taxable dealers; Supply of gas and electric energy certificates; Supply of goods following the cession of a reservation of ownership to an assignee and the exercising of this right by the assignee; Supply of immovable property sold by a judgment debtor in a compulsory sale procedure; Supply of staff engaged in construction and assembly services; Supply of certain telecommunication services.	There is a special method for securing the payment of VAT that can be used when a recipient of a taxable supply wants to avoid being declared joint and severally liable for the unpaid taxes by the supplier. Similarly to the split payment mechanism, for these cases the recipient can pay the VAT due directly to the account of the supplier's tax office.
Denmark	Supply of CO_2 emission allowances;	-

	Supply of scrap metals; Supply of investment gold; Supply of mobile phones, integrated circuit devices, games consoles, tablets PCs and laptops.	
Estonia	Supply of immovable property and investment gold, where the supplier has opted for taxation; Supply of gold material, including semi-finished gold products (purity of at least 325 thousandths); Supply of scrap metal and precious metals.	-
Finland	Supply of taxable investment gold as well as gold material and semi-manufactured gold products of purity equal to or greater than 325 thousandths; Supply of CO_2 emission allowances; Supply of scrap metal and waste; Construction services, including supply of staff engaged in the construction sector.	-
France	Supply of CO_2 emission allowances; Supply of used materials, scrap and waste; Supply of investment gold and gold products of a purity of at least 325 thousandths; Construction services (limited to certain services provided on a building when performed by a subcontractor on behalf of a taxable person); Supply of gas and electric energy to taxable dealers; Supply of certain telecommunication services.	-
Germany	Supplies of pledged assets by the guarantor to the recipient of the security outside the framework of judicial liquidation; Supplies covered by the Real Property Transfer Tax Law (in particular transfers of real estate). If the customer is an entrepreneur: supplies of work or other services serving the construction, repair, maintenance, alteration or removal of structures (except for planning, engineering and supervision) and cleaning of buildings when the customer himself supplies such services; Supply of gold (unwrought or semi-finished of a purity of at least 325 thousandths); Supply of CO_2 emissions allowances; Supply of industrial scrap, ferrous and non-ferrous waste and other waste; Supply of mobile devices, integrated circuit devices, game consoles and tablet PC if the transaction value is or exceeds EUR 5 000; Supply of electricity (generally applicable only if supplier and recipient are both treated as resellers) and supply of gas (generally applicable only if the recipient is to be treated as reseller); Supply of precious metals as well as certain ignoble metals (e.g. copper, nickel, aluminium, lead, zinc), unwrought or semi-manufactured, if the transaction value is or exceeds EUR 5 000.	-
Greece	Construction work on immovable property assigned to public works' contractors by public authorities (that are not necessarily public law entities), provided the public authorities are owners of the works and taxable persons with the right to input tax deduction. Major projects as defined by EU Regulations are exempt from the reverse charge system. Provided the supply is intended for recycling, the following supplies of recyclable waste: Supply of ferrous and non-ferrous waste metals, scrap(clippings) and other used materials Supply of semi-finished products made of ferrous and non-ferrous metals, Supply of residues and other recyclable materials consisting of ferrous and non-ferrous metals, alloys, slag, ash or scale and industrial residues containing metals or metal alloys Supply of parings and scrap (clippings), waste and used recyclable material consisting of cullet, glass, paper, cardboard, rags, bone, leather (natural or artificial), diphtheria, raw hides and skins, tendons and sinews, twine, rope and trawl, cables, rubber and plastic materials,	-

	Supply of scrap (clippings) and waste from the working of base materials Supply of the aforementioned materials after cleaning, polishing, selection, cutting, fragmenting and pressing Supply of greenhouse gas emissions allowances according to EU Directive 2003/87/EC. Supply of mobile phones, videogame consoles, tablets and laptops provided the acquirer is a taxable person entitled to input tax deduction (that is if registered under the normal VAT scheme).	
Hungary	Supply of construction works regarded as a supply of goods; Construction or other alteration or repair activity qualifying as service, directed at the construction, expansion, rearrangement or other modification (including demolition) of immovable property and subject to acquiescence or authorisation by the building authority; Hiring-out of employees and the supply of staff; Supply of scrap and waste products; Supply of a building and the land on which it stands or of an inbuilt plot of land (with certain exceptions) if the supplier opted for taxation; In relation with debtors and creditors, the supply of goods that were pledged as collateral security to cover an overdue claim in execution of that security; Supply of goods with an open market value of more than HUF 100,000 (EUR 334) used by the taxable person for the purposes of his business if the supplier is adjudicated in liquidation proceedings or any similar insolvency proceedings; Supply of CO_2 emissions allowances; Supply of certain specific agricultural products such as wheat and meslin, rye, barley, oats, maize, triticale, soya beans whether or not broken; rape and colza seeds whether or not broken; sunflower seeds whether or not broken. Supply of certain iron and non-alloy steel products such as flat-rolled products of iron or non-alloy steel, bars and rods of iron or non-alloy steel, angles, shapes and sections of iron or non-alloy steel, wire of iron or non-alloy steel, tubes, pipes and hollow profiles of iron or non-alloy steel.	-
Iceland	-	-
Ireland	Supply of construction services supplied by sub-contractors to principal contractors; Supply of immovable property under the option for taxation (including sale by receiver, liquidator or mortgagee in possession; Supply of used material and scrap metal; Supply of CO_2 emissions allowances; Supply of gas and electricity by a business in Ireland to a taxable dealer carrying on business in Ireland; Supply of gas certificates or electricity certificates by a business in Ireland to another business in Ireland.	
Israel[3]	A person not liable for payment of the tax may, with the Director's consent and on conditions prescribed by him, take the payment upon himself, and after the date of that consent he shall be treated as the person liable for its payment; The tax levied on a buyer, if the buyer is a dealer, a non-profit organisation or a financial institution and has committed a real estate sale which is an occasional transaction; Sale of metal debris; A dealer, a non-profit organisation or a financial institution receives services of the types specified below from a person, whose main income is from wage, benefit or pension, shall pay the tax in respect of that service, unless a tax invoice was received from the person rendering the service; these are the services: Artistic performance; construction or preparation of stage sets; preparation, checking, conducting and supervising exams; lectures etc. Services of the following professionals: agronomist, architect, ; practical engineer; private investigator; rabbinical pleader; technician; dental technician; organizational, management, scientific or tax consultant;	

	economist; engineer etc.	
Italy	Supplies carried out by subcontractors in the building sector; Supply of staff engaged in the construction sector; Supply of immovable property under the option for taxation; Supply of used materials, scrap, waste and specific services; Supply of investment gold, including supply of semi-finished products and of gold of a purity of at least 325 thousandths(so called industrial gold); Supply of scrap iron; Supply of mobile phones, tablets, personal computers and integrated circuit devices under certain conditions; Supply of CO_2 emission allowances; Supply of gas and electric energy to taxable dealers; Supply of gas and electric energy certificates.	Supplies of goods and services made to public authorities or government bodies, public owned companies, companies listed on the Italian Stock Market (FITSE-MIB)
Japan		-
Korea	-	For supplies of gold bullion (99.5% or higher purity) and second hand gold products (with 58.5% or higher purity), copper, gold and iron scrap, the supplier must open a bank account designated for the gold or scrap transactions and the purchase price (without VAT) must be transferred to the supplier using the designated bank account. At the same time, the recipient must also deposit the relevant VAT amount into an account designated by the Director of the National Tax Services.
Latvia	Supply of timber and services related to the supply of timber; Supply of construction services; Supply of scrap metals and services related to the supply of scrap metals Supply of mobile telephones, integrated circuit devices, tablet PC's and laptops; Supply of cereals and industrial crops (including oil seeds), including mixtures of these goods, that are not normally used in the unaltered state for final consumption; Supply of raw and semi-finished precious metals, where they are not covered by special scheme for investment gold, raw and semi-finished precious metal alloys and precious metal clad, as well as precious metal or precious metal clad scrap and debris; Supply of game consoles; Supply of metal products; Supply of construction products; Supply of household electronic appliances and household electrical appliances.	-
Lithuania	Supply of timber Supply of construction services Supply of ferrous waste and scrap, residues and other recyclable materials consisting of ferrous and non-ferrous metals Supplies by a taxable person under insolvency procedure Supply of essential (material) improvement to the owner of the building VAT calculated on assets taken over as a contribution in kind or due to reorganisation of another person registered for VAT purposes.	
Luxembourg	Supply of CO_2 emission allowances.	
Mexico	Domestic reverse charge applies to: corporations that receive independent personal services from individuals or rent goods from them; acquire waste to be used for commercial or industrial activities; receive services rendered by commissionaires who are individuals; and receive land motor transportation services of goods lent to both individuals and corporations. credit institutions acquiring assets through payments in kind or through legal or trust adjudication; and individuals or entities acquiring or having temporary use or enjoyment of tangible assets transferred or granted by foreign residents who do not	

	have a permanent establishment in Mexico.	
Netherlands	Supply of construction work (including shipbuilding), including repair, cleaning, maintenance, alteration and demolition services in relation to immovable property, including the handing over of construction works; Supply of staff engaged in the construction sector; Supply of immovable property under the option for taxation; Supply of used materials, scrap, waste and specific services; Supply of goods provided as security by one taxable person to another in execution of that security; Supply of immovable property sold by a judgement debtor in a compulsory sale procedure; Supply of CO_2 emission allowances; Supply of mobile phones, integrated circuit devices, laptops, game consoles and tablet pc's provided that the value of the transactions exceeds EUR 10,000.	-
New Zealand	If the supply of land has been incorrectly zero-rated and the incorrect treatment is discovered after settlement, the recipient of the supply is made responsible for paying GST.	
Norway	Supply of CO_2 emission allowances; Supply of investment gold (with purity equal to or greater than 325 thousandths).	
Poland	Supply of metal scrap, metal waste and metal materials; Supply of CO2 emission allowances; Supply of mobile phones (including smart phones), video game consoles, tablets, notebooks, and laptops; Supply of microprocessors; Construction services supplied by subcontractors; Supply of unwrought non-ferrous metals (aluminium, lead, zinc, tin, nickel); Supply of raw and semi-finished metals, including gold materials and intermediate products containing gold, investment gold and selected steel products.	For B2B supplies, the customer can choose to pay the VAT on a supply on the "VAT account" of the customer (all taxpayers have automatically a VAT account associated with their bank account) separately from the net amount.
Portugal	Supply of used material, scrap metal, waste and specific services; Supply of immovable property under the option for taxation; Work on immovable property (such as repair, cleaning, maintenance, alteration and demolition services, including the handing over of construction works); Supply of taxable investment gold and gold material of purity equal to or greater than 325 thousandths; Supplies of CO_2 emission allowances.	
Slovak Republic	Supply of certain construction works including supply of building (construction) and the supply of certain goods requiring installation or assembly; Supply of immovable property under the option for taxation; Supply of goods which are pledged as a security of a receivable of a creditor within the enforcement of such pledge; Supply of a building or a part of a building in the Slovak Republic which the supplier as a debtor recognised by a court or another relevant state authority sold within the statutory enforcement proceedings; Supply of goods following the cession of a reservation of ownership to an assignee and the exercising of this right by the assignee; Supply of investment gold and of gold material or semi-manufactured products of gold of a purity of at least 325 thousandths between taxable persons; Supply of metal scrap and metal waste; Supply of CO_2 emission allowances; Supply of cereals and oil seeds, grains, straw and fodder crops, which are not typically intended in the unaltered state for final consumption; Supplies of iron and steel; Supply of mobile phones, being devices made or adapted for use in connection with a licensed network and operated on specified frequencies, whether or not they have any other use, if the taxable amount in the	

	invoice for the supply of mobile telephones is EUR 5 000 and more; Supply of integrated circuit devices such as microprocessors and central processing units in a state prior to integration into end user products, if the taxable amount in the invoice for the supply is EUR 5 000 and more; Supply of construction work, including repair, cleaning, maintenance, alteration and demolition services in relation to immovable property as well as the handing over of construction works regarded as a supply of goods.	
Slovenia	Supply of construction work (including repair, cleaning, maintenance, alteration and demolition services in relation to immovable property); Supply of staff engaged in the mentioned activities; Supply of certain immovable property, where the supplier has opted for taxation of the supply; Supply of certain waste, scrap, used material and services; Supply of allowances to emit greenhouse gases.	
Spain	Construction works, including the supply of staff for its performance, in the framework of development, construction or renovation of immovable property; Supply of CO_2 emission allowances; Supply of metal scrap and metal waste; Supply of investment gold and supply of gold material or semi-finished products of a purity of at least 325 thousandths; Supply of buildings in certain situations; Supply of immovable property within bankruptcy proceedings; Supply of immovable property made under enforcement of a security or with the obligation for the acquirer to settle the securitized debt; Supply of mobile phones, videogame consoles, laptop and tablet PCs, only where the customer is a reseller of the goods (traders habitually engaging in the resale of these goods) or, otherwise, where the total amount of supplies to one trader exceeds EUR 10,000. Supply of silver, platinum and palladium.	
Sweden	Supply of construction work, including repair, cleaning, maintenance, alteration and demolition services in relation to immovable property, including the handing over of construction works; Supply of staff engaged in the construction sector; Supply of CO_2 emissions allowances; Supply of used materials, scrap, waste and specific services; Supply of investment gold and gold products of a purity of at least 325 thousandths.	
Switzerland	-	-
Turkey	Supply of lease of movable property by non-taxable persons to taxable persons; Supply of scientific, artistic and literary works provided to taxable persons. Supply of advertisement services provided by non-taxable persons to taxable persons.	Certain recipients of a number of specified services are required to withhold a percentage of the VAT charged to them by the service provider and remit it directly to the tax authorities (*partial withholding*). Among others, these services are (a) supervisory services for building construction, (b) scrap metal, glass, plastic and paper (in cases where the supplier waives the VAT exemption), (c) advisory, supervisory and audit services maintenance and (d) repair services for machinery, equipment and other fixed assets.
United Kingdom	Supply of investment gold and of gold products of a purity of at least 325 thousandths; Supply of CO_2 emissions allowances; Supply of mobile telephones and integrated circuit devices if the value of the goods supplied exceeds GBP 5,000 (VAT inclusive). The value limit does not apply to services; Supply of gas through a natural gas system situated in the United Kingdom or any network connected to such a system and to electricity; Wholesale supply of electronic communication services.	

[1] For the purpose of this table, are considered as a "domestic reverse charge" regime, regimes whereby the customer rather than the supplier of goods, services or intangibles is liable to remit the VAT to the tax authorities on a domestic supply (i.e. a supply where both the supplier and the customer are established in the same jurisdiction, where the supply takes place). The supplier does not charge the VAT to the customer.
[2] For the purpose of this table, a "domestic split payment mechanism" is a mechanism whereby, on a domestic supply of goods, services or intangibles, the supplier remains liable to charge the VAT to the customer, but where (part of) this VAT is directly transferred to the tax authorities or to a specific (blocked) "VAT account" that may belong to the supplier or customer.
Source: national delegates; position as at 1 January 2018

Chapter 3. Selected Excise Duties in OECD Countries

This chapter describes the main features of selected excise duties and their impact on revenue, customer behaviour and markets. It explains the respective impact of ad quantum and ad valorem taxes and how they interact. It shows the detailed excise tax rates on beer, wine, alcoholic beverages, tobacco, and mineral oil products in OECD countries.

3.1. Introduction

Although excise taxes may cover a very wide range of products, excise taxes on alcohol, tobacco and hydrocarbon oils are common to all OECD countries and raise significant revenues for governments. In recent decades, governments have increasingly used these taxes not only as revenue raisers but also to influence customer behaviour where consumption of certain products is considered harmful to health or to the environment.

This chapter presents an overview of the key characteristics of excise duties and the evolution in their use by governments in selected areas (Section 3.2). It then looks in some detail at the excise rates structure for three main categories of products: alcoholic beverages (Section 3.3), tobacco products (Section 3.4) and mineral oil products (Section 3.5). This is followed by a brief description of the impact of differences in excise rates between countries on cross-border trade (Section 3.6) and on their distributional effects (Section 3.7).

3.2. Key characteristics and revenue trends

Excise, unlike other general consumption taxes (incl. value added taxes - VAT[1]) is levied only on specific goods. Although many products can be subject to excise, such as chocolate, coffee and orange juice, this chapter focuses on three principal product groups that are liable to excise in all OECD countries: alcoholic beverages, mineral oils and tobacco products.

Before looking at the key characteristics of these three groups and their comparative treatment by different countries, it is useful to recall the following general characteristics of excise duties:

- Excise duties are generally calculated by reference to the weight, volume, strength, or quantity of the product, combined in some cases with the value, but sometimes on a value basis only.
- Excise duties normally become payable when the goods enter free circulation. Transfers of ownership of excisable goods can take place within a controlled warehousing environment or between registered operators without creating an excise charge.
- The excise system is characterised by small numbers of taxpayers that are active in the manufacturing, wholesale stage or importation of the three main product groups.

Unlike VAT, which is collected through a staged collection process by all the stakeholders in the value chain until the final consumer (see Chapter 2), excise duties are normally collected only once, from one registered operator, at the time the goods are released for consumption. In the European Union, the movement of excisable products between Member States is made under a duty-suspension arrangement until the moment they are released for free circulation. In the United States, where both federal and local excise exist, they are levied by the federal government and by many states and local governments. Federal excise taxes are collected by the Internal Revenue Service while states may impose the tax according to their own rules and rates.

Excise is normally part of the VAT tax base, meaning that VAT is usually levied on the duty-paid value of the excise products. Therefore, an increase of excise duty rates implies an increase of both excise and VAT burden.

The relative share of excise duties in total tax revenue has been subject to a long decline since 1975, when they accounted for 10.5% on average to 7.8% in 2016 (see Annex Table 3.A.9). Behind the OECD average, there are large differences between countries, with excise accounting for 2.6% of total tax revenue in New Zealand and 18.2% in Turkey. In a majority of the OECD countries (20 out of 36), the weight of excise duties is between 5% and 10% of total tax revenue while it accounts for less than 5% in 8 countries (Australia, Canada, Iceland, Israel, New Zealand, Sweden, Switzerland and the United States) and for more than 10% in 8 countries (Estonia, Greece, Latvia, Lithuania, Mexico, Poland, Slovenia and Turkey).

The main characteristics of excise duties and their objectives in terms of revenue raising and consumer behaviour influence are largely shared amongst OECD countries. However, their rates and structure differ significantly and giving an order of magnitude of the tax burden on excise goods is not straightforward. Although taxes (other than VAT) on alcoholic beverages and tobacco consist almost exclusively of excise duties, their structure may vary widely across countries. For example, standard excise rates on beer may be tempered by the application of reduced rates on small breweries. Different duty rates applicable to substitutes (cigarettes and rolling tobacco) may also blur the picture. Excise duties on road fuels show only a part of automotive taxation policy that also includes road tolls, taxes on registration and use of vehicles, taxes on insurance, etc.

The following sections provide some more detail on the main differences in the structure of excise duties and on their increasing use as an instrument to influence behaviour.

3.2.1. Ad valorem vs. ad quantum excises

The level of revenues raised by excise duties and their economic impact depend not only on excise rates and tax bases, but also on their structure. There are two main ways in which excisable products can be taxed: ad valorem and ad quantum. Under an ad quantum excise (also referred to as a "specific" excise), a fixed amount of tax is levied per unit of the product (e.g. USD 1 per litre), which means that this is a tax on the volume of sales. Under an ad valorem excise, the tax is levied as a proportion of the product price (e.g. 20% of the selling price), and it is thus a tax on the value of sales. In a number of instances (e.g. tobacco taxes as presented in Annex Table 3.A.4) excise duties can be levied on the basis of a mix of *ad valorem* and *ad quantum* taxes. *Ad quantum* taxes requires a precise definition of the nature and characteristics of the tax base (e.g. a litre of unleaded gasoline with 94 RON) while an *ad valorem* tax is simply based on the price of the excisable good.

Most excisable products naturally present a bundle of different characteristics (volume, weight, strength, octane, alcoholic or carbon content, etc.). *Ad quantum* taxes remain unaffected by changes in the product characteristics that have not been defined as being relevant for the tax base, whereas *ad valorem* taxes bear on all the characteristics of the product that are reflected in the price. Depending on the structure of the excise, its impact on production and consumption is different. For example, a specific tax on beer (per % absolute alcohol in volume) may encourage brewers to develop varieties of beer, including more luxurious products that could be offered at higher prices while remaining subject to the same level of excise as the cheaper product. On the other hand, ad valorem taxes may discourage costly improvements in product quality or encourage consumers to switch to low-cost products. *Ad quantum* taxes may be easier to administer, because it requires only to determine the physical quantity of the product taxed. *Ad quantum* taxes also produce a more predictable revenue stream than ad valorem taxes, as revenue does not vary with the price of the product (Health Organization Regional Office for Europe, 2015[1]). On the other hand, *ad valorem* taxes may keep pace with inflation better than ad quantum taxes (although it is also possible to adjust *ad quantum* taxes for inflation. It is also noteworthy that empirical suggests that ad quantum tax increases tend to be more than fully passed through to consumers (prices rise by more than the tax increase), whereas *ad valorem* tax increases tend to be less than fully passed through (Sassi, Belloni and Capobianco, 2013[2]).

From a distributional perspective, there may be a case for *ad valorem* rather than *ad quantum* taxation. If one assumes that high-income taxpayers purchase more expensive products than low-income consumers, then an *ad valorem* tax could be assumed to impose a higher tax burden on high-income taxpayers relative to low-income consumers. However, this is not entirely straightforward: the exact distributional impact will depend on consumption patterns, and even with an *ad valorem* tax, high-income taxpayers may still end up paying less tax relative to their income than low-income households. Addressing redistributive goals is likely to be better achieved through the progressive personal income tax which directly links taxes paid to income (Thomas, A. and Brys, B. 2016) (see also Section 3.6 below).

There may be a case for a combination of *ad quantum* and *ad valorem* taxes if the tax is aimed at discouraging consumption of or maximising revenue from, both high and low value products. Where there are large differences in prices of a product, an *ad quantum* tax will be less likely to reduce demand for the high value product, and will raise less revenue from it than an *ad valorem* tax. Additionally, higher income consumers who are more likely to consume high value products may be less responsive than low-income groups to the imposition of a given tax (although *ad quantum* taxes may reduce the price differentials). Imposing a higher aggregate tax on these expensive products will therefore be necessary to affect behaviour. To achieve this, an *ad valorem* tax can be combined with an *ad quantum* tax, which is common with tobacco taxation (see Section 3.3 below).

Setting the "optimal" balance between *ad quantum* and *ad valorem* components of excise will depend of the products concerned, the market structure and the government's objective, hence there is no optimal balance between the two taxes in absolute (KEEN, 1998[3]).

3.2.2. Excises as an instrument to influence behaviour

Whatever the reason for their introduction, excises do affect consumer behaviour. The case put forward in relation to alcoholic beverages and tobacco products, for instance, is that drinking and smoking are health hazards and that increased excise duties help to reduce consumption.

For mineral oils, the policy motivation for levying excises, beyond raising revenue, is increasingly to address energy security concerns and correct social externalities from energy use, particularly environmental and health costs. Over the last decade, environmental and health concerns have played an increasing role in determining the nature and application of taxes on energy use, particularly in the area of transport taxation (see Chapter 4). OECD analysis (OECD, 2010[4]) confirms the advantages of environmental taxes over many other environmental policy instruments in terms of environmental effectiveness, economic efficiency, the ability to raise public revenue, and transparency. In addition, environmental taxes have been successfully used to address a wide range of issues including waste disposal, water pollution and air emissions. It also shows how the way they are designed and implemented is crucial to their success (OECD, 2011[5]).

A related rationale for applying excise duties on energy use is their (cost-)effectiveness in mitigating global warming. While energy use accounted for 80% of total greenhouse gas emissions in 2015 (IEA, 2018[6]), the introduction of excises on fossil-fuel-based energy reduces demand for this energy by increasing its price. If such excise duties are levied proportionally on the carbon content of fuels, they also encourage substitution towards less carbon-intensive forms of energy. Taking electricity as an example, producers can switch from coal to less carbon-intensive natural gas, or carbon-free solar and wind power.

The combination of specific excise duties on energy, carbon taxes (which are often also levied as excise duties) and tradable emission permits, puts a price on the carbon content of energy. This is also known as the effective carbon rate (ECR). A recent study by the OECD on effective carbon rates (OECD, 2018[7]) shows how 42 OECD and G20 countries, representing 80% of world emissions, price carbon emissions from energy use today, and how much progress has been made since 2012. Carbon prices, as measured by the effective carbon rate (ECR) are increasing, albeit slowly. A useful benchmark for measuring progress in this context is the estimated total economic cost of carbon emissions. The low-end estimate of this cost today stands at EUR 30 per ton CO2. The OECD's study indicates that the gap between actual carbon prices and this benchmark cost has reduced from 83% on average in 2012 to 79.5% in 2015, and is estimated to further reduce to 76.5% in 2018. New carbon pricing initiatives have the potential to significantly further reduce this carbon pricing gap. So far, excise duties on energy have been the main contributors to average effective carbon rates.

3.3. Alcoholic beverages

Alcoholic beverages exist in a wide variety across the world and are produced from a wide range of fermented or distilled ingredients (grapes, apples, malt, rice, etc.). The Customs Combined Nomenclature Code (CN) provides a classification of alcoholic beverages with which excise categories are intrinsically linked. The CN includes six main categories of alcoholic beverages: beer made from malt (code 22.03); wine of fresh grapes, including fortified wines (code 22.04); vermouth and other wine of fresh grapes flavoured with plants or aromatic substances (code 22.05); other fermented beverages (for example, cider, perry, mead), mixtures of fermented beverages and mixtures of fermented beverages and non-alcoholic beverages (code 22.06); undenatured ethyl alcohol of an alcoholic strength of 80 % pure alcohol by volume (abv) or higher (code 22.07) and undenatured ethyl alcohol of an alcoholic strength of less than 80 % abv (code 22.08). There are inevitably sub divisions within each of these broad categories but the use of the internationally accepted nomenclature provides for consistency and helps to avoid contradictory definitions in applying rates. Member States of the European Union also apply a harmonised structure for excise duties on alcohol and alcoholic beverages (Council Directive 92/83/EEC). Except otherwise mentioned in country notes, Annex Table 3.A.1 and Annex Table 3.A.1 cover products under CN codes 22.03 and 22.04. Annex Table 3.A.3 covers products not included in Annex Table 3.A.1 and Annex Table 3.A.2.

Given the long history of alcohol taxation, several methods and measures have been developed over time for assessing the alcoholic content of a product. The alcohol by volume (abv) is now the standard measure of the level of alcohol contained in an alcoholic beverage. It is defined as the number of litres of pure ethanol present in 100 litres of solution at 20 °C, expressed as a percentage of the total volume. Annex Table 3.A.1 and Annex Table 3.A.2 provide an overview of excise taxation of beer and wine, whereby the alcoholic content is expressed in % abv. In some countries, the excise taxation of beer calculates the alcoholic content in degree Plato (measuring the density of beer wort in terms of percentage of extract by weight). To allow cross-country comparison, Annex Table 3.A.1 shows the estimated amounts of tax per % abv for these countries based on a conversion from the amounts of tax per degree Plato. There is no precise method to convert from degrees Plato and alcohol per volume but for tax purposes it is assumed that 1% abv is equivalent to 2.5 degrees Plato. The tax amounts per degree Plato have thus been multiplied by 2.5 to obtain the rates in degree abv for the relevant countries in Annex Table 3.A.1.

Excise can be applied to alcoholic beverages in two main ways. The duty can be either *ad quantum* in relation to the alcoholic content of the product or *ad valorem* calculated according to the value of the product. The two methods are generally combined to include both the volume (based on alcohol content) and value. One exception is Mexico where the rate of tax on alcoholic beverages is calculated exclusively on the value of the product, with a graduated rate for beer that takes into account the alcoholic content of the product.

Annex Table 3.A.1, Annex Table 3.A.2 and Annex Table 3.A.3 in respect of excise duties on beer, wine and other alcoholic beverages illustrate the complexity of the computation of excise duties in many instances. The existence of differing sub-categories and specific rates (e.g. for low-alcohol products and for small breweries) and calculations based on both the value and the nature of the product, make it difficult to show an exact estimate of the precise excise tax burden at the consumer level. Nevertheless, Annex Table 3.A.1, Annex Table 3.A.2 and Annex Table 3.A.1 show the large differences of taxation levels between countries. Excise on beer (Annex Table 3.A.1), for instance, varies from about USD 2 per hectolitre per % abv (Germany and Luxembourg) up to USD 39 in Finland and even USD 64 in Israel. Excise on still wine (Annex Table 3.A.2) may vary from zero (Austria, Czech Republic, Germany, Hungary, Israel, Italy, Luxemburg, Portugal, Slovak Republic, Slovenia, Spain and Switzerland) to more than USD 7 per litre (Norway).

3.4. Tobacco products

Historically, as for alcohol taxation, the primary motivation for tobacco taxation was the efficient generation of government revenue. Nearly all OECD countries have taxed tobacco products for many decades and even for centuries in some cases. The relatively low elasticity of demand for tobacco products (i.e. the less than proportionate response of tobacco product consumption to a moderate price increase), the small number of producers and significant consumption made tobacco products a particularly attractive target for excise and other taxation. In light of the clear evidence of the negative health consequences of tobacco use, tobacco taxation has increasingly been used as a tool reduce tobacco use. A recent study by the World Health Organisation provides economic evidence of the effectiveness of increased tobacco taxation and pricing in reducing tobacco use (WHO, 2017[8]).

As with alcohol and mineral oils, there is a sub division of tobacco products into a number of categories – cigarettes, cigars, cigarette rolling tobacco and pipe tobacco. New tobacco products have also emerged in the past decade such as Heated Tobacco Products

(HTP), and Electronic Nicotine Delivery Systems (ENDS), which may be subject to specific tax rates.

Unlike excises on alcoholic beverages and mineral oils, which are almost exclusively *ad quantum*, the majority of countries use a combination of *ad quantum* and *ad valorem* elements to calculate excise on tobacco products.

Table 3.A.4 shows large differences between countries. Differences may also exist within a federal structure such as in the United States where for instance local excise rates on cigarettes (on the top of the federal tax) range from USD 0.17 in Missouri to USD 4.35 in New York per pack of 20 cigarettes (FTA, 2018[9]).

It should be noted that the individual rates or amounts of tax (*ad valorem/ad quantum* excise, VAT, duties, etc.) per type of tobacco product as shown in Annex Table 3.A.4 are not sufficient to assess the overall tax burden on those products. Indeed, a high ad valorem tax on a given product group can be balanced with a low ad quantum excise (or vice versa) when excise is levied on the basis of a mix of both ad valorem and ad quantum taxes for this product group. Ad valorem excises can be assessed on a range of different bases (producer price, import price, retail price). The combined effect of the VAT rate with excise duties needs to be assessed etc.

A better understanding of the relative taxation levels may therefore be gained by calculating the total tax burden (TTB) as a share of the total retail selling price (RSP) of a given product to the final consumer. To illustrate this, Annex Table 3.A.5 shows the total tax burden (*ad quantum* excise + *ad valorem* excise + VAT) for cigarettes as a share of the retail selling price of a pack of 20 cigarettes in OECD countries (for the calculation methodology, see note 1 to Annex Table 3.A.5). This table shows that the total tax burden for a pack of 20 cigarettes varies widely between countries, from 43.01% of the RSP in the United States (national average estimate of federal and local taxes) and 58.89% in Australia to 89.13% in Chile and 85.59% in Greece. The tax burden is above 50% of the RSP in all the OECD countries (except the United States), and above 80% for 8 countries (Chile, Finland, France, Greece, Israel, Poland, Turkey and the United Kingdom).

Annex Table 3.A.5 also shows that there may be substantial differences in the pre-tax prices, depending on the structure of the market, the geographic location (in particular with respect to cross-border shopping) and the relevant tax structure.

Determining the rate for tobacco taxation depends on the policy objectives of the tax. If the tax is primarily intended to raise revenue then the tax rate will be determined in light of the revenue targets and the elasticity of the demand for the taxed products. A moderate rate may be sufficient to generate stable revenue without creating significant political economy difficulties. If the tax is intended to have a significant impact on customer behaviour then a higher tax rate is likely to be required to achieve the desired health outcomes. In the specific case of tobacco, research (Goodchild, Perucic and Nargis, 2016[10]) has shown that higher taxes and prices on tobacco reduce both prevalence (i.e. users quitting) and intensity of tobacco use (i.e. users consuming less), in particular for vulnerable populations (young people and low-income households). The monetary burden of higher tobacco taxes also appears to fall more heavily on the wealthiest users, whose tobacco use declines less, while most of the health and economic benefits from reductions in tobacco use accrue to the most disadvantaged populations, whose tobacco use declines more when taxes increase (WHO 2015). Political economy factors (e.g., industry lobbying, public opposition) may make imposing a high rate difficult to achieve. Earmarking (part of) the revenue from the taxes for specific health related purposes such as funding health programmes and/or tobacco control activities may increase public support, although it reduces the flexibility in government budgeting (OECD, 2016a). Concerns about cross-border trade and bootlegging between countries with high price differentials may also make it difficult to impose a high tax rate in some countries in the absence of efficient regional co-operation.

3.5. Mineral oil products

Mineral oils are usually sub divided into product categories on the basis of technical specifications. The main product categories are unleaded gasoline, diesel oil, and heavy fuel oil. Some OECD countries also tax other energy products such as natural gas, electricity and coal through excises or specific taxes on energy products, such as carbon taxes.

The revenues raised from these taxes are significant in OECD countries, as a result of the considerable level of consumption and high tax rates in many of these countries. Although there are large differences between countries, the level of taxation for fuel relative to the base is very high compared to other taxes within the overall economy. For premium unleaded gasoline, for instance, the total tax burden (mainly excise plus VAT) exceeds 100% of pre-tax prices in all the OECD countries, except Australia, Canada, Chile, Japan, Mexico, New Zealand and the United States (Annex Table 3.A.6).

In the European Union (EU), the Energy Taxation Directive (2003/96/EC) sets out common rules for the taxation of energy products in EU member states. This Directive aims to reduce distortions of competition between mineral oils and other energy products, as well as tax competition between member states from rate differentiation in energy taxation. It also aims to incentivise more efficient energy use. The Directive sets common taxation rules for a range of fuels, including many oil products, coal and natural gas, and for electricity consumption. For each, it sets a minimum level of tax expressed in terms of the volume, weight, or energy content of the fuel. For example, minimum rates on road fuels are as follows: EUR 0.359/l for unleaded gasoline; EUR 0.330/l for gas oil and EUR 0.125/kg for LPG. The Directive does not specify which taxes should be used to reach the minimum level of taxation. These may include a diversity of specific taxes such as excise, carbon tax, energy tax, etc.

The OECD's Taxing Energy Use publication (OECD, 2018b) provides a comprehensive overview of specific taxes on energy for 42 OECD and G20 countries. It shows that these taxes are strongly heterogeneous and are in general too low from an environmental point of view. Taxes on road transport are much higher than taxes in other sectors, but they are still too low to cover the external costs of road transportation in nearly all cases. They also tend to be higher where GDP per capita is higher. Between 2012 and 2015, the first steps towards removing lower tax rates on diesel compared to gasoline have been taken in some countries. Apart from this, however, there are no signs that the polluter-pays principle has determined the energy tax landscape more strongly in 2015 than in 2012.

A significant feature of excise on mineral oils is the fact that it has been used to influence consumer behaviour to a greater degree than in other areas. Although excise on transport fuels has been around for many years, it was originally motivated primarily if not exclusively by non-environmental objectives, such as general revenue generation or to finance infrastructure spending in some cases. When the more environmentally-friendly unleaded gasoline appeared on the market, it was not commercially competitive with leaded gasoline as a retail product because it was more expensive to produce. Energy taxation was used to overcome this handicap by making unleaded gasoline cheaper at the pump. Today, leaded gasoline has disappeared and is even not allowed any more on the market. Lower taxes on Liquefied Petroleum Gas (LPG) used as propellant had a much less significant effect on consumer behaviour. The characteristics of this fuel (not liquid at standard temperature and atmospheric pressure; more difficult to stock; need for specifically equipped stations) have hindered its development. The use of LPG is globally very low compared to diesel and gasoline.

Excise taxes on transport fuels are usually much higher than on mineral oils and, more generally, than on fossil fuels used in other sectors (OECD, $2013_{[11]}$). This can be for various reasons, including a lower elasticity of the tax base in transport; the use of excises to cover (more or less directly) external costs that are relevant only in the transportation context (most notably congestion); and equity concerns. Equity considerations have notably motivated the differences in taxation of diesel used for household heating compared to diesel used for transportation (Flues and Thomas, $2015_{[12]}$). The vast majority of OECD countries (except Greece, Hungary, Israel and the Netherlands) tax heating oil for households at a lower rate than diesel for transport use even though both products are more or less identical (see Annex Table 3.A.8).

Excise levels for diesel fuel are still lower than those for gasoline in most countries. Only Switzerland levies a higher excise duty on diesel than on gasoline and only two countries apply the same excise rate to both fuels (Australia and United Kingdom). From an environmental point of view, this is peculiar, as diesel consumption in vehicles has a much greater environmental impact than unleaded gasoline, largely due to the significant differences in NOx[2] and particulate emissions. With more stringent motor vehicle regulations, the difference is becoming less pronounced for new vehicles, although there are concerns about differences between test cycle and on-road performance and the stock of vehicles is still weighted toward older, more polluting diesel vehicles (Harding, $2014_{[13]}$).

Excise rates on automotive fuels should not be considered in isolation in assessing the overall tax burden on automotive transport. Vehicles may also be subject to distance-based taxes, parking taxes, road tolls, registration taxes and recurrent circulation taxes and many countries differentiate those taxes according to the type of fuel used or according to CO2 emissions per unit distance (see Chapter 4). Furthermore, the tax treatment of company car use is often more favourable – sometimes considerably so – than that of other car use (Harding, $2014_{[14]}$).

The rates shown in Annex Table 3.A.6 to Annex Table 3.A.8 are taken from the International Energy Agency and do not reflect excise duties exclusively but also include in some countries a number of taxes such as contributions to emergency stock funds.

3.6. Impact on cross-border trade

Differences in excise rates between countries often result from national traditions, social, environmental and health policy, local production and government financing needs. Such differences are not without impact on the cross-border movement of goods. The development of integrated markets (e.g. the European Union) and elimination of border controls at frontiers have shed light on the disparate excise rates between neighbouring countries to the extent that market forces are affected. In such circumstances, the effects of cross border shopping can have a significant economic impact on businesses and put pressure on the relevant tax authorities to seek closer approximation of excise duty rates with their neighbours. Differences between certain neighbouring countries may also encourage cross-border "bootlegging" activities (McKee Laura MacLehose Ellen Nolte et al., 2004[15]). Although some would argue that market forces should encourage moves towards convergence of rates, this is contradictory with other policy factors when issues such as health are taken into account in setting the rates.

3.7. Distributional impact of excise

The distributional impact of excise taxes is a concern to many policy makers. Knowing the distributional effects of excise duties allows for better fine-tuning of the distributional impacts of the overall system. While excise taxes reduce the demand for the taxed goods and thus the money households spend on them over time, they can increase immediate budgetary pressure, if introduced without further support measures. The effect of excise taxation on the poorer households depends on having the right policies in place. Flues and Van Dender (Flues and van Dender, 2017[16]) show that by taking just one-third of the additional revenues raised through stronger excise taxes on energy to fund cash transfers, policy makers can make it easier for households to pay their energy bills, not harder.

The distributional impact of excise taxes varies across the goods on which they are imposed. A recent study for 20 mainly European OECD countries showed that the combined impact of excise taxes on alcohol, tobacco and transport fuels tends to be regressive whether measured as a percentage of income or expenditure (OECD/KIPF, 2014[17]). On the other hand, research on the distributional impact of excise taxes on transport fuels has shown that these taxes are not regressive as a whole (Flues and Thomas, 2015[12]). These results imply that as households earn more they spend a smaller proportion of their income and total expenditure on excise taxes on alcohol and tobacco. Exact burdens can vary depending on tax design. For example, if richer households consume more expensive alcohol and tobacco than poorer households, richer households will face relatively higher tax burdens with an ad-valorem tax that taxes the value of the product compared to an ad quantum tax that taxes the quantity consumed. The non-regressive nature of taxes on transport fuels can be explained both by a smaller likelihood of lower income households owning a car and by driving less if they own a car.

Notes

[1] VAT may also be referred to as Goods and Services Tax (GST). For ease of reading, all value added taxes will be referred to as VAT in this chapter.

[2] NOx is a generic term for the various nitrogen oxides produced during combustion. These are considered to be important air pollutants.

References

Flues, F. and A. Thomas (2015), "The distributional effects of energy taxes", *OECD Taxation Working Papers*, No. 23, OECD Publishing, Paris, https://dx.doi.org/10.1787/5js1qwkqqrbv-en. [12]

Flues, F. and K. van Dender (2017), "The impact of energy taxes on the affordability of domestic energy", *OECD Taxation Working Papers*, No. 30, OECD Publishing, Paris, https://dx.doi.org/10.1787/08705547-en. [16]

FTA (2018), "State excise taxes rates on cigarettes FTA", https://www.taxadmin.org/assets/docs/Research/Rates/cigarette.pdf. [9]

Goodchild, M., A. Perucic and N. Nargis (2016), "Modelling the impact of raising tobacco taxes on public health and finance", *Bulletin of the World Health Organization*, Vol. 94/4, pp. 250-257, http://dx.doi.org/10.2471/blt.15.164707. [10]

Harding, M. (2014), "Personal Tax Treatment of Company Cars and Commuting Expenses: Estimating the Fiscal and Environmental Costs", *OECD Taxation Working Papers*, No. 20, OECD Publishing, Paris, https://dx.doi.org/10.1787/5jz14cg1s7vl-en. [14]

Harding, M. (2014), "The Diesel Differential: Differences in the Tax Treatment of Gasoline and Diesel for Road Use", *OECD Taxation Working Papers*, No. 21, OECD Publishing, Paris, https://dx.doi.org/10.1787/5jz14cd7hk6b-en. [13]

Health Organization Regional Office for Europe, W. (2015), *AK Using price policies to promote healthier diets*, http://www.euro.who.int/pubrequest. [1]

IEA (2018), *CO2 Emissions from Fuel Combustion 2018*, IEA, Paris, https://dx.doi.org/10.1787/co2_fuel-2018-en. [6]

KEEN, M. (1998), "The Balance between Specific and Ad Valorem Taxation", *Fiscal Studies*, Vol. 19/1, pp. 1-37, http://dx.doi.org/10.1111/j.1475-5890.1998.tb00274.x. [3]

McKee Laura MacLehose Ellen Nolte, M. et al. (2004), *Health policy and European Union enlargement*, http://www.openup.co.uk. [15]

OECD (2018), *Effective Carbon Rates 2018: Pricing Carbon Emissions Through Taxes and Emissions Trading*, OECD Publishing, Paris, https://dx.doi.org/10.1787/9789264305304-en. [7]

OECD (2013), *Taxing Energy Use: A Graphical Analysis*, OECD Publishing, Paris, https://dx.doi.org/10.1787/9789264183933-en. [11]

OECD (2011), *Environmental Taxation A Guide for Policy Makers*, OECD, http://www.oecd.org/env/tools-evaluation/48164926.pdf. [5]

OECD (2010), *Taxation, Innovation and the Environment*, OECD Publishing, Paris, https://dx.doi.org/10.1787/9789264087637-en. [4]

OECD/KIPF (2014), *The Distributional Effects of Consumption Taxes in OECD Countries*, OECD Tax Policy Studies, No. 22, OECD Publishing, Paris, https://dx.doi.org/10.1787/9789264224520-en. [17]

Sassi, F., A. Belloni and C. Capobianco (2013), "The Role of Fiscal Policies in Health Promotion", *OECD Health Working Papers*, No. 66, OECD Publishing, Paris, https://dx.doi.org/10.1787/5k3twr94kvzx-en. [2]

WHO (2017), *Report on the global tobacco epidemic 2017*, https://www.who.int/tobacco/global_report/2017/en/. [8]

Annex 3.A. Tables

Annex Table 3.A.1. Taxation of beer

Country	Currency	Specific excise per hectolitre per % abv[1]		Lower excise for small independent breweries			Excise duty on low alcohol beer Excise per hectolitre of product		VAT rate	Excise rates progressive by strength
		National currency	USD	Annual production (hl)	National currency	USD	National currency	USD	%	
Australia*	AUD	Country note		Country note			Country note		10.0	Yes
Austria	EUR	5.00	5.62	< 12 500	3	3.37	_	_	20.0	No
				< 25 000	3.5	3.93			20.0	
				< 37 500	4	4.49			20.0	
				= 50 000	4.5	5.06			20.0	
Belgium	EUR	5.01	5.63	≤ 12 500	4.36	4.90	_	_	21.0	No
				≤ 25 000	4.50	5.06			21.0	
				≤ 50 000	4.65	5.22			21.0	
				≤ 75 000	4.79	5.38			21.0	
				≤ 200 000	4.94	5.55			21.0	
Canada*	CAD	Country note		Country note			Country note		5.0/13.0 15.0	Yes
Chile*	CLP	Country note		Country note			Country note		19.0	No
Czech Republic	CZK	80.00	3.42	≤ 10 000	40.00	1.71	_	_	21.0	No
				≤ 50 000	48.00	2.06			21.0	
				≤ 100 000	56.00	2.39			21.0	
				≤ 150 000	64.00	2.74			21.0	
				≤ 200 000	72.00	3.08			21.0	
Denmark*	DKK	56.02	8.49	≤ 3 700	Country note		0.00	0.00	25.0	No
				≤ 20 000	Country note				25.0	
				< 200 000	Country note				25.0	
Estonia	EUR	16.92	19.01	≤ 6 000	8.46	9.51	_	_	20.0	No
Finland*	EUR	35.55	39.94	≤ 5 000	17.78	19.98	8.00	8.88	24.0	No
				≤ 30 000	24.89	27.97			24.0	
				≤ 55 000	28.44	31.96			24.0	
				≤ 100 000	32.00	35.96			24.0	
France*	EUR	7.42	8.34	≤ 200 000	3.71	4.17	3.70	4.16	20.0	No
Germany	EUR	1.97	2.21	≤ 5 000	1.10	1.24	_	_	19.0	No
				≤ 10 000	1.32	1.48			19.0	
				≤ 20 000	1.54	1.73			19.0	
				≤ 40 000	1.65	1.85			19.0	
Greece	EUR	12.50	14.04	≤ 200 000	6.25	7.02	_	_	24.0	No
Hungary	HUF	1620.00	5.90	≤ 200 000	810.00	2.95	-	-	27.0	No
Iceland*	ISK	Country note		_	_	_	Country note	_	11.0	Yes
Ireland*	EUR	22.55	25.34		Country note		Country note		23.0	Yes

Israel*	ILS	231.00	64.17	_	_	_	Country note		17.0	No
Italy*	EUR	7.55	8.48	_	_	_	Country note	_	22.0	No
Japan*	JPY	Country note					_	_	8.0	No
Korea*	KRW	Country note					Country note		10.0	No
Latvia*	EUR	4.50	5.06	≤ 10 000	2.25	2.53	-	-	21.0	No
Lithuania	EUR	7.11	7.99	-	-	-	-	-	21.0	No
Luxembourg *	EUR	1.98	2.22	≤ 50 000	0.98	1.10	_	_	17.0	No
				≤ 200 000	1.12	1.26	_	_	17.0	
Mexico*	MXN	26.50%					_	_	16.0	Yes
Netherlands *	EUR	Country note		_	_	_	_	_	21.0	Yes
New Zealand*	NZD	29.05	20.61				Country note		15.0	No
Norway*	NOK	See note					Country note		25.0	Yes
Poland*	PLN	19.48	5.15	Country note			_	_	23.0	No
Portugal*	EUR	See note		Country note			Country note		23.0	Yes
Slovak Republic	EUR	3.59	4.03	≤ 200 000	2.65	2.98	_	_	20.0	No
Slovenia*	EUR	12.10	13.60	20 000	6.05	6.80	_	_	22.0	No
Spain*	EUR	Country note		_	_	_	Country note		21.0	Yes
Sweden	SEK	202.00	23.63	_	_	_	_	_	25.0	No
Switzerland*	CHF	Country note					Country note		7.7	Yes
Turkey*	TRY	134.98	2.37	_	_	_	_	_	18.0	No
United Kingdom*	GBP	19.08	24.46	Country note			8.42	10.79	20.0	No
United States*	USD	Country note					_	_		No

* See Country notes to Annex Table 3.A.1.

Note: Conversion of national currency in USD: conversion rates are average market rates (2017) published in OECD Monthly Monetary Statistics (*stats.oecd.org*).

1. % abv = percentage of pure alcohol by volume at 20°C. In some countries, the excise rate on beer is calculated per hectolitre per degree Plato. For ease of reading, all amounts have been converted in % abv. There is no precise conversion between degrees Plato and % abv but for tax purposes it is often assumed that 1% abv is equivalent to 2.5 degrees Plato. As a result, tax rates expressed in degree Plato have been multiplied by 2.5 to obtain the % abv.

Source: national delegates; position as at 1 January 2018.

StatLink https://doi.org/10.1787/888933890198

Country notes to Annex Table 3.A.1

Australia. The excise rates for beer in individual containers not exceeding 48 litres are: AUD 42.84 per litre of alcohol where volume of alcohol does not exceed 3%, AUD 49.90 where volume of alcohol exceeds 3% but does not exceed 3.5% and AUD 49.90 where volume exceeds 3.5%. The rates for beer in individual containers exceeding 48 litres are: AUD 8.57 per litre of alcohol where volume of alcohol does not exceed 3%, AUD 26.83 where volume of alcohol exceeds 3% by volume of alcohol but not more than 3.5%, and AUD 33.15 where volume exceeds 3.5%. These rates apply as of 1 August 2018. Lower rates also apply for beer produced for non-commercial purposes using commercial equipment being AUD 3.01 per litre of alcohol for beer not exceeding 3% and 3.48 per litre of alcohol for beer exceeding 3% Each rate is calculated on the amount by which the alcohol content exceeds 1.15% by volume of alcohol. Beer that does not contain more than 1.15% cent by volume of alcohol is free of excise. These rates are indexed to inflation in February and August each year. Independent brewers receive an excise refund of 60% of the excise paid up to a maximum of AUD 30 000 per financial year for beer sold directly from the brewery.

Canada. Excise duty rates for beer are imposed per hectolitre of product (not per hectolitre per degree alcohol). Provincial and territorial governments also charge taxes and mark-ups on beer. Federal excise duty rates, on all beer or malt liquor containing: (1) more than 2.5% abv, CAD 31.84 per hectolitre; (2) more than 1.2% abv but not more than 2.5% abv, CAD 15.92 per hectolitre; (3) not more than 1.2% abv, CAD 2.643 per hectolitre. Reduced rates of excise duty apply on the first 75 000 hectolitres of beer and malt liquor brewed in Canada per year by licensed brewers: the aforementioned rates are reduced by (1) 90%, on the first 2 000 hectolitres, (2) 80%, on the next 3 000 hectolitres, (3) 60%, on the next 10 000 hectolitres, (4) 30%, on the next 35 000 hectolitres, and (4) 15%, on the next 25 000 hectolitres.

Chile. The sale of alcoholic beverages (including wine, beer, distilled alcoholic beverages and other alcoholic beverages) is subject to 19% VAT and also to a surtax on the sale or import of alcoholic beverages. The rate applied to beer is of 20.5% and does not depend upon the degree of alcohol that the beer contains. The tax is applied to the VAT base, that is the sale`s price (excluding VAT itself) and levies sales made between wholesale dealers. For sales between wholesalers, the tax paid to the vendor is creditable against the tax applied on sales at each stage of the value chain (including imports) until the last sale to the final retailer. The sale from the retailer to the final consumer is not subject to the surtax and the retailer cannot deduct the input tax.

Denmark. Lower rates on small independent breweries: production ⩽ 3 700 hl receives a tax reduction of DKK 77.08 per hl; production ⩽ 20 000 (X) receives a tax reduction of DKK 259.81/X + 6.83 per hl; production < 200 000 hl receives a tax reduction of DKK 22.02 - X/9083 per hl. An additional duty is placed on products which contain a mixture of beer and non-alcoholic drinks. Rates: DKK 9.38/l. of mixture with alcohol content ⩽ 10% vol. in the final product and DKK 16.39/l. of mixture with alcohol content >10% vol. in the final product. Beer with alcohol content less than 2.8% vol. is free of excise tax.

Finland. Beer with an alcoholic content less than 0.5 % vol. is free of excise.

France. Beer with alcoholic content above 18% support an additional taxation for social budget : EUR 2.97/degree of alcohol/hectolitre

Iceland. The duty in Iceland is ISK 119.6 per centilitre of alcohol per litre minus 2.25 centilitres. For example, one litre of beer that has 6% abv has 6 centilitres alcohol per litre. Therefore, the duty for one litre of beer that contains 6% abv would be as follows: (6-2.25) * 119.6 = ISK 448.5 per litre. As a result of this formula, beer with less than 2.25% abv is not taxed.

Ireland. There is remission or repayment of 50% alcohol products tax (excise duty) on beer brewed in independent small breweries producing up to 30 000 hl a year. Budget 2017 increased the qualifying production level from 30 000 to 40 000 hectolitres but maintained the current 30 000 hectolitre limit for remission/repayment of APT. For low alcohol beer, the rate is 0.00 (beer ⩽ 1.2% abv) and EUR 11.27 (beer > 1.2% abv up to 2.8% abv).

Israel. The duty was set as ILS 231 on 1 January 2018. The amount is updated each year according to the change in the Consumer Price Index (CPI). There is no duty on beer under 2% alcohol (or under 3.8% alcohol if marketed in reusable bottles). The statistical data for Israel are supplied by and under the responsibility of the relevant Israeli authorities. The use of such data by the OECD is without prejudice to the status of the Golan Heights, East Jerusalem and Israeli settlements in the West Bank under the terms of international law.

Italy. Beer with volume of alcohol does not exceed 0.5 percent is not taxed.

Japan. Excise rates are JPY 22 000 per hl of product. Reduced rates for small brewers (annual production of liquor up to 100 000 hl) apply for the first 2 000 hl of beer per year at the following rates: (a) if annual production of beer is less than or equal to 10 000 hl JPY 18 700/hl; (b) if annual production of beer is more than 10 000 hl or less than or equal to 13 000 hl, JPY 20 350/hl (temporary measure).

Korea. The rate of Liquor Tax on beer is 72% of the manufacturer's price. In addition, Education Tax (30% on the amount of Liquor Tax levied) is also levied.

Latvia. Starting from 1 March 2018 the excise per hectolitre per % abv is EUR 6.8; excise per hectolitre per % abv for small independent breweries is EUR 3.4 (not less than EUR 12.5 per hectolitre of beer). The reduced rate for small independent breweries (annual production up to 50 000 hl) is applied for the first produced 10 000 hl of beer.

Lithuania. Beer with an alcoholic content of less than 0.5% vol. is free of excise.

Luxembourg. Rates for small breweries (annual production up to 200 000 hl) range from EUR 0.40 to EUR 0.45. Additional rate for alcopops: EUR 600 per hectolitre.

Mexico. The rates apply to the value of the goods as follows: 26.5% for beer and other alcoholic beverages up to 14° Gay-Lussac (GL); 30% for beverages above 14° G.L. and up to 20° G.L.; 53% for beverages above 20° G.L. As a mechanism to discourage the use of disposable containers, taxpayers should pay the greater amount between the result of applying the corresponding rate to the value or a MXN 3 per litre fee (taxpayers that use re-usable containers can reduce an amount of MXN 1.26 per litre).

Netherlands. Most beers in the Netherlands are in the range 11°-15° Plato, usually 12° Plato, with an excise duty of EUR 37.96:12 = EUR 3.16 per degree Plato. Excise duty rates are as follows per hectolitre of product: a) Up to 7° Plato EUR 8.83; b) 7°-11° Plato EUR 28.49; c) 11°-15° Plato EUR 37.96; d) 15 or more degrees Plato EUR 47.48. Rates for small breweries (annual production up to 200 000 hl) are as follows: a) up to 7° Plato the above mentioned rate; b) 7°-11° Plato EUR 26.35; c) 11-15 degrees Plato EUR 35.11; d) 15 or more degrees Plato EUR 43.92. For beer with a maximum alcohol content of 0.5% a consumer tax of EUR 8.83 per hectolitre is applicable and a VAT rate of 6%.

New Zealand. The excise rate for beer containing more than 2.5% abv is NZD 29.054 per litre of alcohol in finished product. The rate for beer containing more than 1.15% abv but not more than 2.5% abv is NZD 0.43573 per litre of product. There is no excise duty on beer containing less than 1.15% abv.

Norway. Excise rates are as follows per hectolitre of product: a) 0.0-0.7% abv: NOK 0; b) 0.7-2.7% abv: NOK 339; c) 2.7-3.7% abv: NOK 1 274; d) 3.7-4.7% abv: NOK 2 207. The excise rate for beer with an alcoholic content of more than 4.7% abv is NOK 494 per degree of alcohol and hectolitre.

Poland. Exemptions from excise for small breweries: 1) production ≤ 200 000 hl a year – 50% of the amount of excise duty calculated with the standard rate of excise duty on beer; if producers produce more than 200 000 hl a year – to all beer produced in a year is applied the standard rate of excise duty on beer with no possibility of excise tax exemption; the above rules also apply to producers who cooperate with each others; 2) intra-Community purchase or import of beer by entities that meet the conditions specified in law – 50% of the amount of excise duty calculated with the standard rate of excise duty on beer.

Portugal. Excise rates for beer are as follows per hectolitre of product: (a) >0.5. ⩽ 1.2% abv EUR 8.34; (b) >1.2 ⩽2.8% abv EUR 10.44; (c) > 2.8 ⩽ 4.4% abv EUR 16.70; (d) > 4.4 ⩽ 5.2% abv EUR 20.89; (e) > 5.2 ⩽ 6% abv EUR 25.06; (f) >6% abv EUR 29.30 (rates as at 31 May 2018). Rates for small breweries (annual production up to 200 000 hl) are 50% of the normal rates.

Slovenia. Reduced rate for small breweries (yearly production <= 20 000 hl): EUR 6.05 per hl per % abv. Exemption for natural person use of beer if yearly production is less than 500 l.

Spain. Excise rate according to strength is: beer < 1.2% abv is free of excise; beer between 1.2% and 2.8% abv is EUR 2.75/hl; beer between 2.8% abv and 11° Plato is EUR 7.48/hl; beer with a degree Plato > 11 and not > 15 = EUR 9.96/hl; beer with a degree Plato > 15 and not > 19 = EUR 13.56/hl; beer with a degree Plato > 19 = EUR 0.91/hl and per degree Plato. There is no tax on Beer in Ceuta and Melilla (Spanish cities situated in the North of Africa).

Switzerland. Rates per hectolitre: light beer (up to 10.0° Plato): CHF 16.88, regular and special beer (10.1 to 14.0° Plato): CHF 25.32, strong beer (from 14.1° Plato): CHF 33.76. Reductions for small breweries from 40 % (annual production max. 15 000 hl) to 0 % (annual production min. 55 000 hl). Beer with more than 15 % vol. is taxed as an alcoholic beverage (CHF 2900 per hectolitre of absolute alcohol).

Turkey. The minimum tax amount is TL 134.98 per hectolitre/degree. If the amount computed according to the tax rate (63%) is lower than the minimum tax amount, the minimum tax amount is paid.

United Kingdom. Beer with an alcoholic content below 1.2% abv is free of excise duty.
Lower strength beer duty applies to beer with a strength between 1.2% to 2.8% abv.
High strength beer duty was introduced on 1 October 2011 and is a duty applied to all beer exceeding 7.5% abv. It is charged in addition to general beer duty.
Reduced duty rates apply for independent breweries making 'Small Brewery Beer'. The rates are as follows;

- producing no more than 5,000 hls: 50% of the standard duty rate of duty
- producing more than 5,000 hls but no more than 30,000 hls – duty is calculated using the formula: Annual production minus 2500 /annual production x standard rate of duty
- producing more than 30,000 hls but no more than 60,000 hls – duty is calculated using the formula: Annual production minus (2500 minus 8.33% of annual production in excess of 30,000 hls)/annual production x standard rate of duty

Breweries making 'Small Brewery Beer' cannot claim a reduction in the rate of lower strength beer duty'.

United States. The weighted average Federal and State excise tax rate is USD 22 per hectolitre of product. The Federal tax is USD 18.00 per barrel (31 gallons). 1 barrel = 1.1735 hectolitres. Small domestic brewers who produce less than 2 million barrels of beer per calendar year pay USD 7.00 in federal tax per barrel on the first 60 000 barrels. There is no progressive rate structure based on alcohol content and no Federal VAT.

European Union. According to Directive 92/83/EEC, beer with an alcoholic content less than 0.5% abv is not a beer and is not taxed in the EU.

Annex Table 3.A.2. Taxation of wine

	Currency	Still wine			Sparkling wine			Low-alcohol wine (< 8.5% abv)		
		Excise per hectolitre of product		VAT	Excise per hectolitre of product		VAT	Excise per hectolitre of product		VAT
		National currency	USD	%	National currency	USD	%	National currency	USD	%
Australia*	AUD	Country note	-	10.00	Country note	-	10.00	Country note	-	10.00
Austria	EUR	0.00	0.00	20.00	100.00	112.36	20.00	0.00	0.00	20.00
Belgium	EUR	74.91	84.17	21.00	256.32	288.40	21.00	23.91	26.87	21.00
Canada*	CAD	63.00	48.46	5.0/13.0 15.0	63.00	48.46	5.0/13.0 15.0	Country note	-	5.0/13.0 15.0
Chile*	CLP	Country note	-	19.00	Country note	-	19.00	Country note	-	19.00
Czech Republic	CZK	0.00	0.00	21.00	2340.00	100.04	21.00	0.00	0.00	21.00
Denmark*	DKK	1161.00	175.91	25.00	1496.00	226.67	25.00	534.00	80.91	25.00
Estonia*	EUR	147.82	166.09	20.00	147.82	166.09	20.00	84.41	94.84	20.00
Finland*	EUR	383.00	430.34	24.00	383.00	430.34	24.00	Country note	-	24.00
France*	EUR	3.78	4.25	20.00	9.35	10.51	20.00	3.78	4.25	20.00
Germany*	EUR	0.00	0.00	19.00	136.00	152.81	19.00	0.00	0.00	19.00
Greece	EUR	20.00	22.47	24.00	20.00	22.47	24.00	20.00	22.47	24.00
Hungary*	HUF	0.00	0.00	27.00	16460.00	59.97	27.00	0.00	0.00	27.00
Iceland*	ISK	Country note	-	11.00	Country note	-	11.00	Country note	-	11.00
Ireland*	EUR	424.84	477.35	23.00	849.68	954.70	23.00	141.57	159.07	23.00
Israel*	ILS	0.00	0.00	17.00	See note	-	17.00	0.00	0.00	17.00
Italy	EUR	0.00	0.00	22.00	0.00	0.00	22.00	0.00	0.00	22.00
Japan	JPY	8000.00	71.31	8.00	8000.00	71.31	8.00	8000.00	71.31	8.00
Korea*	KRW	Country note	-	10.00	Country note	-	10.00	Country note	-	10.00
Latvia*	EUR	78.00	87.64	21.00	78.00	87.64	21.00	Country note		21.00
Lithuania*	EUR	164.67	185.02	21.00	164.67	185.02	21.00	65.46	73.55	21.00
Luxembourg*	EUR	0.00	0.00	14 or 17	0.00	0.00	17.00	0.00	0.00	14.00
Mexico*	MXN	26.5%/30%	-	16.00	26.5%/30%	-	16.00	26.5%	-	16.00
Netherlands*	EUR	88.30	99.21	21.00	88.30	99.21	21.00	44.24	49.71	21.00
New Zealand*	NZD	Country note	-	15.00	Country note	-	15.00	Country note	-	15.00
Norway*	NOK	5928.00	716.81	25.00	5928.00	716.81	25.00	Country note	-	25.00
Poland	PLN	158.00	41.80	23.00	158.00	41.80	23.00	158.00	41.80	23.00
Portugal	EUR	0.00	0.00	13.00	0.00	0.00	23.00	0.00	0.00	23.00
Slovak Republic*	EUR	0.00	0.00	20.00	79.65	89.49	20.00	0.00	0.00	20.00
Slovenia	EUR	0.00	0.00	22.00	0.00	0.00	22.00	0.00	0.00	22.00
Spain*	EUR	0.00	0.00	21.00	0.00	0.00	21.00	0.00	0.00	21.00
Sweden*	SEK	Country note	-	25.00	Country note	-	25.00	Country note	-	25.00
Switzerland*	CHF	0.00	0.00	7.70	0.00	0.00	7.70	0.00	0.00	7.70
Turkey*	TRY	663.63	181.82	18.00	4483.51	1228.36	18.00	663.63	181.82	18.00

United Kingdom*	GBP		288.65	370.06	20.00		369.72	474.00	20.00		88.93	114.01	20.00
United States*	USD	47.00		47.00	-	116.00		116.00	-	Country note	-		-

* See Country notes to Annex Table 3.A.2.
Note: Conversion of national currency in USD: conversion rates are average market rates (2017) published in OECD Monthly Monetary Statistics (*stats.oecd.org*).
Source: National delegates; position as at 1 January 2018.

StatLink https://doi.org/10.1787/888933890217

Country notes to Annex Table 3.A.2

Australia. All wine (including still, sparkling and low alcohol wine) is liable for the wine equalisation tax (WET). WET applies at 29% of the value of the wine at the last wholesale sale (before adding GST). A rebate of WET paid, or the amount of WET that would have been paid had the buyer not quoted, applies to eligible producers, up to a maximum of AUD 350 000 each financial year.

Canada. (1) A rate of CAD 0.63 per litre applies to wine with more than 7% abv. The rate is CAD 0.301 per litre on wine of more than 1.2% abv, but not more than 7%abv; and for all wine with 1.2% abv or less the rate is CAD 0.0209 per litre. (2) Fortified wine in excess of 22.9% abv would not be included in the definition of "wine" (and, therefore, fall within the definition of "spirits"). Provincial and territorial governments also charge taxes and mark-ups on wine.

Chile. The sale of alcoholic beverages is subject to a surtax of 20.5% on the sale or import of wine, sparkling wine, champagne, cider and other alcoholic beverages (among others). The tax is applied to the VAT base, that is the sale`s price (excluding VAT itself), and levies sales made between wholesale dealers. For sales between wholesalers, the tax paid to the vendor is creditable against the tax applied on sales at each stage of the value chain (including imports) until the last sale to the final retailer. The sale from the retailer to the final consumer is not subject to this surtax and the retailer cannot deduct the input tax nor is levied with this tax the sale of wine in bulk made by producers to a taxpayer seller subject to this surtax.

Denmark. The rate for high-alcohol wine > 15 % abv – maximum 22 % abv is DKK 1 555 per hectolitre. Medium-alcohol wine < 6% abv – maximum 15 % abv is DKK 1 161 per hectolitre. Low-alcohol wine < 1.2 % abv – maximum 6 % abv is DKK 534 per hectolitre. The rates for sparkling wine correspond to the rates for still wine plus DKK 335 per hectolitre. An additional duty is placed on products that contain a mixture of wine and non-alcoholic drinks. Rates: DKK 7.13 per litre of mixture with alcohol content ⩽10 % abv in the final product and DKK 11.50 per litre of mixture with alcohol content > 10 % abv in the final product.

Estonia. Low alcohol wine means wine with alcohol content up to 6% abv.

Finland. Excise rates for low alcohol wine are as follows: a) over 1.2% abv and up to 2.8% abv EUR 24.00; b) over 2.8% abv and up to 5.5% abv EUR 187.00; c) over 5.5% abv and up to 8.0% abv EUR 268.00.

France. A reduced rate applies to the following categories of low-alcohol wine: cider, perry, mead, grapes juice lightly sparking.

Germany. Excise rate for low alcohol sparkling wine < 6 % abv is EUR 51.00. Intermediate products with a volume of alcoholic degree between 1.2 % and 22 % abv are taxed according to the following rates: > 15 % abv - 22 % abv = EUR 153/hl; <= 15 % abv = EUR 102/hl; <= 15 % abv and sparkling = EUR 136/hl.

Hungary. The rates for other fermented beverages (mostly fruit wines) are as follows: a) still: HUF 9870 per hectolitre of product, b) sparkling: HUF 16460 per hectolitre of product. c) low alcohol: HUF 0 per hectolitre of still blend of more than 50% wine and sparkling mineral water without added flavouring and not exceeding 8.5% vol. The rate for intermediate products is HUF 25520 per hectolitre of product.

Iceland. The duty rate is ISK 108.95 per centilitre of alcohol per litre minus 2.25 centilitres for wine up to 15% abv. For example, one litre of wine that has 15% abv has 15 centilitres alcohol per litre. So the duty for one litre of wine that contains 15% abv would be as follows: (15-2.25) * 108.65 = ISK 1 389.11 per litre.

Ireland. The rate for low alcohol wine applies to wine with an alcoholic content of less than 5.5% abv. The rate for still wine with alcoholic content > 15% abv is EUR 616.45. The rate for still wine exceeding 5.5% vol but not exceeding 15% volume is EUR 424.84.

Israel. The statistical data for Israel are supplied by and under the responsibility of the relevant Israeli authorities. The use of such data by the OECD is without prejudice to the status of the Golan Heights, East Jerusalem and Israeli settlements in the West Bank under the terms of international law.

Korea. The rate of liquor tax on wine is 30% on the manufacturer's price (or imported price). In addition, Education Tax (10% of the amount of Liquor tax levied) is also levied. These rates are applicable to both still and sparkling wine regardless of alcohol content.

Latvia. Starting from 1 March 2018 the excise for wine (still and sparkling) is EUR 92 per hectolitre. There is no specific rate for low-alcohol (still) wine (<8.5% abv).

Lithuania. Low-alcohol wine covers still and sparkling wine < 8.5% abv.

Luxembourg. The reduced VAT rate (14%) applies to still wine with alcoholic content ⩽ 13% abv. Additional rate for alcopops: EUR 600 per hectolitre.

Mexico. All rates apply to the value of the goods, and not per hectolitre of product, as follows: 26.5% for beer and other alcoholic beverages up to 14° Gay-Lussac (GL); 30% for beverages above 14° G.L. and up to 20° G.L.; 53% for beverages above 20° G.L.

Netherlands. For low alcohol wine < 1.2% abv the VAT rate is 6%.

New Zealand. The excise rate for unfortified wine is NZD 2.9054 per litre of product.

Norway. The rate shown in the table is the rate for wine with an alcoholic content of 12% abv. Excise rates for wine with an alcoholic content of 4.7%-22% abv = NOK 494 per vol. pct. alcohol and per hectolitre.

Slovak Republic. The rate of EUR 54.16/hl applies to sparkling fermented beverages with an alcoholic strength by volume not exceeding 8.5 % abv. The rate for intermediate products is EUR 84.24/hl.

Spain. Intermediate products - products to which distilled alcohol has been added - and with a volume of alcoholic degree between 1.2% abv and less than 22% abv are taxed according to the following rates: alcoholic degree > 1.2% abv and less than 15% abv = EUR 36.65/hl. Others = EUR 61.08/hl.

Sweden. Excise rates for alcohol wine (still and sparkling) are as follows: a) < 2.25%abv SEK 0; b) 2.25%-4.5% abv SEK 919; c) 4.5%-7% abv SEK 1358; d) 7%-8.5% abv SEK 1869; e) 8,5-15% abv SEK 2618; f) 15,0-18,0% abv SEK 5479.

Switzerland. In general natural wines made from fresh grapes with more than 18% abv and other wines with more than 15% abv are taxed as an alcoholic beverage (CHF 1 450 per hectolitre of absolute alcohol). All wines with more than 22% abv are taxed as an alcoholic beverage (CHF 2 900 per hectolitre of absolute alcohol).

Turkey. The excise rate is 0%.

United Kingdom. Reduced Rates for lower strength drinks (wine categories)are as follows; 5A exceeding 1.2% but not exceeding 4% abv = GBP 88.93; (b) exceeding 4% but not exceeding 5.5% abv = GBP 122.30; (c) low strength sparkling wine exceeding 5.5% but less than 8.5% abv = GBP 279.46; (d) sparkling wine and made wine at least 8.5% abv but not exceeding 15% abv = GBP 369.72. Rate for the band exceeding 15% abv but not exceeding 22% abv = GBP 384.82. The duty rates on wine changed on 13 March 2017 to excise duty rate on still wine 288.65, reduced rate for lower strength drinks (wine categories) (a) exceeding 1.2% but not exceeding 4% abv = GBP 88.93 (b)exceeding 4% but not exceeding 5.5% abv = GBP 122.30 and (c) low strength sparkling wine exceeding 5.5% but less than 8.5% abv = 279.46 (d) sparkling wine and made wine at least 8.5% abv but not exceeding 15% abv = 369.72. Rate in the band exceeding 15% abv but not exceeding 22% abv = GBP 384.82.

United States. The weighted average Federal and State excise tax rate is USD 47 per hectolitre of product for still wine up to 14% abv and USD 116 for sparkling wine. The Federal excise rates are as follows: a) up to 14% abv: USD 1.07 per gallon; b) 14%-21% abv: USD 1.57 per gallon; c) 21%-24% abv: USD 3.15 per gallon; d) artificially carbonated wine USD 3.30 per gallon; and e) sparkling wine USD 3.40 per gallon. 26.42 US gallons = 1 hectolitre. There is no Federal VAT.

Annex Table 3.A.3. Taxation of alcoholic beverages[1]

Currency		Tax per hectolitre of absolute alcohol			
		Excise		VAT rate	Small distillery rate
		National currency	USD	%	
Australia*	AUD	8105.00	6187.02	10.00	No
Austria*	EUR	1200.00	1348.31	20.00	Yes
Belgium	EUR	2992.79	3362.69	21.00	No
Canada*	CAD	1193.00	917.69	5.0/13.0/15.0	No
Chile*	CLP	Country note	-	19.00	No
Czech Republic	CZK	28500.00	1218.47	21.00	No
Denmark*	DKK	15000.00	2272.73	25.00	No
Estonia	EUR	2508.00	2817.98	20.00	No
Finland*	EUR	4785.00	5376.40	24.00	No
France*	EUR	1741.04	1956.22	20.00	No
Germany*	EUR	1303.00	1464.04	19.00	Yes
Greece*	EUR	2450.00	2752.81	24.00	No
Hungary*	HUF	333385.00	1214.61	27.00	Yes
Iceland*	ISK	1474000.00	13798.91	11.00	No
Ireland*	EUR	4257.00	4783.15	23.00	No
Israel*	ILS	8424.00	2340	17.00	No
Italy*	EUR	1032.52	1160.13	22.00	No
Japan*	JPY	Country note	-	8.00	No
Korea*	KRW	See note	-	10.00	No
Latvia*	EUR	1450.00	1629.21	21.00	No
Lithuania*	EUR	1665.04	1870.83	21.00	No
Luxembourg	EUR	1041.15	1169.83	17.00	No
Mexico*	MXN	53%	-	16.00	No
Netherlands*	EUR	1686.00	1894.38	6.0/21.0	No
New Zealand*	NZD	Country note	-	15.00	No
Norway	NOK	75800.00	9165.66	25.00	No
Poland	PLN	5704.00	1508.99	23.00	No
Portugal*	EUR	1386.93	1558.35	23.00	Yes
Slovak Republic*	EUR	1080.00	1213.48	20.00	No
Slovenia*	EUR	1320.00	1483.15	22.00	Yes
Spain*	EUR	913.28	1026.16	21.00	Yes
Sweden	SEK	51659.00	6031.46	25.00	No
Switzerland*	CHF	2900.00	2929.29	7.70	Yes
Turkey*	TRY	18439.82	5052.01	18.00	No
United Kingdom*	GBP	2874.00	3684.62	20.00	No
United States*	USD	995.00	995.00	-	No

* See Country notes to Annex Table 3.A.3.

Note: Conversion of national currency in USD: conversion rates are average market rates (2017) published in OECD Monthly Monetary Statistics (*stats.oecd.org*).

1. Alcoholic beverages other than those included in Annex Table 3.A.1. and Annex Table 3.A.2.

Source: national delegates. Position as at 1 January 2018.

StatLink https://doi.org/10.1787/888933890236

Country notes to Annex Table 3.A.3

Australia. The excise duty of AUD 84.51 per litre of alcohol applies to spirits and other excisable beverages (except beer). A lower rate of AUD 78.93 per litre of alcohol applies to brandy (distilled from grape wine). These rates apply as of 1 August 2018 and are indexed to inflation in February and August of each year. Independent distillers receive an excise refund of 60% of the excise paid up to a maximum of AUD 30 000 per financial year.

Austria. For small distilleries producing not more than 4hl pure alcohol per year the rate is EUR 648.(54% of the standard rate).

Canada. (1) Spirits are subject to excise duty at the rate of CAD 11.930 per litre abv. Spirits containing not more than 7% abv are subject to excise duty at the rate of CAD 0.301 per litre. (2) Beer with an alcoholic strength in excess of 11.9% abv is deemed to be Spirits. Provincial and territorial governments also charge taxes and mark-ups on spirits.

Chile. Alcoholic beverages are subject to a surtax on the sale or import. The rates applied are the following: 31.5% on liquors, brandy, vermouth, pisco, whiskey and other distilled alcoholic beverages; 20.5% on beer, wine, sparkling wine, champagne, cider and other alcoholic beverages. The tax is applied to the VAT base, that is the sale`s price (excluding VAT itself) and levies sales made between wholesale dealers. For sales between wholesalers, the tax paid to the vendor is creditable against the tax applied on sales at each stage of the value chain (including imports) until the last sale to the final retailer. The sale from this retailer to the final consumer is not subject to the surtax and the retailer cannot deduct the input tax nor is levied with this tax the sale of wine in bulk made by producers to a taxpayer seller subject to this surtax.

Czech Republic. The reduced rate of CZK 14 300 per hectolitre of pure alcohol applies for small fruit grower's distilleries producing no more than 30 litres of fruit spirit per year per household. The excise duty of CZK 2 340 per hectolitre of product is applicable for intermediate products.

Denmark. An additional duty is placed on products which contain a mixture of spirits and non-alcoholic drinks, Rates: DKK 4.21 per litre of mixture.

Finland. Excise rates are as follows: (a) CN - code 2208 alcoholic content between 1.2% abv and 2.8% abv. EUR 880; (b) Other products EUR 4 785.

France. Additional taxation for social budget : EUR 559.02 per hectolitre of absolute alcohol.

Germany. The rates for small distilleries are EUR 730 or EUR 1 022. Additional rate for alcopops: EUR 5 550 per hectolitre of absolute alcohol.

Greece. The rate for ouzo is EUR 1225 per hectolitre of pure alcohol.

Hungary. A reduced rate of 50% applies to ethyl-alcohol produced by fruit growers' distilleries from fruit supplied to them by private fruit growers. The application of reduced rate is limited to 43 litres of pure alcohol for private consumption per fruit grower household per year.

Iceland. Excise rate shown in the table is the rate for other alcohol than beer or wine up to 15% abv. The rate is ISK 147 per each centilitre of alcohol.

Ireland. This table illustrates the tax per hectolitre of absolute alcohol for spirits. However, other fermented beverages and intermediate beverages are taxed as follows: other fermented beverages (cider and perry) still and sparkling ≤ 2.8% abv EUR 47.23/hl; still and sparkling > 2.8% avb but not exceeding 6.0% avb EUR 94.46/hl; still and sparkling >6.0% avb but not exceeding 8.5% avb EUR 218.44/hl; still >8.5% avb EUR 309.84/hl and sparkling >8.5% avb EUR 619.70/hl. Other fermented beverages (other than cider and perry) still and sparkling ≤ 5.5% abv EUR 141.57/hl; still >5.5% avb EUR 424.84/hl and sparkling >5.5% avb EUR 849.68/hl. Intermediate beverages: still ≤ 15% abv EUR 424.84/hl; still >15% avb EUR 616.45/hl; sparkling EUR 849.68/hl.

Israel. The statistical data for Israel are supplied by and under the responsibility of the relevant Israeli authorities. The use of such data by the OECD is without prejudice to the status of the Golan Heights, East Jerusalem and Israeli settlements in the West Bank under the terms of international law.

Italy. Taxation applies for beverages of alcoholic strength exceeding 1.2% abv. The rate of EUR 88.67 applies to intermediate products.

Japan. Excise rates are as follows: a) Whiskey and brandy (40% abv) JPY 40 000; b) Spirits (37% abv) JPY 37 000; c) Shochu Group A and B (25% abv) JPY 25 000.

Korea. As Excise Tax for liquor is based on the value of the product, the rate does not vary with alcohol content. For whiskey, brandy, general distilled spirits, liquor, diluted soju and distilled soju, the Liquor tax is 72% and the Education tax is 30%.

Latvia. Starting from 1 March 2018 the excise rate is EUR 1670 per hectolitre of absolute alcohol.

Lithuania. Intermediate products below 15% abv are taxed at 185.82 per hectolitre of product; intermediate products above 15% abv are taxed at 264.52 per hectolitre of product.

Luxembourg. Additional rate for alcopops: EUR 600 per hectolitre.

Mexico. The excise tax is set at an ad valorem rate and not per hectolitre of product. The rates for alcoholic beverages apply to the value of the goods as follows: 26.5% up to 14° Gay-Lussac (G.L.); 30% above 14° G.L. and up to 20° G.L.; 53% above 20° G.L.

Netherlands. For low alcohol spirits with an alcoholic content <1.2% the VAT rate is 6%.

New Zealand. For alcoholic beverages with 9-14% abv, the excise rate is NZD 2.9054 per litre. For alcoholic beverages above 14% abv, the excise rate is NZD 52.916 per litre of absolute alcohol (with the exception of unfortified wine and vermouth which has the rate of NZD 2.7870 per litre of product).

Portugal. Intermediate products are taxed at EUR 76,10/hl; Ethyl alcohol/spirits: EUR 1 386,93/hl (rates applicable as at 31 May 2018). A reduced rate of 50% applies to small distilleries.

Slovak Republic. A reduced rate of 50 % of the national rate of excise duty on ethyl alcohol, applies to ethyl alcohol produced by fruit growers′ distilleries. The application of the reduced rate is limited to 43 litres of ethyl alcohol for personal consumption of the fruit growers′ household per year.

Slovenia. Tax per hectolitre of absolute alcohol is EUR 1 320. For small producers not producing more than 150 litres of spirits per year, the rate is EUR 660 per hl.

Spain. The excise rate in the Canary Islands is EUR 714.63 per Hl of pure alcohol. There is a special regime for small distilleries for which the rate is EUR 799.19 per hl (or EUR 622.23 in the Canary Islands).

Switzerland. Under certain conditions farmers do not pay tax on the alcohol produced for their personal consumption. A reduced rate of 30 % is applied to the first 30 litres of pure alcohol produced per year by small producers. Normal rate: CHF 2900 per hectolitre. Special rate for certain types of wines: CHF 1450 per hectolitre. Special rate for alcopops: CHF 11 600 per hectolitre (Alcopop -also called ready to drink (RTD) or designer drink) is a mix of alcohol and soda.

Turkey. The excise rate is 0%. If the tax amount computed according to the tax rate is lower than the minimum tax amount specified in the table, then the minimum tax amount is paid.

United Kingdom. All drinks over 22% are taxed as spirits. Most other mixtures of spirits with other types of alcohol are also taxed as spirits. The duty rates for cider and perry are: still cider and perry exceeding 1.2% but not exceeding 7.5% abv =GBP 40.38; still cider and perry exceeding 7.5% but less than 8.5% abv = GBP 61.04; sparkling cider and perry exceeding 1.2% abv but not exceeding 5.5% abv = GBP 279.46; sparkling cider and perry exceeding 5.5% but not exceeding 8.5% abv = GBP 279.46.

United States. The weighted average Federal and State excise tax rate is USD 995 per hectolitre. The Federal excise rate is USD 13.50 per proof gallon. A proof gallon is a US gallon (3.785 litres) containing 50% alcohol. There is no Federal VAT.

Annex Table 3.A.4. Taxation of tobacco

	Currency	Cigarettes			Cigars[2]			Rolling tobacco for cigarettes			VAT
		Specific excise per 1 000		Excise on value	Specific excise per 1 000		Excise on value	Specific excise per 1 000 grams		Excise on value	
		National currency	USD	% of RSP[1]	National currency	USD	% of RSP[1]	National currency	USD	% of RSP[1]	%
Australia*	AUD	530.96	405.31	0.00	Country note	-	0.00	663.72	506.66	0.00	10.00
Austria*	EUR	58.00	65.17	37.50	0.00	0.00	13.00	0.00	0.00	56.00	20.00
Belgium	EUR	64.60	72.58	40.04	0.00	0.00	10.00	42.35	47.58	31.50	21.00
Canada*	CAD	107.80	82.92	00.00	Country note	-	Country note	134.75	103.65	00.00	5.0/13.0/15.0
Chile*	CLP	46323.00	71.41	30.00	0.00	0.00	52.60	0.00	0.00	59.70	19.00
Czech Republic	CZK	1460.00	62.42	27.00	1710.00	73.11	-	2236.00	95.60	-	21.00
Denmark*	DKK	1182.50	179.17	1.00	500.00	75.76	10.00	788.50	119.47	0.00	25.00
Estonia*	EUR	69.50	78.09	30.00	151.00	169.66	10.00	76.84	86.34	0.00	20.00
Finland*	EUR	53.75	60.39	52.00	10.00	11.24	34.00	36.25	40.73	52.00	24.00
France	EUR	48.75	54.78	49.70	19.00	21.35	23.00	67.50	75.84	37.74	20.00
Germany	EUR	98.20	110.34	21.69	14.00	15.73	1.47	48.49	54.48	14.76	19.00
Greece	EUR	82.50	92.70	26.00	0.00	0.00	35.00	170.00	191.01	0.00	24.00
Hungary*	HUF	15700.00	57.20	25.00	0.00	0.00	14.00	14000.00	51.01	0.00	27.00
Iceland*	ISK	24552.50	229.85	0.00	Country note	-	0.00	27300.00	255.57	0.00	24.00
Ireland*	EUR	309.04	347.24	9.04	Country note	-	0.00	335.34	376.79	0.00	23.00
Israel*	ILS	395.00	109.72	Country note	0.00	0.00	Country note	454.02	126.12	0.00	17.00
Italy	EUR	19.36	21.75	59.10	0.00	0.00	23.00	0.00	0.00	58.50	22.00
Japan*	JPY	12244.00	109.15	0.00	12244.00	109.15	0.00	12244.00	109.15	0.00	8.00
Korea*	KRW	145450.00	128.64	64.64	Country note	-	0.00	103200.00	91.28	0.00	10.00
Latvia*	EUR	67.00	75.28	20.00	73.00	82.02	-	66.00	74.16	-	21.00
Lithuania*	EUR	56.00	62.92	25.00	33.00	37.08	-	60.24	67.69	-	21.00
Luxembourg	EUR	18.89	20.22	46.65	0.00	0.00	10.00	15.85	17.81	33.15	17.00
Mexico*	MXN	350.00	18.55	40.28	Country note	-	Country note	Country note	-	Country note	16.00
Netherlands	EUR	173.10	194.49	5.00	0.00	0.00	6.00	106.65	119.83	0.00	21.00
New Zealand*	NZD	Country note	-	0.00	Country note	-	0.00	Country note	-	0.00	15.00

Norway	NOK	2590.00	313.18	0.00	2590.00	313.18	0.00	2590.00	313.18	0.00	25.00
Poland*	PLN	206.76	54.70	31.41	393.00	103.97	-	141.29	37.38	31.41	23.00
Portugal*	EUR	94.89	106.62	15.00	0.00	0.00	25.00	80.00	89.89	15.00	23.00
Slovak Republic*	EUR	61.80	69.44	23.00	71.11	79.90	-	73.90	83.03	0.00	20.00
Slovenia*	EUR	71.32	80.13	22.61	0.00	0.00	6.30	42.00	46.62	37.00	22.00
Spain	EUR	24.10	27.08	51.00	0.00	0.00	15.80	22.00	24.72	41.50	21.00
Sweden	SEK	1540.00	180.12	1.00	1360.00	159.06	0.00	1884.00	220.35	0.00	25.00
Switzerland*	CHF	118.32	119.52	25.00	5.60	5.66	1.00	38.00	38.38	25.00	7.70
Turkey*	TRY	242.90	66.55	65.25	242.90	66.55	40.00	242.90	66.55	65.25	18.00
United Kingdom*	GBP	217.23	278.50	16.50	270.96	347.38	0.00	221.18	283.56	0.00	20.00
United States*	USD	135.00	135.00	Country note	Country note	-	-	Country note	-	-	-

* See Country notes to Annex Table 3.A.4.

Note: Conversion of national currency in USD: conversion rates are average market rates (2015) published in OECD Monthly Monetary Statistics (*stats.oecd.org*).

1. RSP. Retail selling price.

2. Cigars. Denmark and Japan tax cigars at a rate per 1 000 pieces and not according to weight. In Denmark it is assumed that a cigar weighs 3 grams and in Japan 1 gram.

Source: national delegates. Position as at 1 January 2018.

StatLink https://doi.org/10.1787/888933890255

Country notes to Annex Table 3.A.4

Australia. The excise rate of AUD 0.80726 per stick applies to cigarettes or cigars (in stick form) not exceeding in weight 0.8 grams per stick actual tobacco content. Other tobacco products are subject to an excise rate of AUD 1076.35.72 per kilogram of tobacco content. These rates apply from 1 January 2018.

Austria. The excise duty on cigars is 13% of RSP, at least EUR 100 for 1 000 pieces. Minimum excise duty on rolling tobacco for cigarettes is EUR 100 per kg. The minimum excise duty on cigarettes is 98% of the total excise duty burden on cigarettes falling under the WAP.

Canada. The excise duty on cigars is CAD 23.46235 per 1 000 cigars plus an additional excise duty based on the greater of CAN 0.08434 per cigar and 84% of the sale price. Each province and territory also levies a tobacco tax at varying rates on all tobacco products. Retail sales prices are subject to GST/HST and, in some cases, when the HST is not applicable, to a provincial sales tax.

Chile. The sale of tobacco products is subject to 19% VAT and to a tax on the sale or import of processed tobacco, cigarettes and cigars. The tax applied to processed tobacco is of 59.7% on the sales` price. Cigarettes are taxed at a rate of 30% over the pack` sales price and with an additional rate of 0,0010304240 of a Monthly Tax Unit per cigarette contained in the pack (a Monthly Tax Unit equals approximately CLP 47 019 or USD 76.48). Cigars are taxed at a rate of 52.6%. The tax base of the excise tax is the sale` price to the final consumer, including VAT and the tax levied on tobacco, cigarettes and cigars.

Denmark. The excise tax for other smoking tobaccos is DKK 738.5 / 1 000 g. for coarse-cut tobacco

Estonia. For cigarettes, the minimal excise amount to be paid is EUR 113.38 per 1000 items. For cigars and cigarillos, the minimal excise amount to be paid is EUR 211 per 1000 items.

Finland. Excise rates shown as of 1 January 2018. Cigarette paper: excise 60% of RSP. Other smoking tobacco: EUR 46.50 /kg and 48 % of RSP. Minimum excise tax for cigarettes is EUR 235.50 per 1000 pieces and EUR 143.50 /kg for fine cut rolling tobacco for cigarettes. As of 1 July 2018, the excise tax on cigarettes is EUR 58.00 per 1000 cigarettes and 52% of RSP. Minimum excise tax is EUR 248 per 1000 cigarettes. For cigars excise tax is EUR 15 per 1000 cigars and 34% of RSP. For fine cut rolling tobacco for cigarettes EUR 39.00 /kg and 52% of RSP. Minimum excise tax for fine cut rolling tobacco is EUR 151/kg. Other smoking tobacco: EUR 51.50 /kg and 48 % of RSP.

France. The minimal excise amounts to be paid are EUR 210 per 1000 items for cigarettes, EUR 92 per 1000 items for cigars and EUR 167 per 1000 g for rolling tobacco for cigarettes.

Hungary. Minimum excise tax is HUF 28 000 per 1000 pieces for cigarettes, HUF 4 000 per 1000 pieces for cigar and cigarillo. VAT as % of tax included retail selling price is 21.26%.

Iceland. There is no specific excise rate for a piece of cigar. The rate is ISK 27 300 per 1000 grams of cigars (i.e. the same rate as for rolling tobacco).

Ireland. The rate of excise duty on cigarettes is EUR 309.04 per 1000 cigarettes together with an amount equal to 9.04% of the price at which the cigarettes are sold by retail or EUR 344.07 per 1000 cigarettes, whichever is the greater. The rate of excise duty on cigars is EUR 355.238 per kilogram. The rate of excise duty on fine-cut tobacco for the rolling of cigarettes is EUR 335.238 per kilogram. The rate of excise duty on fine-cut tobacco for the rolling of cigarettes is EUR 335.342 per kilogram. Other smoking tobacco is subject to excise duty at a rate of EUR 246.449 per kilogram.

Israel. Excises on value for cigarettes and for cigars are 270% and 90% of the wholesale price, respectively. The statistical data for Israel are supplied by and under the responsibility of the relevant Israeli authorities. The use of such data by the OECD is without prejudice to the status of the Golan Heights, East Jerusalem and Israeli settlements in the West Bank under the terms of international law.

Japan. The tax consists of a national element, a prefectural element and a municipal element. As of 1 October 2018, the excise rate is JPY 13 244 per 1 000 pieces (cigarettes, cigars) or per 1 000 grams (rolling tobacco for cigarettes).

Korea. The excise tax on cigars is KRW 294800/1000g. National tax (Individual Consumption Tax) levies on tobacco since 2015.

Latvia. Starting from 1 July 2018 the specific excise is EUR 74.60 per 1000 cigarettes and 20% of RSP. Minimum excise EUR 109.20 per 1000 cigarettes.

Lithuania. Minimum excise for cigarettes is EUR 90.00 per 1000 pieces. Starting from 1 March 2018 the specific excise for cigarettes is EUR 59.00 per 1000 pieces; minimum excise is EUR 96 per 1000 cigarettes. The excise rate for cigars and cigarillos is set per kilogram. Starting from 1 March 2018 excise for cigars and cigarillos is EUR 37.00 per kilogram.

Luxembourg. Change of excise duties on tobacco products is generally applicable starting 1st February. Minimum excise duty is EUR 116 per 1 000 cigarettes. Minimum excise duty is EUR 50 per kilo of rolling tobacco for cigarettes. Minimum excise duty for cigars is EUR 23.50 per 1 000.

Mexico. An ad-valorem rate of 160% on the producer or importer price applies for all categories. A reduced rate of 30.4% applies for cigars or rolling tobacco as long as these products are fully handmade. The ad-valorem tax applies at the stage of the producer or importer but on the retail price. In addition a charge of MXN 0.35 should be paid for each sold or imported cigarette. This charge also applies for cigars and other tobacco (MXN 0.35 per each 0.75 grams), with the exemption of those that are fully handmade.

New Zealand. The excise rate for 1 000 cigarettes with actual tobacco content not exceeding in weight of 0.8 kg is NZD 738.13. The excise rate for Cigarettes exceeding 0.8 kg in actual tobacco content per 1 000 cigarettes is NZD 1051.83 The excise rate per kilo of tobacco content for other tobacco products, such as snuff, cigars, cheroots and cigarillos is NZD 922.64.

Poland. Since 1 January 2015 the excise duty rate for cigars is calculated on per kilogramme basis.

Portugal. Rates applicable since 1 January 2018. Excise tax on cigarettes is reduced to (1) EUR 34.00 and 40% for cigarettes sold in Azores Islands and made by small producers from the Azores and Madeira Islands; (2) 78.37 and 20% for cigarettes sold in Madeira Island and made by small producers from the Azores and Madeira Islands.

Slovak Republic. Tax on rolling tobacco for cigarettes includes other smoking tobacco. The excise for cigars is EUR 71.11/kg.

Slovenia. Minimum excise duty is EUR 111 per 1 000 cigarettes. Minimum excise duty is EUR 92 per kilo of rolling tobacco for cigarettes. Minimum excise duty for cigars is EUR 42 per kilo.

Switzerland. If the Retail Selling Price for 1 000 cigarettes is CHF 375.00 or less, minimum excise duty (specific + on value) yields CHF 212.10 for 1 000 pieces. Specific excise per 1 000 grams of rolling tobacco for cigarettes: the minimum excise duty (specific + on value) yields CHF 80.00 per 1 000 grams.

Turkey. Minimum tax amount per 1000 cigarettes is TL 242.90. Specific tax amount is TL 0.3246 for 1 pack of cigarettes. Tax on cigarettes and other tobacco products computed according to the tax rate cannot be less than the minimum tax amount. After calculating the tax according to minimum tax amount system, specific tax amount is added to the tax for 1 pack of cigarettes.

United Kingdom. Specific excise rate for cigars is given per kilogramme and not for 1 000 units. Specific rates exist for "other smoking tobacco" and "other chewing tobacco" which are currently both set at GBP 119.13 per kilo.

United States. State taxes vary widely. The weighted average of Federal and State taxes per thousand cigarettes is USD 135.00. Federal specific excise tax rates on tobacco are: USD 50.33 per thousand for small cigarettes (no more than 3 pounds per thousand); USD 105.69 per thousand for large cigarettes; USD 50.33 per thousand for small cigars weighing no more than 3 pounds per thousand; 52.75% of the manufacturers price but not more than USD 402.60 per thousand for large cigars; and USD 24.78 per pound (54.63 per kg) for roll-your-own tobacco. Some states also tax on an ad valorem basis.

Annex Table 3.A.5. Tax burden as a share of total price for cigarettes[1]

Country	Ex-tax price USD[2]	Specific excise % RSP[3]	Excise on value % RSP[4]	VAT/GST/RST % RSP[5]	Total tax share % RSP	Price of a 20 cigarettes pack[6]		
						Currency	Price (RSP in local currency)	Price (RSP in USD)
Australia	6.62	49.80	0.00	9.09	58.89	AUD	21.00	16.09
Austria	1.13	24.36	37.50	16.67	78.52	EUR	4.76	5.27
Belgium	1.57	14.33	45.84	17.36	77.53	EUR	6.32	6.99
Canada*	2.62	57.24	0.00	8.97	66.21	CAD	10.29	7.77
Chile	0.35	43.16	30.00	15.97	89.13	CLP	2178.00	3.22
Czech Republic	0.76	33.95	27.00	17.36	78.31	CZK	86.00	3.52
Denmark	1.65	53.75	1.00	20.00	74.75	DKK	44.00	6.54
Estonia	0.96	30.53	30.00	16.67	77.20	EUR	3.80	4.20
Finland	1.02	13.56	52.00	19.35	84.91	EUR	6.12	6.77
France	1.53	13.93	49.70	16.67	80.30	EUR	7.00	7.74
Germany	1.79	32.73	21.69	15.97	70.39	EUR	5.47	6.05
Greece	0.65	40.24	26.00	19.35	85.59	EUR	4.10	4.54
Hungary	1.08	27.26	25.00	21.26	73.52	HUF	1152.00	4.09
Iceland	4.56	36.18	0.00	19.35	55.53	ISK	1240.00	10.26
Ireland	2.60	50.36	9.20	18.70	78.26	EUR	10.80	11.95
Israel*	1.58	22.19	46.18	14.53	82.90	ILS	35.60	9.27
Italy	1.38	6.88	51.03	18.03	75.94	EUR	5.20	5.75
Japan	1.49	55.65	0.00	7.41	63.06	JPY	440.00	4.04
Korea	1.01	64.76	0.00	9.03	73.85	KRW	4500.00	3.88
Latvia	0.67	37.47	25.00	17.36	79.83	EUR	3.00	3.32
Lithuania	0.86	32.70	25.00	17.36	75.06	EUR	3.10	3.44
Luxembourg	1.68	7.07	46.65	17.00	70.72	EUR	5.20	5.75
Mexico	0.90	13.50	40.28	13.79	67.58	MXN	51.84	2.78
Netherlands	2.04	54.01	0.83	17.36	72.20	EUR	6.63	7.33
New Zealand	5.51	58.81	0.00	13.04	71.85	NZD	28.11	19.56

Norway	4.39	46.04	0.00	20.00	66.04	NOK	108.60	12.93
Poland	0.74	31.13	31.41	18.67	81.25	PLN	13.28	3.93
Portugal	1.40	37.85	17.00	18.70	73.55	EUR	4.80	5.31
Slovak Republic	0.71	39.54	23.00	16.67	79.21	EUR	3.10	3.43
Slovenia	1.10	35.29	21.18	18.03	74.51	EUR	3.90	4.31
Spain	1.16	9.94	51.00	17.36	78.29	EUR	4.85	5.37
Sweden	2.32	47.50	1.00	20.00	68.50	SEK	63.16	7.38
Switzerland	3.38	28.45	25.00	7.41	60.86	CHF	8.50	8.63
Turkey	0.79	1.89	65.25	15.25	82.39	TRY	13.50	4.47
United Kingdom	2.18	47.33	16.50	16.67	80.50	GBP	8.30	11.20
United States	3.66	37.81	0.00	5.20	43.01	USD	6.43	6.43

* Canada and the United States, national average estimates calculated for prices and taxes reflect the fact that different rates are applied by state/province over and above the applicable federal tax.

* Israel: The statistical data are supplied by and under the responsibility of the relevant Israeli authorities. The use of such data by the OECD is without prejudice to the status of the Golan Heights, East Jerusalem and Israeli settlements in the West Bank under the terms of international law.

Notes:

1. The share of taxes are presented as a % of Retail Selling Price (RSP) for a pack of 20 cigarettes. The RSP is defined as the Weighted Average Price (WAP) i.e. the average consumer price of a tobacco product based on the prices of individual brands and weighted by sales of each brand in the country. Where the WAP is not available, the RSP is defined as the average price of the most sold brand of cigarettes on the market (MSB - see Annex C). This table reflects the situation in 2016 since it is based on annual average prices and taxes (as at 1 July 2016) that are not available for the year 2017 at the time of this publication.
2. The pre-tax price includes the producer and distributor margins. It is estimated by the deduction of the total tax share from the RSP.
3. Specific excise: a specific excise tax is a tax on a specific good produced or imported in a country charged as a fixed amount per unit of the product. The amount shown in this table is as a percentage of RSP.
4. Excise on value: an excise on value or ad valorem is a tax on a product produced or imported in a country charged as a percentage of the value of a transaction. Example: 50% of the RSP.
5. VAT/GST: Value added tax or Goods and services tax (see Chapter 1). RST: Retail sales taxes for Canada (in some provinces) and the United States. The amount is shown as a percentage of RSP.
6. Price of a 20 cigarettes pack of the Most Sold Brand (see Annex C).
7. In this table, amounts in local currency are converted in USD using the average market exchange rate 2016 published in OECD Monthly Monetary Statistics (*stats.oecd.org*).

Source: World Health Organisation and national delegates.

StatLink https://doi.org/10.1787/888933890274

Annex Table 3.A.6. Taxation of premium unleaded gasoline (per litre) 2017[1]

Country	Currency	Ex-tax price[2]		Excise[3]		VAT rate[4]	VAT amount	Total tax	Total price	Total tax as % of total price
		National currency	USD	National currency	USD	%	USD	USD	USD	
Australia	AUD	0.948	0.726	0.403	0.309	10.00	0.104	0.412	1.139	36.2
Austria*	EUR	0.499	0.563	0.493	0.556	20.00	0.224	0.779	1.342	58.1
Belgium	EUR	0.571	0.644	0.605	0.682	21.00	0.278	0.960	1.604	59.9
Canada*	CAD	0.812	0.626	0.255	0.196	11.97	0.098	0.295	0.920	32.0
Chile*	CLP	372.97	0.575	289.76	0.447	19.00	0.109	0.556	1.130	49.1
Czech Republic	CZK	12.170	0.521	12.840	0.549	21.00	0.225	0.774	1.295	59.8
Denmark*	DKK	4.428	0.671	4.594	0.696	25.00	0.342	1.037	1.708	60.7
Estonia	EUR	0.529	0.596	0.512	0.579	20.00	0.235	0.812	1.408	57.7
Finland*	EUR	0.474	0.534	0.696	0.785	24.00	0.317	1.109	1.636	67.3
France*	EUR	0.498	0.561	0.651	0.734	20.00	0.259	0.993	1.554	63.9
Germany*	EUR	0.500	0.564	0.655	0.738	19.00	0.247	0.986	1.550	63.6
Greece	EUR	0.517	0.583	0.700	0.789	24.00	0.329	1.118	1.701	65.7
Hungary*	HUF	157.990	0.576	122.674	0.447	27.00	0.276	0.723	1.299	55.7
Iceland*	ISK	92.060	0.862	75.550	0.707	24.00	0.376	1.084	1.945	55.7
Ireland	EUR	0.531	0.599	0.588	0.663	23.00	0.290	0.953	1.552	61.4
Israel*	ILS	2.180	0.606	3.016	0.838	17.00	0.224	1.062	1.667	63.7
Italy	EUR	0.531	0.599	0.728	0.821	22.00	0.312	1.133	1.732	65.4
Japan*	JPY	71.500	0.637	56.600	0.505	8.00	0.091	0.596	1.233	48.3
Korea	KRW	896.350	0.793	781.890	0.692	10.00	0.148	0.840	1.633	51.4
Latvia	EUR	0.524	0.591	0.436	0.492	21.00	0.227	0.719	1.310	54.9
Lithuania*	EUR	0,500	0.562	0.434	0.488	21.00	0.220	0.708	1.270	55.8
Luxembourg*	EUR	0.539	0.608	0.462	0.521	17.00	0.192	0.713	1.320	54.0
Mexico*	MXN	15.380	0.813	0.000	0.000	16.00	0.130	0.130	0.943	13.8
Netherlands	EUR	0.509	0.574	0.786	0.886	21.00	0.305	1.185	1.758	67.5
New Zealand*	NZD	1.025	0.729	0.665	0.473	15.00	0.180	0.653	1.381	47.3
Norway*	NOK	5.350	0.647	6.230	0.753	25.00	0.350	1.103	1.750	63.0
Poland*	PLN	2.102	0.556	1.669	0.442	23.00	0.230	0.671	1.227	54.7

Portugal	EUR	0.548	0.618	0.652	0.735	23.00	0.311	1.046	1.664	62.9
Slovak Republic*	EUR	0.579	0.653	0.514	0.579	20.00	0.246	0.826	1.479	55.9
Slovenia*	EUR	0.471	0.531	0.564	0.636	22.00	0.257	0.893	1.424	62.7
Spain*	EUR	0.552	0.622	0.461	0.520	21.00	0.240	0.760	1.382	55.0
Sweden*	SEK	4.988	0.583	6.175	0.722	25.00	0.326	1.049	1.632	64.3
Switzerland	CHF	0.704	0.715	0.731	0.742	8.0	0.117	0.859	1.573	54.6
Turkey	TRY	2.332	0.639	2.377	0.652	18.00	0.232	0.884	1.523	58.0
United Kingdom	GBP	0.410	0.528	0.580	0.746	20.00	0.255	1.001	1.529	65.5
United States*	USD	0.492	0.591	0.147	0.147	-	-	0.147	0.738	19.9

* See Country notes to Table Annex Table 3.A.6.

Note: Conversion of national currency in USD: conversion rates are average market rates (2017) published in OECD Monthly Monetary Statistics (stats.oecd.org). See also Annex B.

1. Prices and taxes as at 4th Quarter 2017.
2. Ex-tax price is the price excluding VAT and excise.
3. Excise taxes are expressed in local currency/USD per litre. They include all non-VAT taxes levied on the product. For the purposes of this table, payments made to specific bodies that use all the amounts collected to accomplish specific missions (e.g. some emergency stock fees) are not considered as "taxes" and are included in the ex-tax price. When different rates apply to the same product depending e.g. on its biofuel or sulphur content, the rate shown is the one applicable to the most commonly used fuel in the country.
4. GST for Australia, and New Zealand; volume-weighted GST-HST/retail sales taxes for Canada; sales taxes for the United States and Consumption Tax for Japan. VAT for all other countries.

Source: International Energy Agency, Energy Prices and Taxes and national delegates.

StatLink https://doi.org/10.1787/888933890293

Country notes to Annex Table 3.A.6

Austria. The excise amount of EUR 0.482/l applies to unleaded gasoline with minimum 4.6% biofuel content and sulphur content ⩽ 10mg/kg. Otherwise the excise duty is EUR 0.515/l.

Canada. The excise rate includes federal and provincial taxes (the federal excise rate is CAD 0.1 per litre). The federal GST rate is 5%. The volume weighted GST rate including provincial GST rates was 10.58% and the volume weighted GST/retail sales tax rate was 11.97%. Municipal taxes and carbon pollution pricing are not included in the excise taxes.

Chile. The Consumer Protection System of IEC Taxpayers (Sistema de Protección al Contribuyente del Impuesto Especifico a los Combustibles - SIPCO) introduced in 2011 provides for the variable component of the excise and acts weekly either as a tax or a tax credit to stabilize consumer price. The variable component is added to the fixed component of the excise. The excise is not included in the VAT base.

Denmark. The excise amount is for fuel with a minimum amount of 4.8% of biofuels. It includes the Excise Tax, the Environment Tax and the NOx Tax.

Finland. The excise amount for premium unleaded gasoline includes taxes of energy and CO2 components. Strategic stockpile fee of EUR 0.0068/l is included in the ex-tax price.

France. A rate is determined for each region ranging from EUR 0.407/l up to EUR 0.6682. An additional tax of max. EUR 0.0073/l can be applied by region councils or in Corse to finance sustainable, railway or river navigation substructure.

Germany. The excise amount is for unleaded gasoline with sulphur content ⩽ 10mg/kg. Otherwise the excise amount is EUR 0.6698/l.

Hungary. Excise amount depends on the world market price of crude oil. If the world market price of crude oil is higher than 50 USD/barrel the excise amount is HUF 122.674/l (including the excise duty of HUF 120/l and the strategic stock fee of HUF 2.674/l). If the world market price of crude oil is 50 USD/barrel or less the excise amount is HUF 127.674/l (including the excise duty of HUF 125/l and the strategic stock fee of HUF 2.674/l).

Iceland. Since this country is not member of the IEA or the EU, price data is taken from European Automobile Manufacturers Association. The excise rate of ISK 75.55/l includes the general excise on petrol (ISK 26.8/l), the special excise on petrol (ISK 43.25/l) and the carbon tax (ISK 5.5/l).

Ireland. The 'Ex-tax price' includes a National Oil Reserves Agency (NORA) levy which is charged at a rate of EUR 0.02 per litre.

Israel. The statistical data for Israel are supplied by and under the responsibility of the relevant Israeli authorities. The use of such data by the OECD is without prejudice to the status of the Golan Heights, East Jerusalem and Israeli settlements in the West Bank under the terms of international law.

Japan. This amount includes the Gasoline Tax, the Local Gasoline Tax, and the Petroleum and Coal Tax.

Lithuania. Quarterly 'Ex-tax price is calculated as arithmetic average of weekly Euro-super 95 prices (Data published in the Weekly Oil Bulletin, DG Energy and Transport, European Commission).

Luxembourg. The excise amount is for unleaded gasoline with sulphur content ⩽ 10mg/kg. Otherwise the excise amount is EUR 0.464/l.

Mexico. There are no excise duties on volume. A tax (Impuesto Especial de Productos y Servicios) is charged as a percentage of the value of the product at wholesale level. It is included in the ex-tax price.

Netherlands. The amount of EUR 0.786/l excise includes the excise tax of 0.778/l and the stockpiling tax of 0.008/l.

New Zealand. The excise amount includes the National Land Transport Management Fund excise tax, the Accident Compensation Commission Levy, the Petroleum or Engine Fuels Monitoring Levy and the Local Authority Fuel Tax.

Norway. The excise amount includes the Excise tax and the CO2 tax.

Poland. The excise amount includes excise tax and fuel charge.

Slovak Republic. The excise amount is EUR 0.554/l for gasoline with biofuel content lower than the minimum of 5.9%.

Slovenia. The excise duty amount of EUR 564.06 per 1000 litres includes: the excise duty of EUR 507.80; EUR 7.36 surcharge on energy end-use efficiency on petrol; EUR 9.11 surcharge for the promotion of electricity generation from renewable energy sources and high-efficiency cogeneration on petrol and EUR 39.79 CO_2-tax.

Spain. The excise amount of EUR 0.462/l includes the Excise tax (EUR O.424/l) and the average Regional authorities tax (EUR 0.038/l).

Sweden. The actual excise amount is SEK 6.500/l (SEK 3.880 Gasoline tax + SEK 2.620 CO_2 tax). However, the amount shown in the table (SEK 6.175) is 95% of this amount to account for the tax-exempt ethanol content (5%) of gasoline.

United States. Average federal and state taxes - there is no VAT

European Union. Directive 2003/96/EC sets minimal excise rates for energy products and electricity

Annex Table 3.A.7. Taxation of automotive diesel (per litre) 2017[1]

Country	Currency	Ex-tax price[2]		Excise[3]		VAT rate[4]	VAT amount	Total tax	Total price	Total tax as % of total price
		National currency	USD	National currency	USD	%	USD	USD	USD	
Australia	AUD	0.744	0.570	0.403	0.309	10.00	0.088	0.397	0.967	41.0
Austria*	EUR	0.390	0.440	0.410	0.462	20.00	0.180	0.643	1.082	59.4
Belgium	EUR	0.600	0.676	0.530	0.598	21.00	0.268	0.865	1.541	56.1
Canada*	CAD	0.861	0.663	0.194	0.149	11.97	0.097	0.247	0.945	27.1
Chile*	CLP	373.910	0.576	75.780	0.117	19.00	0.109	0.226	0.802	28.2
Czech Republic	CZK	13.430	0.575	10.950	0.468	21.00	0.219	0.687	1.262	54.5
Denmark	DKK	4.480	0.678	3.132	0.474	25.00	0.288	0.763	1.441	52.9
Estonia	EUR	0.623	0.702	0.493	0.556	20.00	0.252	0.807	1.510	53.5
Finland*	EUR	0.607	0.684	0.447	0.504	24.00	0.285	0.884	1.475	53.6
France*	EUR	0.507	0.572	0.531	0.599	20.00	0.234	0.833	1.404	59.3
Germany*	EUR	0.541	0.610	0.470	0.530	19.00	0.217	0.746	1.356	55.0
Greece	EUR	0.618	0.697	0.410	0.462	24.00	0.267	0.729	1.426	51.1
Hungary*	HUF	176.020	0.641	112.588	0.410	27.00	0.284	0.694	1.336	52.0
Iceland*	ISK	96.110	0.900	66.400	0.621	24.00	0.365	0.987	1.886	52..3
Ireland	EUR	0.553	0.623	0.479	0.540	23.00	0.268	0.808	1.431	56.4
Israel*	ILS	2.290	0.636	2.890	0.803	17.00	0.245	1.047	1.684	62.2
Italy	EUR	0.533	0.601	0.617	0.696	22.00	0.285	0.981	1.582	62.0
Japan	JPY	75.300	0.671	34.900	0.311	8.00	0.079	0.390	1.061	36.7
Korea	KRW	665.500	0.589	528.750	0.468	10.00	0.106	0.573	1.162	49.3
Latvia	EUR	0.538	0.607	0.341	0.384	21.00	0.208	0.593	1.199	49.4
Lithuania	EUR	0.517	0.581	0.330	0.371	21.00	0.200	0.571	1.152	49.6
Luxembourg*	EUR	0.540	0.609	0.335	0.378	17.00	0.168	0.545	1.154	47.3
Mexico*	MXN	14.720	0.778	0.000	0.000	16.00	0.124	0.124	0.902	13.8
Netherlands	EUR	0.543	0.612	0.498	0.561	21.00	0.246	0.802	1.415	56.9
New Zealand	NZD	1.077	0.766	0.006	0.004	15.00	0.116	0.120	0.886	13.5
Norway	NOK	5.750	0.695	5.000	0.604	25.00	0.325	0.929	1.624	57.2
Poland*	PLN	2.207	0.584	1.459	0.386	23.00	0.223	0.609	1.193	51.1

Portugal*	EUR	0.565	0.637	0.466	0.525	23.00	0.267	0.793	1.430	55.4
Slovak Republic*	EUR	0.612	0.690	0.368	0.415	20.00	0.221	0.636	1.326	48.0
Slovenia*	EUR	0.497	0.560	0.491	0.554	22.00	0.245	0.799	1.359	58.8
Spain*	EUR	0.563	0.635	0.367	0.414	21.00	0.220	0.634	1.269	50.0
Sweden*	SEK	6.111	0.715	5.727	0.670	25.00	0.346	1.016	1.731	58.7
Switzerland*	CHF	0.751	0.762	0.759	0.771	8.00	0.123	0.893	1.656	53.9
Turkey	TRY	2.433	0.667	1.795	0.492	18.00	0.209	0.701	1.368	51.2
United Kingdom	GBP	0.439	0.565	0.580	0.746	20.00	0.262	1.009	1.574	64.1
United States*	USD	0.605	0.605	0.153	0.153	-	-	0.153	0.758	20.2

* See Country notes to Annex Table 3.A.7.

Note: Conversion of national currency in USD: conversion rates are average market rates (2017) published in OECD Monthly Monetary Statistics (stats.oecd.org). See also Annex B.

1. Prices and taxes as at 4th Quarter 2017.
2. Ex-tax price is the price excluding VAT and excise.
3. Excise taxes are expressed in local currency/USD per litre. They include all non-VAT taxes levied on the product. For the purposes of this table, payments made to specific bodies that use all the amounts collected to accomplish specific missions (e.g. some emergency stock fees) are not considered as "taxes" and are included in the ex-tax price. When different rates apply to the same product depending e.g. on its biofuel or sulphur content, the rate shown is the one applicable to the most commonly used fuel in the country.
4. GST for Australia, and New Zealand; volume-weighted GST-HST/retail sales taxes for Canada; sales taxes for the United States and Consumption Tax for Japan. VAT for all other countries.

Source: International Energy Agency, Energy Prices and Taxes and national delegates.

StatLink https://doi.org/10.1787/888933890312

Country notes to Annex Table 3.A.7

Austria. The excise amount of EUR 0.397/l applies to automotive diesel with minimum 6.6% of biofuel and sulphur content ⩽ 10mg/kg). Otherwise the excise amount is EUR 0.425/l.

Canada. The excise rate includes federal and provincial taxes (the federal rate is CAD 0.04 per litre). The federal GST rate is 5%. The volume weighted GST rate, including provincial GST rates, was 10.58% and the volume weighted GST/sales tax rate was 11.97%. Municipal taxes and carbon pollution pricing are not included in the excise taxes.

Chile. The Fuel Price Stabilisation Mechanism (Mechanisme de Estabilisacion de Precios de los Combustibles MEPCO) introduced in July 2014 is the variable component of the excise, and acts weekly either as a tax or a tax credit to stabilise consumer price compared to international market price variations. The excise is not included in the VAT base.

Finland. The excise amount of EUR 0.447/l is for paraffinic diesel and it includes the Energy Content tax and CO_2 tax. Excise duty for non-paraffinic diesel is EUR 0.527/l. Precautionary stock fee EUR 0.0035/l is included in the ex-tax price.

France. A rate is determined for each region ranging from EUR 0.5307/l up to EUR 0.5631. An additional tax of max. EUR 0.0135/l can be applied by region councils or in Corse to finance sustainable, railway or river navigation substructure.

Germany. The excise amount is for unleaded gasoline with sulphur content ⩽ 10mg/kg. Otherwise the excise amount is EUR 0.48517/l.

Hungary. Excise amount depends on the world market price of crude oil. If the world market price of crude oil is higher than 50 USD/barrel the excise amount is HUF 112.588/l (including the excise duty of HUF 110.35/l and the strategic stock fee of HUF 2.505/l). If the world market price of crude oil is 50 USD/barrel or less the excise amount is HUF 122.588/l (including the excise duty of HUF 120.35/l and the strategic stock fee of HUF 2.505/l).

Iceland. Since this country is not member of the IEA or the EU, price data is taken from European Automobile Manufacturers. The excise rate of ISK 66.40/l includes the excise on diesel (ISK 60.1/l) and the carbon tax (ISK 6.3/l).

Ireland. The 'Ex-tax price' includes a National Oil Reserves Agency (NORA) levy which is charged at a rate of EUR 0.02 per litre.

Israel. The statistical data for Israel are supplied by and under the responsibility of the relevant Israeli authorities. The use of such data by the OECD is without prejudice to the status of the Golan Heights, East Jerusalem and Israeli settlements in the West Bank under the terms of international law.

Lithuania. Automotive diesel used for agriculture is taxed at a lower excise rate (EUR 0.021/l). As of 1st January, 2018 there was an increase in excise rate: rate for automotive diesel used for agriculture was set at EUR 0.056/l, normal rate for automotive diesel was set at EUR 0.347/l. Quarterly 'Ex-tax price is calculated as arithmetic average of weekly gas oil prices (Data published in the Weekly Oil Bulletin, DG Energy and

Transport, European Commission).

Luxembourg. The excise amount is for unleaded gasoline with sulphur content ⩽ 10mg/kg. Otherwise the excise amount is EUR 0.338/l.

Mexico. Excise taxes on gasoline and diesel in 2015 had three components: (1) the excise-carbon tax, set proportionally to the carbon content of the fuel and implemented through a fixed amount per litre, whose main purpose is to send a carbon price signal to contribute to Climate Change commitments; (2) the excise tax specifically earmarked as transfers to the State's governments, proportional to their consumption, also implemented as a fixed amount per litre; and (3) the main excise tax, which, changed each month in value according to a set of criteria which essentially subtracted from the fuel's controlled price the cost of importing or producing fuel, plus the costs of distribution, logistics, related items, and the retail profit for gas station owners. This general excise tax could even become a negative tax (a subsidy) if domestic prices for fuel were low and international reference prices were high, and this was the case for the first 3 years of the decade. The 2016 excise tax reforms changed completely this latter component. Now, the general excise tax on gasoline and diesel is also a fixed quota tax per litre. During the transition period before full price liberalisation of fuels in 2018, the fixed quota of the excise tax will have a complementary quota component (positive or negative) to ensure that the final fuel prices do not vary outside a price band of +/- 3% of the price they had in 2015. This complementary quota can never become equal in size to the excise tax, so general fossil fuel subsidies would be precluded from happening again.

Netherlands. The amount of EUR 0.498/l excise includes the excise tax of 0.490/l and the stockpiling tax of 0.008/l.

Poland. The excise amount includes excise tax and fuel charge.

Portugal. Automotive diesel used for agriculture is taxed at a lower VAT rate of 13%.

Slovak Republic. The excise amount is EUR 0.394/l for diesel with biofuel content lower than minimum of 6.9%.

Slovenia. The excise duty of EUR 491 per 1000 litres includes the excise duty of EUR 426.05; EUR 8.00 surcharge on energy end-use efficiency on gasoil used as propellant, EUR 9.90 surcharge for the promotion of electricity generation from renewable energy sources and high-efficiency cogeneration on gasoil used as propellant, EUR 46.71 CO_2 tax.

Spain. The excise amount of EUR 0.368/l includes the Excise tax (EUR O.331/l) and the average Regional authorities tax (EUR 0.037/l).

Sweden. The tax amount of SEK 5.727/l relates to Class 1 automotive diesel (aromatic content < 5%vol.; max sulphur content of 10 wppm. Higher taxes apply to Class 2 (SEK 6.015/l) and Class 3 (SEK 6.164/l) diesel.

United States. Average federal and state taxes - there is no VAT

European Union. Directive 2003/96/EC sets minimal excise rates for energy products and electricity.

Annex Table 3.A.8. Taxation of fuel oil for households (2017)[1]

Country	Currency	Ex-tax price[2]		Excise[3]		VAT rate[4]	VAT amount	Total tax	Total price	Total tax as % of total price
		National currency	USD	National currency	USD	%	USD	USD	USD	
Australia*	AUD	See note				10.00				
Austria*	EUR	0.484	0.546	0.109	0.123	20.00	0.134	0.257	0.802	32.0
Belgium	EUR	0.477	0.538	0.019	0.021	21.00	0.117	0.138	0.676	20.4
Canada*	CAD	0.939	0.733	0.000	0.000	9.83	0.071	0.071	0.795	8.9
Chile*	CLP	508.000	0.783	0.000	0.000	19.00	0.149	0.149	0.932	16.0
Czech Republic*	CZK	12.058	0.516	0.660	0.028	21.00	0.114	0.142	0.658	21.6
Denmark*	DKK	4.734	0.717	2.448	0.371	25.00	0.272	0.643	1.360	47.3
Estonia	EUR	0.492	0.555	0.493	0.556	20.00	0.222	0.778	1.333	58.4
Finland*	EUR	0.508	0.573	0.229	0.258	24.00	0.199	0.458	1.030	44.4
France	EUR	0.526	0.593	0.119	0.134	20.00	0.145	0.280	0.873	32.0
Germany*	EUR	0.440	0.496	0.061	0.069	19.00	0.107	0.177	0.673	26.2
Greece*	EUR	0.427	0.481	0.280	0.316	24.00	0.183	0.499	0.980	50.9
Hungary*	HUF	177.588	0.647	112.588	0.410	27.00	0.285	0.696	1.343	51.8
Iceland*	ISK	Country note								
Ireland*	EUR	0.467	0.526	0.102	0.115	13.50	0.087	0.202	0.728	27.7
Israel*	ILS	2.110	0.586	2.890	0.803	17.00	0.236	1.039	1.625	63.9
Italy	EUR	0.570	0.643	0.403	0.454	22.00	0.241	0.696	1.338	52.0
Japan*	JPY	72.149	0.643	2.800	0.025	8.00	0.053	0.078	0.722	10.9
Korea*	KRW	714.722	0.632	72.450	0.064	10.00	0.070	0.134	0.766	17.5
Latvia	EUR	0.541	0.610	0.057	0.064	21.00	0.142	0.206	0.816	25.2
Lithuania	EUR	0.445	0.500	0.021	0.024	21.00	0.110	0.134	0.634	21.1
Luxembourg*	EUR	0.487	0.549	0.010	0.011	14.00	0.078	0.090	0.639	14.0
Mexico*	MXN	Country note								
Netherlands	EUR	0.357	0.402	0.498	0.561	21.00	0.201	0.758	1.161	65.5
New Zealand*	NZD	Country note								
Norway	NOK	4.648	0.562	2.803	0.339	25.00	0.225	0.564	1.126	50.1
Poland	PLN	2.202	0.583	0.232	0.061	23.00	0.148	0.210	0.792	26.4
Portugal	EUR	0.530	0.598	0.347	0.391	13.00	0.129	0.520	1.117	46.5

Slovak Republic*	EUR	Country note								
Slovenia	EUR	0.452	0.510	0.222	0.250	22.00	0.167	0.417	0.927	45.0
Spain*	EUR	0.463	0.522	0.089	0.100	21.00	0.131	0.231	0.753	30.7
Sweden*	SEK	4.910	0.574	4.092	0.479	25.00	0.263	0.742	1.316	56.4
Switzerland	CHF	0.567	0.576	0.226	0.229	8.00	0.064	0.294	0.869	33.8
Turkey*	TRY	2.398	0.657	1.137	0.312	18.00	0.174	0.486	1.143	42.5
United Kingdom	GBP	0.393	0.506	0.111	0.143	20.00	0.130	0.273	0.778	35.0
United States*	USD	0.719	0.719	0.035	0.035	0.00	0.000	0.035	0.754	4.6

* See Country notes to Annex Table 3.A.8.

Note: Conversion of national currency in USD: conversion rates are average market rates (2017) published in OECD Monthly Monetary Statistics (stats.oecd.org). See also Annex B.

1. Prices and taxes as at 4th Quarter 2017.
2. Ex-tax price is the price excluding VAT and excise.
3. Excise taxes are expressed in local currency/USD per litre. They include all non-VAT taxes levied on the product. For the purposes of this table, payments made to specific bodies that use all the amounts collected to accomplish specific missions (e.g. some emergency stock fees) are not considered as "taxes" and are included in the ex-tax price. When different rates apply to the same product depending e.g. on its biofuel or sulphur content, the rate shown is the one applicable to the most commonly used fuel in the country.
4. GST for Australia, and New Zealand; volume-weighted GST-HST/retail sales taxes for Canada; sales taxes for the United States and Consumption Tax for Japan. VAT for all other countries.

Source: International Energy Agency, Energy Prices and Taxes and country delegates.

StatLink https://doi.org/10.1787/888933890331

Country notes to Annex Table 3.A.8

Australia. No data is available.

Austria. Tax amount of EUR 0.098/l applies to light fuel oil with sulphur content ⩽ 10mg/kg. Otherwise the excise duty is EUR 0.128/l.

Canada. Fuel oil is assumed to be heating oil. There is no federal or provincial fuel tax on heating oil. The federal GST rate is 5%. Most provinces do not apply their provincial GST/retail sales tax on heating oil. The volume weighted GST/sales tax rate was 9.83%. Municipal taxes and carbon pollution pricing are not included in the excise taxes.

Chile. Domestic Kerosene is covered weekly by the Oil Price Stabilisation Fund (Fundo de Estabilisacion de Preicos del Petroleo FEPP) which applies a tax or a fiscal credit/subsidy, measured in USD per m3. The tax is not included in the VAT base at the stage of the import, production, refining, distribution or sale to the consumer, and the fiscal credit is deductible from the taxable base on the first sale or importation.

Czech Republic. Fuel oil marked in accordance with Directive 95/60/EC is subject to reimbursement of an excise duty amount of CZK 10 290/1000l when it has been duly proved that the fuel oil has been used for heating purposes. The excise amount shown in the table includes the reimbursement.

Denmark. The amount of DKK 2.406/l includes the Excise tax of DKK 1.955/l; the Environment tax of DKK 0.455/l and the NOx tax of DKK 0.0009/l.

Finland. The excise amount of EUR 0.1874/l includes the Excise tax Energy/CO_2 tax (EUR 0.1839/l) and the Precautionary stock fee (EUR 0.00353/l).

Germany. The excise amount is for properly marked gas oil with a sulphur content ⩽ 50mg/kg. Otherwise the excise amount is EUR 0.0764/l.

Greece. The excise of EUR 0.280/l for heating oil for households applies during the winter season (15 October - 30 April). Otherwise the excise is 0.410/l.

Hungary. Excise amount depends on the world market price of crude oil. If the world market price of crude oil is higher than 50 USD/barrel the excise amount is HUF 112.588/l (including the excise duty of HUF 110.35/l and the strategic stock fee of HUF 2.505/l). If the world market price of crude oil is 50 USD/barrel or less the excise amount is HUF 122.588 (including the excise duty of HUF 125/l and the strategic stock fee of HUF 2.505/l).

Iceland. No data is available

Ireland. The 'Ex-tax price' includes a National Oil Reserves Agency (NORA) levy which is charged at a rate of EUR 0.02 per litre. The Excise rate of 0.102/litre applies to marked gas oil (marked diesel). Marked kerosene is also widely used for heating (including domestic heating) and the rate for that is EUR 0.05073/litre.

Israel. The statistical data for Israel are supplied by and under the responsibility of the relevant Israeli authorities. The use of such data by the OECD is without prejudice to the status of the Golan Heights, East Jerusalem and Israeli settlements in the West Bank under the terms of international law.

Japan. Kerosene for households.

Korea. Kerosene for households

Latvia. Excise tax of EUR 0.021/litre for marked fuel for heating purposes applies if it contains at least 5% biodiesel of total volume of product.

Lithuania. Quarterly 'Ex-tax price is calculated as arithmetic average of weekly Heating gas oil prices (Data published in the Weekly Oil Bulletin, DG Energy and Transport, European Commission).

Luxembourg. A reduced VAT rate of 14% applies to heating gas oil.

Mexico. No data is available

Netherlands. The amount of EUR 0.498/l excise includes the excise tax of 0.490/l and the stockpiling tax of 0.008/l.

New Zealand. No data is provided because the product is not consumed in significant quantities.

Norway. The amount of NOK 2.803/l includes base tax of NOK 1.603/l and CO_2 tax of NOK 1.20/l.

Slovak Republic. No data is provided because the product is not consumed in significant quantities.

Slovenia. The amount of EUR 222 per hectolitre includes the excise duty of EUR 157.50, EUR 8.00 surcharge on energy end-use efficiency on gasoil used for heating purposes, EUR 9.90 surcharge for the promotion of electricity generation from renewable energy sources and high-efficiency cogeneration on gasoil used for heating purposes, and EUR 46.71 CO_2-tax.

Spain. The excise amount of EUR 0.088/l includes the Excise tax (EUR 0.085/l) and the average Regional authorities' tax (EUR 0.003/l).

Sweden. Price data are not available in IEA statistics. Price data is extracted from economic information available on ec.europa.eu/energy/observatory/reports. Excise tax includes the Energy Tax (SEK 0.855/l) and CO_2 Tax (SEK 3.237/l).

Turkey. Kerosene for households.

United States. Average federal and state taxes - there is no VAT

European Union. Directive 2003/96/EC sets minimal excise rates for energy products and electricity.

Annex Table 3.A.9. Excises (5121) as percentage of GDP and Total Taxes

	Tax revenue as % of GDP					Tax revenue as % of total taxation				
	1975	2005	2010	2015	2016	1975	2005	2010	2015	2016
Australia	3.0	2.3	1.9	1.4	1.3	11.8	7.6	7.5	4.9	4.7
Austria	2.9	2.6	2.3	2.2	2.2	7.9	6.3	5.7	5.2	5.3
Belgium	2.6	2.3	2.1	2.1	2.2	6.6	5.3	5.0	4.7	5.1
Canada	2.0	1.6	1.4	1.3	1.3	6.3	4.9	4.5	3.9	3.9
Chile	..	1.6	1.4	1.5	1.5	..	7.8	7.1	7.4	7.5
Czech Republic	..	3.4	3.5	3.3	3.3	..	9.8	10.8	10.0	9.7
Denmark	5.1	4.9	4.1	3.9	4.0	13.8	10.3	9.1	8.5	8.6
Estonia	..	3.6	4.2	4.2	4.6	..	12.2	12.6	12.6	13.6
Finland	4.2	3.6	3.4	3.7	3.8	11.5	8.6	8.2	8.3	8.6
France	2.3	2.4	2.3	2.6	2.6	6.5	5.7	5.4	5.7	5.8
Germany	3.0	2.8	2.5	2.1	2.1	8.8	8.4	7.0	5.8	5.5
Greece	2.5	2.6	3.3	3.9	4.1	13.6	8.2	10.5	10.7	10.5
Hungary	..	3.5	3.4	3.3	3.2	..	9.7	9.2	8.4	8.3
Iceland	0.9	3.6	2.9	2.5	2.5	3.0	9.2	8.6	7.0	4.9
Ireland	7.2	3.2	2.9	2.1	2.1	26.0	10.8	10.7	9.0	9.0
Israel[1]	..	1.5	1.8	1.5	1.5	..	4.5	5.8	4.8	4.8
Italy	2.5	2.2	2.3	2.8	2.9	10.2	5.6	5.4	6.5	6.8
Japan	2.3	1.8	1.7	1.6	1.5	11.3	6.9	6.5	5.1	5.0
Korea	3.3	2.7	2.5	2.0	2.1	22.0	12.0	10.6	8.1	8.1
Latvia	..	3.5	3.6	3.3	3.5	..	12.6	12.7	11.4	11.5
Lithuania	..	2.9	3.2	3.1	3.2	..	10.0	11.4	10.8	10.7
Luxembourg	2.3	4.5	3.5	2.6	2.7	7.3	11.8	9.3	7.1	7.0
Mexico	..	0.6	0.6	2.0	2.1	..	5.1	5.0	12.2	12.6
Netherlands	2.4	3.1	2.9	2.6	2.7	6.3	8.7	8.1	7.1	7.0
New Zealand	2.8	1.4	0.9	0.9	0.8	9.4	3.9	2.9	2.8	2.6
Norway	4.0	3.2	2.9	2.5	2.5	10.3	7.4	7.0	6.6	6.6
Poland	..	4.3	4.3	3.9	4.1	..	13.0	13.7	12.1	12.2
Portugal	2.5	3.7	3.1	2.9	3.1	13.0	11.9	10.4	8.4	9.1
Slovak Republic	..	3.6	2.9	2.7	2.7	..	11.4	10.2	8.3	8.3
Slovenia	..	3.4	4.3	4.2	4.1	..	9.0	11.6	11.5	11.3
Spain	0.4	2.5	2.2	2.4	2.3	2.2	7.0	7.0	7.0	6.8
Sweden	3.4	2.8	2.6	2.2	2.2	8.8	6.1	6.0	5.1	4.9
Switzerland	1.7	1.4	1.4	1.2	1.2	7.7	5.4	5.1	4.5	4.4
Turkey	2.0	4.9	4.9	4.5	4.6	17.6	21.2	19.9	18.1	18.2
United Kingdom	4.3	2.8	2.9	2.5	2.4	12.7	8.7	8.9	7.8	7.4
United States	1.9	1.0	1.0	0.9	0.8	7.6	3.9	4.1	3.3	3.3
Unweighted average[2]										
OECD Average	2.9	2.8	2.7	2.6	2.6	10.5	8.6	8.4	7.8	7.8

Notes 1. Israel: The statistical data for Israel are supplied by and under the responsibility of the relevant Israeli authorities. The use of such data by the OECD is without prejudice to the status of the Golan Heights, East Jerusalem and Israeli settlements in the West Bank under the terms of international law.

2. The 2016 OECD average excludes the one-off revenues from stability contributions in Iceland.

Source: *Revenue Statistics 2018.*

StatLink https://doi.org/10.1787/888933890350

Chapter 4. Taxing vehicles

This chapter describes the main features of vehicle taxes and their use for influencing customer behaviour, in particular within the context of environmental policies. It looks at the taxes on the sale and registration of vehicles and recurrent taxes on the use of motor vehicles and their components and provides comparative statistics on the level of these taxes

4.1. Introduction

Taxes on vehicles were introduced in most OECD countries in the first half of the 20th century and have become an important source of tax revenue for many governments. All member countries rely on a range of tax instruments to ensure significant revenue from both private and commercial road users. Vehicle taxation in its widest definition represents a prime example of the use of the whole spectrum of consumption taxes for taxing vehicles, including VAT as well as specific or *ad valorem* taxes (see definitions in Chapter 3). These taxes have progressively been adapted to influence consumer behaviour and curb transport externalities, in particular environmental externalities.

Taxes and charges on vehicles include:

- Taxes (including VAT and retail sales taxes) on the purchase and registration of motor vehicles, payable once at the time of acquisition and/or first putting into service of a vehicle (see Table 4.A.1).
- Periodic taxes payable in connection with the ownership or use of the vehicles (see Table 4.A.2).
- Taxes on fuels (see Tables 3.A.6 and 3.A.7 in Chapter 3).
- Any other taxes and charges that are directly or indirectly connected with the use or ownership of vehicles, such as insurance taxes, road tolls, distance charges, congestion charges, company car taxation, etc.

The sale and use of motor vehicles generate considerable VAT or retail sales tax revenues. These taxes are levied on the import and sale of vehicles (in the latter case by application to the full selling price or, for used cars, to the margin between the buying and the selling price). VAT or retail sales tax will generally also apply to general maintenance and running costs. In addition, they are levied in most cases on the final duty-paid value (e.g. VAT on fuel is levied on the excise-inclusive price - see Tables 3.A.6 and 3.A.7 in Chapter 3).

Taxes on vehicles reflect a variety of influences beyond the obvious need to raise revenue. Geographic, industrial, social, energy, transport, urban and environmental policy considerations have all had an influence on the level and structure of taxation. Many taxes on vehicles were instituted in a time when cars were considered luxury items. Wider ownership of cars in recent decades has reduced the progressivity of those taxes (many low-income households have at least one car today). Currently, taxation schemes are increasingly used to influence consumer or business behaviour. Energy and environmental considerations have led to an adjustment of taxation according to the fuel efficiency of vehicles, CO_2 and other polluting emissions. Taxes on road use have also been introduced to manage the external cost of transport and raise additional revenue.

In most countries total taxes on vehicles result from a combination of one-off (on purchase or import) and recurrent (on ownership or use) taxes as well as from a mix between *ad valorem* (on the price) and specific taxes (taking into account polluting emissions, weight, engine power, number of axles, age, fuel efficiency, equipment, suspension, cylinder capacity, number of seats, type of fuel, electric propulsion and distance covered).

Taxes on the sale/registration and use of motor vehicles (Table 4.A.1 and Table 4.A.2) cannot be considered in isolation from other tax bases and rates. A number of other elements should also be taken into account when considering the taxation of vehicles such as insurance premium taxes, specific road tolls (bridge or motorway tolls, congestion charges, distance charges), fuel taxes (see Chapter 3), energy taxes and a number of direct tax components such as the personal tax treatment of company cars (Harding, 2014[1]).

4.2. Car taxation used to curb transport externalities

Taxation has increasingly been used over the last decades to influence customer behaviour and encourage the purchase of low polluting or more fuel-efficient vehicles. In 2018, more than three quarters (29 out of 36) of OECD member countries take environmental or fuel efficiency criteria into account when determining the level of taxation for the purchase or use of vehicles (see Table 4.A.1 and Table 4.A.2). Amongst these countries, 15 determine the levels of taxation on polluting emissions (for example, the level of CO, CO_2, NOx or particulate matter per kilometre) or CO_2 emissions and 24 apply tax rebates or exemptions for electric or hybrid vehicles. A number of EU Member States use the polluting emission norms set by European legislation (Directive 2007/46/EC and subsequent regulations) as a benchmark for their vehicle taxes although there is currently no European rule regarding car taxation.

Differentiating motor vehicle purchase taxes according to the fuel-efficiency or polluting emissions can give potential vehicle purchasers an immediate incentive to buy a vehicle that pollutes less, is more fuel-efficient, or both. Differentiation of purchase or annual registration charges on motor vehicles can also provide such an incentive, but somewhat less directly. One approach is to estimate vehicles' usage over their lifetime, and to calculate tax rates based on the estimated tonnes of CO_2 a vehicle is estimated to emit over its lifetime. Research in this context show that tax rates applied per tonne CO_2 emitted over a vehicle's estimated lifetime vary significantly between countries (for an in-depth study on this topic, see (Nils Axel Braathen, 2009[2])

High registration taxes are also likely to reduce the number of new motor vehicles purchase. However, while this would, at first sight, appear to favour environmental objectives, higher purchase taxes on vehicles can not only reduce the size of the vehicle fleet but also cause some purchasers to defer their purchase or to purchase a used vehicle, increasing the population of older, more polluting, cars.

Many of the tax systems discussed above define tax bases and rates assuming compliance with the CO_2 or polluting emissions standards.

At the local level, other taxes and charges have been implemented or have been considered to reduce local air pollution and other social costs of vehicle usage more generally, particularly in urban areas (Van Dender, Forthcoming[3]). Local traffic emits air pollutants in addition to CO_2 emissions, especially fine particulates, which create health damages whose economic costs can be estimated. Expressed per vehicle-kilometre, these external environmental costs of car traffic have been estimated at up to EUR 0.01 (gasoline cars) to EUR 0.037 (diesel cars). Traffic congestion also creates marginal external costs that are estimated to range from EUR 0.30 to EUR 2.42 per vehicle/kilometre when traffic volumes exceed road capacity. Other vehicle transport externalities include traffic accidents (costs estimated at up to EUR 0.03 per vehicle kilometre), noise (up to EUR 0.36/km for heavy goods vehicles in urban areas) and road damage (from EUR 0.05 per vehicle kilometre for cars to 0.52 for heavy trucks). Taxes can efficiently internalise these external costs and ensure their cost-effective reduction (OECD, 2017[4]), provided that they are carefully targeted. While fuel taxes are well suited to reflect external costs from CO_2 emissions (see Chapter 3), distance-based taxes and, to some extent, parking charges have the potential to effectively reflect specific costs such as congestion, road damage and other infrastructure-related costs. Distance-based taxes that take into account vehicle characteristics can also help address air pollution (Van Dender, Forthcoming[3]).

In addition to tax policies, governments generally operate rules for reducing motor vehicle pollution by imposing technical norms to the car industry. For example, in the European Union (EU) polluting emissions have been regulated since 1970 and a series of amendments have been issued since then to gradually tighten the limit values. The current norms set maximum emissions of carbon monoxide (CO), Volatile Organic Compounds (VOC), nitrogen oxides (NOx) and particles. These are reflected in the Euro 6 (setting lower emission limits for the registration and sale of new types of cars and vans as of 1 September 2015) and in the Euro VI standards for heavy duty vehicles. Emissions of carbon dioxide (CO_2) have also been targeted by the European Commission since 2007 and the EU has put in place a comprehensive legal framework to reduce CO_2 emissions from new light duty vehicles as part of its efforts to ensure it meets its greenhouse gas emission reduction targets. EU regulation (333/2014), sets a CO_2 emissions standard at 95g/km, phased in for 95 % of vehicles in 2020, with a 100 % compliance target in 2021. The target for 2021 represents a reduction of 40% compared with the 2007 fleet average of 158.7 g/ km. Mandatory standards for heavy-duty vehicles (busses, trucks, etc.) are also being developed as part of a comprehensive strategy to reduce CO_2 emissions.

4.3. Taxes on purchase and registration of motor vehicles

Taxes on the acquisition and registration of motor vehicles may include VAT, sales taxes, excise duties and other fees and charges associated with the registration of a vehicle. These taxes may vary considerably from one country to another (see Table 4.A.1). They are based on a large diversity of criteria or on a combination of these criteria. There are five main criteria against which the tax can be assessed:

- The price or value of the vehicle;
- The engine power or cylinder capacity;
- Environmental impact, incl. polluting emissions, CO_2 emissions and the type of fuel used;
- Social considerations incl. preferential treatment of emergency vehicles, ambulances, vehicles for disabled people, vehicles for public transport, etc.;
- The use of the vehicle incl. specific criteria apply to commercial vehicles such as number of axles, cargo room, number of seats, etc.

A number of specific elements can further be taken in consideration for determining the tax burden, such as weight, presence of safety equipment, air conditioning, etc. A specific tax applies to tyres in the United States. Taxation depends on the age of the vehicle in several countries.

The burden of these taxes varies considerably from one country to another and differs between states, provinces, cities or regions within a country. For example, a VAT rate of 8% and a 3% acquisition tax apply in Japan whereas a 25% VAT and a 150% registration tax is applied in Denmark.

The international differences in taxation of sales and registration of motor vehicles do not give rise to considerable cross-border shopping as motor vehicles need to be registered with a unique identification number in the principal country of use. Similarly VAT levied on the importation of a vehicle (or on its "acquisition" for sales within the EU) will generally be due in the country of registration. Even in the integrated market of the EU there has been no harmonisation or even approximation of taxes or tax rates on motor vehicles.

Nevertheless, motor vehicle taxation can affect the functioning of the motor vehicle market. This may notably be the case for registration taxes. Generally, registration tax paid in the country of first registration is not paid back when a car is transferred from one country to another (e.g. when the owner moves from one country to another). When registration tax has to be paid (again) in the country of destination where the car is to remain permanently, double taxation occurs. In addition, large differences in tax systems reinforce car market fragmentation. Cars marketed in one country with specifications designed to meet the national tax structure (e.g. brackets of fiscal horsepower, tax policy regarding diesel) are imperfect substitutes and may not effectively compete with cars sold in another country with different tax requirements. Also pre-tax prices appear to be influenced by tax considerations. Significant tax differentials may encourage consumers in some cases to buy cars in countries where registration taxes are very high and where car manufacturers tend to offer lower prices net of taxes by compensation and import and register them in their own country. This may undermine the benefits that should derive from a competitive market for both consumers and industry.

4.4. Periodic taxes in connection with ownership or use of motor vehicles

Taxes on the use of vehicles include recurring charges levied on the right to drive on public roads, usually in the form of an annual motor tax (see Table 4.A.2). Taxes on the operation of motor vehicles also include excise duties on fuel (see Chapter 3) and motorway charges or other road user tolls and motor fuel taxation. Recurring taxes on the ownership of motor vehicles can take many forms. The main elements used to assess these kinds of taxes are very similar to those used for assessing taxes on sale and registration such as use (commercial or not), vehicle type, type of fuel, engine size, age, emissions of pollutants and fuel efficiency.

References

Harding, M. (2014), "Personal Tax Treatment of Company Cars and Commuting Expenses: Estimating the Fiscal and Environmental Costs", *OECD Taxation Working Papers*, No. 20, OECD Publishing, Paris, https://dx.doi.org/10.1787/5jz14cg1s7vl-en. [1]

Nils Axel Braathen (2009), *Incentives for CO2 Emission Reductions in Current Motor Vehicle Taxes*, http://www.oecd.org/env/transport.. [2]

OECD (2017), *Environmental Fiscal Reform PROGRESS, PROSPECTS AND PITFALLS*, http://www.oecd.org/tax/tax-policy/tax-and-environment.htm.. [4]

Van Dender, K. (Forthcoming), *Taxing Vehicles, Fuel and Road Use: Opportunities for Improving Transport Tax Practice*, OECD. [3]

Annex 4.A. Data on Car Taxation

Table 4.A.1. Taxes on sale and registration of motor vehicles[1]

Country	Taxes	Criteria	Rebates/Exemptions
Australia	GST: 10% Luxury Car Tax: 33% calculated on the value of most cars that exceed the luxury car tax threshold. The luxury car tax threshold is generally AUD 66 311 (in 2018-19), tax inclusive (including GST) or AUD 75 526, tax inclusive (including GST) if the car's fuel consumption is less than 7 litres per 100 kilometres. Registration fee – varies between states/territories – may be calculated on the tare weight, value or type of vehicle Stamp duty - varies between states/territories - calculated on the tare weight (heavy vehicles) or value (light vehicles)	Value Fuel efficiency Weight (registration or stamp duty only)	Some exemptions apply from luxury car tax including: - emergency vehicles such as ambulances etc - sale of vehicle is more than 2 years after manufacture or importation - vehicles modified to transport a person in a wheelchair (provided it is not GST-free) - commercial vehicles primarily used for carrying goods in business or trade - imported by museum for public display Eligible tourism operators and primary producers are eligible to claim a refund of Luxury Car Tax paid up to AUD 3 000 for certain cars. GST: exemption is provided to veterans and persons with a disability that fulfil legal requirements.
Austria	VAT: 20%. New Car Registration Tax: while the tax base is the selling price, the tax rate depends on the CO2-emissions of the car: (CO2 emissions in gram/km, reduced by 90 grams), divided by 5. The rate cannot exceed 32% (which corresponds to 250g CO2/km). For CO2 emissions above 250g/km, the tax increases by 20 EUR for each g/km exceeding the limit of 250g/km. An amount of up to 300 EUR (no bonus possible) has to be deducted from the amount of tax calculated following the above rules. Registration fee (tax): fixed rate of Registration fee: motor vehicles registered for the state or local authorities EUR 119.80 per motor vehicle (+ up to 45 Euro processing fee for the registration office + approx. EUR 20 for other expenditures)	Value CO2 emissions	New Car Registration Tax: exemptions for demonstration vehicles, motor vehicles for driving schools, vehicles that are hired, used for guests or as taxis, motor vehicles used for short time hiring out, motor vehicles used for the transport of sick persons and for rescue services, vehicles used for the transport of corpses, vehicles used by fire brigades and accompanying vehicles for special transports. Registration fee: exemption for motor vehicles registered for the state or local authorities

Belgium	**VAT**: 21% **Entry into Service Tax** *Flemish Region*: for non-leasing passenger cars, the tax rate depends on vehicle age, environmental characteristics (including CO2 emissions), the type of fuel and the euro standard. The tax for leased vehicles is still calculated based on the engine power of the vehicle. *Walloon Region*: the tax rate depends on engine power and is set according to a degressive scale based on the age of the vehicle. For motorcycles the amount is calculated with respect to the kilowatt. For electric cars, the tax is set at EUR 61.50 as of fiscal year 2018. If the engine power corresponds to different amounts expressed in h.p. than in kilowatt, the highest amount has to be taken into consideration. *Brussels Capital Region*: the tax rate depends on fiscal horsepower and cylinder capacity and is set according to a progressive scale based on the age of the vehicle (fuel and gasoil from EUR 61.50 to EUR 4.957 and Liquefied Gas Petroleum from EUR 61.50 to EUR 4.659).	Age Engine power Cylinder capacity Environmental characteristics (incl. CO_2 emissions) Type of fuel/gas	*Flemish Region*: exemption for certain fuel types (pure electric, hydrogen-powered, plug-in hybrid (until 2021), powered by CNG/LNG (until 2021). Vehicles of more than 15 years old are subject to a uniform rate of EUR 61.50. Rebates will be accorded for used cars (in a progressive scale from 90% to 10% of the registration tax or a lump sum depending on the age of the vehicle), and for cars entirely or partially powered by Liquefied Gas Petroleum. All regions provide exemptions for some vehicles used by public authorities and vehicles for disabled people and war invalids.
Canada	**GST**: 5% **HST**: 13% or 15% for sales in the participating provinces. The following provinces have harmonized their provincial sales taxes with the federal Goods and Services Tax and therefore levy a rate of GST/HST of: New Brunswick, Newfoundland and Labrador, Prince Edward Island, Nova Scotia 15%; Ontario: 13%; Québec applies GST at a rate of 5% and Québec Sales Tax at a rate of 9.975%. **Provincial rates** are applicable for sales made in provinces not applying HST **Automotive Air Conditioning Tax**: CAD 100 per unit. **Excise tax on Fuel Inefficient Vehicles**: vehicles with a weighted fuel consumption rating of 13 or more litres per 100 kilometres (55 % city and 45% highway) are subject to an excise tax at the following rates: at least 13 but less than 14 litres per 100 kilometres, CAD 1 000; at least 14 but less than 15 litres per 100 kilometres, CAD 2 000; at least 15 but less than 16 litres per 100 kilometres, CAD 3 000; and 16 or more litres per 100 kilometres, CAD 4 000.	Value Fuel efficiency Air conditioning	**Rebate of GST/HST** – Specially Equipped Motor Vehicle: to purchasers of specially equipped motor vehicles for persons with disabilities. The rebate is only available on the GST/HST paid on the portion of the purchase price that is attributable to the special features. **Rebate of Excise Tax on Fuel Inefficient Vehicles** – Specially Equipped Van: to end-users of vans equipped with a device designed exclusively to assist in placing a wheelchair in the van without having to collapse the wheelchair
Chile	**VAT**: 19% (used cars are exempt with some exceptions) **Registration fees** payable to Civil Registry: first registration fee, new plate fee, fee for transfer and registration of vehicles. **Tax on transfer of used motor vehicles** (levied by municipalities): 1.5% of the value of the vehicle.	Value Fixed fee	

Czech Republic	**VAT**: 21% **Registration fee**: motorcycles CZK 300 or 500 (depending on cylinder capacity); other motor vehicles CZK 800. The fee includes the registration plate. Permit fee on non-standard motor vehicles	Value Cylinder capacity	
Denmark	**VAT**: 25% **Vehicle registration tax:** payable on first registration of the vehicle. Graduated tax rates according to the value of the vehicle (with lower rates for commercial vehicles) from 105% to 150% (on the remainder above DKK 82 800) for private vehicles and from 0% to 50% (on the remainder above DKK 17 500) for commercial vehicles.	Value Utilisation Safety equipment Anti-pollution equipment	**Rebate for low fuel consumption vehicles**: Registration tax is reduced by DKK 4 000 for every kilometre the vehicle can run in excess of 16 km with 1 litre of petrol or in excess of 18 km with 1 litre of diesel. A supplement of DKK 1 000 is payable for cars for every kilometre less than 16 km (petrol) or 18 km (diesel) they can run on one litre of fuel. **Traffic Safety Equipment:** Motor vehicles with major traffic safety equipment receive a deduction in the value liable to registration duty up to DKK 13 370. Motor vehicles with minor traffic safety equipment receive a deduction between DKK 200 and DKK 600.
Estonia	**VAT:** 20% **Vehicle registration fee (State fee):** Vehicle- EUR 130; Temporarily imported vehicle- EUR 335	Value Type of vehicle	
Finland	**VAT**: 24% **Vehicle Registration Tax** is based on CO_2 emissions. Rates vary from 3.3% of the general consumer price of the vehicle for cars emitting 0g/km or less to 50% for cars emitting 360g/km or more. **For delivery vans** there is a deduction based on maximum laden weight of the vehicle for vans over 2 500 kg. **For motor cycles** rates vary according to the cylinder capacity, between 9.8% and 24.4%, and the base is general retail value.	Value CO^2 emissions Utilisation Cylinder capacity Type	Exemption for disabled people, taxis, motor homes, cars used for veterinary purposes, rescue vehicles and funeral cars.
France	**VAT**: 20% **Tax on Registration Certificates** or regional tax on certificates **is** based on horsepower. Rates vary between EUR 27 and EUR 46 per horsepower according to the region. The rate is reduced by half for some vehicles depending on their nature (trucks weighing more than 3.5 tons, motorcycles) or age (more than 10 years old). **Additional tax on Registration certificates for first registration in France:** CO_2 emission component of the tax varies from EUR 0 for vehicles emitting less than 120g CO_2/km to EUR 10 500 for vehicles emitting more than 185g CO_2/km. Horsepower component of the tax (vehicles that have not been subject to a Community-type approval) varies from EUR 3000 (6HP) to EUR 10 500 (16HP). The tax is not applicable to vehicles belonging to disabled people. **Additional tax on Registration certificates for registration after first**	Value Engine power Weight Utilisation Age CO_2 emissions Type of fuel Electric propulsion Bonus-malus	**Exemption for new demonstration models** weighing less than 3.5 tons, state vehicles, certain motorcycles **Rebate for electricity or gas propelled cars:** from 50% to 100% of the Tax on Registration Certificates. **Rebate for Ethanol propelled cars:** the Tax on Registration Certificates is reduced by 50%for cars that run with E85 fuel (super ethanol). **Bonus-malus system:** a premium is granted for the purchase of a new car when its CO_2 emissions are 125 g/km or less. The maximum premium is EUR 5000 (below 60 g/km). A malus is payable for the purchase of a car emitting more than 155 g CO_2/km. The maximum tax amounts to EUR 2,600 (above 245 g/km).

	registration in France: the tax is based on horsepower. Horsepower component of the tax varies from EUR 100 (10HP) up to EUR 1000 (15HP) The tax is not applicable to vehicles belonging to disabled people. **Additional tax on Registration certificates for cars with horsepower of 36HP or more**: the tax is EUR 500 per horsepower from 36HP with a maximum of EUR 8 000. Collection vehicles are exempt from this tax. **Additional Lorries Tax** is levied on the regional certificate tax for lorries according to their weight (from EUR 38 for less than 3.5 tons to EUR 305 for more than 11 tons or trailers and buses for public transport of passengers); **Company car tax** is based on CO_2 emissions. Tax rates vary from EUR 1 for each gram emitted for cars emitting 20g CO_2/km or less to EUR 29 for each gram emitted for cars emitting more than 250g CO_2/km.		
Germany	**VAT**: 19%	Value	
Greece	**VAT**: 24% **Registration tax:** rate varies • from 3.8% up to 64,00% of the taxable value, according to the retail price before taxes and to the CO_2 emissions for passenger cars that belong to the current emissions standard. • from 5.7% to 96.00% of the taxable value, according to the retail price before taxes and to the CO_2 emissions for passenger cars that belong to the previous emissions standard. • from 11.40% to 192.00% of the taxable value, according to the retail price before taxes and to the CO_2emissions for passenger cars that belong to other emissions standard. • from 48.00% to 384.00% of the taxable value, according to the retail price before taxes and to the CO_2 emissions for conventional technology cars. • from 5% to 13% of the taxable value, for lorries-trucks etc (less or more than 3.5 tones), according to emissions standard. • from 0% to 25% of the taxable value for motorcycles according to cylinder capacity. **Registration tax for buses** depends on the number of seats etc.	**Cars:** value (retail price before taxes), CO_2 emissions, "Euro" emissions standards, **Lorries:** weight, emissions standards, body type. **Motorcycles:** cylinder capacity	**Exemptions from registration tax:** Hybrid cars are relieved from the registration tax by 50%. Electric cars are not subjected to registration tax Cars used by public authorities Cars used by disabled persons. Cars used by parents having at least three (3) children. Ambulances used by public hospitals Cars used by people who have moved their normal residence to Greece Cars donated to the Greek Police, Fire Brigade or Greek Coast Guards.
Hungary	VAT: 27% Registration Tax: from HUF 45 000 to HUF 400 000 on new passenger cars according to engine type (diesel or petrol) and engine cylinder capacity, and from HUF 20 000 to HUF 230 000 on motorcycles according to engine cylinder capacity. For cars with lower environmental category of engine higher rates are levied (400, 600, 800 or 1200% higher), but rate is reduced according to a scale	Engine type Cylinder capacity Engine power Polluting emissions Type of fuel	**Reduced registration tax** for cars with hybrid engines or with gas-powered engines (HUF 76 000) and for cars with electric engines (HUF 0).

	based on age (until 90%). Reduced rate is levied to hybrid cars and HUF 0 is levied to electric cars. Transfer of motor vehicles: the rate of duty shall be determined based on the capacity of motor vehicle's engine (in kW). The tax rate is from HUF 300/kW to HUF 850/kW depending on the age of the vehicle (the older the vehicle, the less is due).	Age Electric propulsion	
Iceland	**VAT**: 24% **Vehicle Registration Fee** of ISK 5 000 on initial registration and ISK 2 130 for subsequent changes. **Motor vehicle excise duty:** based on CO_2 emissions ranging from 0-65% **Excise duties on motor vehicles other than private automobiles:** % of value **Large goods vehicles**, large special purpose vehicles, tractors, agriculture trailers, large snow-mobiles, amphibious vehicles, competition cars and motorbikes, vehicles for transport of disabled persons, rescue vehicles and large coaches is exempt. **Small goods vehicles**, small special purpose vehicles, vehicles over 40 years old, motor vehicle bodies 13% **Small coaches**, motorbikes, other vehicles 30%.	Value CO_2 emissions Electric propulsion	**Temporary VAT exemption** with a cap at import and domestic sales of electric-, hydrogen or plug-in hybrid vehicles, including busses.
Ireland	**VAT**: 23% **Registration Tax**: based on CO_2 emissions for passenger vehicles with not more than 9 seating positions and certain commercial vehicles with greater than 4 seats. Rates vary from 14% of the value of such a vehicle with CO_2 emissions of up to 80 g/km to 36% for such a vehicle with CO_2 emissions above 225 g/km. Flat rate applies to vehicles designed and constructed for the carriage of goods and having a maximum laden mass not exceeding 3.5 tonnes not included above and motor caravans (13.30% of the value). Motor cycles are charged EUR 2 per cc up to and including 350cc and EUR 1 per cc above. Large vehicles designed and constructed for the carriage of goods (maximum laden mass over 3.5 tonnes), buses, tractors and "vintage" (over 30 years old) vehicles are charged EUR 200. Special purpose vehicles such as ambulances and fire engines (NIL Rate).	Value CO_2 emissions Type Age Max laden mass Body type	**Relief for hybrid electric vehicles**: age dependent with a maximum tax relief of EUR 1500 for a new vehicle. **Relief for plug-in hybrid electric vehicles**: age dependent with a maximum tax relief of EUR 2500 for a new vehicle. **Relief for new series production electric vehicles**: subject to a maximum of EUR 5000 **Remission/repayment for vehicles specially adapted for persons with certain severe and permanent physical disabilities:** subject to a maximum of EUR 10 000, EUR 16 000 and EUR 22 000 for a disabled driver and EUR 16 000 and EUR 22 000 for a disabled passenger. The amount is depended on the adaptations carried out on the vehicle. Relief for certain charitable organisations is subject to a maximum of EUR 16 000 when the vehicle is adapted to carry less than five such persons. **Exemptions:** Transfers of permanent residence, transfers of permanent business undertakings, inheritances, donations by certain organisations, international air services, diplomatic agents and EU officials, vehicles for use by EU or UN organisations

Israel[2]	**VAT**:17% **Purchase Tax**: private and commercial vehicle weight not exceeding 3500 kg are taxed at 83% of the value; Additional luxury tax is levied on the value of the vehicle that exceeds 300 000 NIS, according to the following formula: 20%*(vehicle price - 300 000)/vehicle price; Taxi < 3 500 kg – 8%; Taxi >3 500 kg – 0%; Commercial vehicles over 3500 kg are taxed at 72% of their value but not eligible for a grant.	Weight Polluting emissions Electric propulsion Safety system Engine power	**Rebates according to the polluting emissions:** vehicles weighing up to 3500 kg benefit of a rebate on the Purchase Tax according to their degree of pollution. There are 15 levels of polluting emissions according to a "Green Score" (weighting the emission of five major pollutants). Rebate is up to the amount of NIS 16 383 **Hybrid vehicles** - Pollution level 1 or 2 – battery capacity > 3 KWH and green score < 100 – 20% others are taxed at a rate of 30%. **Electricity powered vehicles** are taxed a rate of 10% of their value depending on the customs and purchase tax rate. There is no luxury tax on hybrid vehicles and electronic vehicles. Vehicles weighing up to 3500 kg benefit of a rebate on the Purchase Tax (up to 2400 NIS) according to their safety level. There are 9 safety levels (0-8) depending on the number of safety systems.
Italy	**VAT**: 22% **Stamp duty** for registration with the Public Automotive Registry (PRA): EUR 32.00; for the issue of the registration certificate: EUR 32.00 **Provincial Transcription Tax (IPT)**: cars up to 53 kw; buses and tractors up to 110 kw: EUR 150.81; cars over 53 kw: EUR 3.5119 per kw. Provinces may increase the rate up to a maximum of 30%	Engine power	**Exemption from the IPT**: sale of vehicles from private individuals to dealers/dealers of used vehicles; vehicles for special categories of disabled people; vehicles for voluntary associations. **IPT reduction** of 25% for historic vehicles and special vehicles (e.g. cement mixer, milk transport, etc.).
Japan	**VAT:** 8% **Automobile Acquisition Tax (Prefecture):** 3% of aquisition price (2% for commercial and light vehicles)	Value	Special measures of reduced automobile acquisition tax Vehicles with small burden of environment, barrier-free buses and taxis, trucks with collision damage alleviation brake control device, etc., buses for ordinary passengers used on the bus routes provided for in prefectural ordinance.
Korea	**VAT**: 10% **Special Excise Tax:** from zero to 5% of the manufacturer's price according to cylinder capacity **Education Tax**: 30% on the amount of Excise Tax **Acquisition Tax**: 2-7% of the retail price excluding VAT	Value Cylinder capacity Electric propulsion	**Exemptions from special excise tax and education tax** Cars used by disabled persons; ambulances used by hospitals; cars used for transportation business(public passenger transportation only); cars used for car-rental business. **Exemptions from acquisition tax** Cars used by disabled persons, cars used by parents having at least 3 children, small cars for non-commercial activities **Rebate for hybrid and electricity powered vehicles** : relief of the Special excise tax(not exceed KRW 1 000 000(hybrid), KRW 2 000 000(electricity powered).

Latvia	**VAT:** 21% **Vehicle registration (state fee):** for registration, registration certificate and registration number plates - EUR 43.93 **Natural resource tax:** EUR 55 per vehicle	Value	-
Lithuania	**VAT**: 21 % **Registration fee**: a flat rate fee of EUR 14.48 is payable on the first registration of new vehicle (passenger cars, heavy vehicles) and a flat rate fee of EUR 12.45 is payable on the first registration of other vehicle – e.g. used cars (passenger cars, heavy vehicles) in the Republic of Lithuania.	Value Age of vehicle	**Rebate for disabled people** (only owners of passenger cars (once every 3 years): -90% rebate on registration fee for owner who has a disability percentage of 75-100% -75% rebate on registration fee for owner who has a disability percentage of 60-70% -50% rebate on registration fee for owner who has a disability percentage of 45-55%
Luxembourg	**VAT**: 17% **Registration Tax**: the tax is calculated per 100 cm3 according to the following formula: Tax = a * b * c, where a = CO_2 emissions component; b = multiplier (= 0.9 for cars using gasoil & 0.6 for cars not using gasoil). c= additional multiplier when CO_2 emissions >90 g/km (= 0.5 plus 0.1 per additional 10 g/km).	Value CO_2 Emissions Type of fuel Electric propulsion	**Bonus system** : purchasers of new hybrid cars emitting less than 60g CO_2/km and electricity powered vehicles are entitled to a bonus of EUR 5 000.
Mexico	**VAT**: 16% **New vehicles tax**: from 2% to 17% plus a no movable fee according to vehicle value. For vehicles whose price is higher than MXN 723 804.80 (for 2018), there is an additional discount consisting in the reduction of the tax according to the 7% of the difference between the sales price and the threshold mentioned above. The update of the limits of the tax tariff is made every year.	Value Electric propulsion	Exemption of 100% in New Vehicles Tax to vehicles with value up to MXN 244 565.77 Exemption of 50% in New Vehicles Tax to vehicles with value from MXN 244 565.78 to MXN 309 783.32 Exemption of 100% in New Vehicles Tax for hybrid electricity powered vehicles.
Netherlands	**VAT**: 21% **Registration Tax:** for passenger cars, it is fully based on CO_2 emissions and the type of motor fuel used. Vehicles with a CO_2 emission of 0g/km are in any case exempt from the registration tax. For passenger cars, the registration tax is progressive and varies between EUR 356 and EUR 458 per g/km exceeding the level of 1g/km. Passenger cars using diesel are charged with an additional EUR 86.43 per g/km exceeding the level of 67 g/km. Registration tax for motorcycles and delivery vans is based on the value of the vehicle	CO_2 Emissions Motor fuel Value Electric propulsion	**Zero-emission (e.g. electricity powered vehicles)** are exempt from Registration Tax **Other examples of exemption are:** delivery vans owned by entrepreneurs and used for business purposes for at least 10%;. **Tax refunds are provided for vehicles such as**: vehicles used by fire brigades, vehicles used by the police, funerary vehicles, vehicles used for the transport of prisoners, vans used by disabled persons, (animal) ambulances, taxis and vehicles that are used for secure transport

New Zealand	**GST: 15%** **Registration Fee on initial registration:** the registration fee varies depending on the type of vehicle being registered. The base registration fee for a private passenger vehicle varies from NZD 74.00 to NZD 232.00 depending on the size of the engine. **Road user charges:** all diesel vehicles and any vehicle with a GVM of 3.5 tonnes or more are required to pay road user charges. Road user charges are distance based (purchased in 1000 kilometre increments) and charges vary based on the weight and configuration of the vehicle.	**Vehicle type** **Cylinder capacity** **Electric propulsion**	**Electric vehicles are currently exempt from road user charges.**
Norway	**VAT**: 25% **Registration Tax**: rates vary according to weight, CO_2-emissions and NOx-emissions. When CO_2-emissions information is not stated, the tax is calculated based on cylinder capacity instead of CO_2-emissions.	Weight CO_2 emissions NOx emissions Type of fuel Electric range	**Electricity powered vehicles** are exempt from the Registration Tax Plug-in hybrid vehicles (both electric and combustion engine, with external charging) have a rebate in the Registration Tax. 23% of the total weight is not included in the tax base. From 1 July 2018 the weight deduction is differentiated by electric range. **Flexifuel vehicles** (can use fuel with at least 85 pct. Ethanol) have a rebate of NOK 10 000 NOK per vehicle.
Poland	**VAT**: 23% **Excise-Duty** is levied on passenger cars prior to their first registration due to their sale, intra-community acquisition and import. The excise tax base is the sale price or the customs value (in case of import). Rates for passenger cars depend on engine capacity i.e. 18.6% for cars with engine cubic capacity over 2000 cm^3 and 3.1% for the others.	Value Cylinder capacity Electric/hydrogen propulsion	Are exempt from the Excise duty: certain types of ambulance vehicles; electric, hybrid and hydrogen fueled vehicles (the exemption for hybrid vehicles is temporary and shall apply until 1 January 2021; passenger cars introduced in Poland for permanent stay or returning from a temporary stay in the EU or EFTA (under certain conditions).
Portugal	**VAT**: 23% **Motor vehicle tax release for consumption (ISV)** is based on cylinder capacity and CO_2 emissions,(light passengers vehicles) or only on cylinder capacity (other light vehicles, and cycles with two, three or four wheels). There are other rate brackets for light commercial vehicles and some segments of combined (passenger and freight) vehicles.	Value Engine capacity CO_2 Emissions Particles emissions Electric propulsion	Are exempt: vehicles owned by the State (central, regional or local administration), fire brigades, foreign States, diplomatic and consular missions, international organisations and European agencies. Are also exempt: vehicles for disable persons, passenger vehicles for rental or taxi services. Non-motorized vehicles that are purely electric vehicles or moved by renewable energies, and ambulances and heavy vehicles (above 3.500 kg) are out of motor vehicle tax incidence.

Slovak Republic	VAT: **20%** **Administrative fees:** registration in the vehicle register is subject to a registration fee payable by the holder of a motor vehicle (applies to new, imported and used cars). The fee is calculated by formula with given parameters: RP = Pkw x RV1-n where RP is fee rate, Pkw is power of engine, RV1-n is coefficient of vehicle residual value, but the rate shall not be lower than EUR 33. Pkw values vary in 16 brackets from EUR 33 (engine capacity up to 80kw) to EUR 3900 (engine capacity above 254kw). RV1-n coefficient varies in 17 brackets from 1 (first registration) to 0.06 (vehicles over 16 years old). First record of electric car in the cars register is subject to a fee of EUR 33 payable by the holder of the vehicle. Plate fee: release of a licence plate number: EUR 16.50 per plate i.e. EUR 33 for 1 vehicle.	Value Engine power Residual value Type of fuel Electric propulsion	Disabled persons: 50% rebate (max. 100 EUR) in administrative fee are applied for disabled persons. Hybrids, CNG, LNG vehicles: 50% rebate in administrative fee for vehicle holder. Family vans: 50% rebate in administrative fee for vehicle holder with maximum power of engine of 110 kW; holder has at least 4 children in parenting. Other exemptions: 100% rebate for state authorities, higher territorial units, budget organisation, diplomats, court of justice, prosecution, police, Slovak red cross and legal person owned by state authority (100% of shares).
Slovenia	**VAT: 22%** **Motor vehicle** tax is paid for passenger motor vehicles, motorcycles and camper vans, which are put into circulation in Slovenia for the first time; imports and acquisitions from other EU Member States are also taxed. The tax base is the selling price of an individual motor vehicle, excluding VAT and this tax. The tax rate is determined according to environmental criteria (CO_2, Euro emission standards) and the rates are determined from 0.5% to 28% for petrol cars and from 1% to 31% for diesel cars. Passenger cars with cylinder capacity over 2500 cm^3 are subject to the additional tax. Rates vary from 8% (2500 cm^3 and more) to 16% (4000 cm^3 and more). For diesel cars particulate matter (PM) emissions are also considered. Tax rates for motorcycles and camper vans are set upon engine power in the range from 1.5% to 5% for motorcycles and 6% to 18% for camper vans. Motorcycles with cylinder capacity over 1000 cm^3 are subject to the additional tax of 5%. Motor vehicle tax is levied only at the time of first registration of a vehicle and not on an annual basis. **Environmental tax** for pollution of the environment with used motor vehicles is paid for passenger motor vehicles, motorcycles, camper vans and vehicles for the carriage of goods, which are put into circulation in Slovenia for the first time; imports and acquisitions from other EU Member States and imports from third countries are also taxed. The basis for calculating the environmental tax is the mass of a motor vehicle. The amount of tax is determined by the government each year according to the costs of handling used motor vehicles deregistered from traffic on the territory of Slovenia in the previous year. The environmental tax is paid in certain amount per kilo of vehicle and is a precondition for registration. For the year 2015 the amount of tax hasn`t been determined and it amounts to 0 EUR/kg. Environmental tax is levied only at the time of first registration of a	Value Selling price CO_2 emissions Particulate matter emissions EURO emissions standards Engine power Cylinder capacity Weight	**Motor vehicle tax exemptions:** vehicles acquired for transport of families with three or more children; vehicles purchased for carrying disabled people; vehicles intended for (1) official use by diplomatic and consular representations accredited to Slovenia; (2) official use by international organisations, if so stipulated by international treaties binding on Slovenia; (3) personal use by foreign staff of diplomatic and consular missions, accredited to Slovenia, including their family members; (4) personal use by foreign staff of international organisations, including their family members, if so stipulated by international treaties binding on Slovenia. **Are also exempt:** used vehicles (old-timers); vehicles imported on a temporary basis (the temporary change of residence of the vehicle's proprietor who does not maintain his permanent residence in Slovenia); sports vehicles that have not been adapted for road use and are intended only for driving on circuits; transfer of vehicles in the case of reorganizations of vehicle's proprietor; emergency rescue motor vehicles used for transport of victims and patients; financial leasing of the vehicles (All of listed tax exemptions in this box can be used for financial leasing of the vehicles) **Environmental tax**: no exemptions

	vehicle and not on an annual basis. The environmental tax is no longer payable from 12 May 2018.		
Spain	VAT: 21% Vehicle Registration Tax (VRT) is based on CO_2 emissions. Rates vary from 0% (up to 120 g CO_2/km) to 14.75% (200 g CO_2/km and more).	Value CO_2 emissions	VRT exemptions: taxis, driving school vehicles, rental service vehicles; vehicles acquired and used by disabled people; vehicles with special diplomatic registration; transfer of vehicles in the case of change of residence of vehicle's proprietor.
Sweden	VAT: 25%	Value	
Switzerland	VAT: 7.7% Automobile duty: 4% of the vehicle's value is levied on light commercial vehicles with a unit weight of no more than 1600 kg, as well as on passenger vehicles. The duty is payable on the importation of automobiles into the domestic territory and the delivery and own use of automobiles produced domestically. No registration tax (but small fees for number plates and registration papers)	Value Electric propulsion	Electrically powered vehicles are exempt from acquisition tax
Turkey	VAT: 18%. Special Consumption Tax (SCT) is collected once on first acquisition of vehicles. Criteria: engine capacity, SCT tax base, motor power for electric and hybrid vehicles in kw.	Value Cylinder capacity Electric propulsion	Exemption: vehicles for diplomatic use, vehicles for people with disabilities, acquisition of aircraft and helicopters by T.A.A., the first acquisition of vehicles by the headquarters of the Prime Ministry, the vehicles acquired exclusively for use in petroleum exploration activities, the exemption for vehicle purchases of relatives of martyrs, exemption for renewed of commercial vehicles. Rebate: discounted SCT rate applied for only electric vehicles in the 87.03 and 87.11 tariff positions and motor vehicles that have electric motors along with fuel engines (hybrids) in the 87.03 tariff position.
United Kingdom	VAT: 20% Vehicle First Registration Fee: a flat rate fee of GBP 55.0 is payable on the first registration or licensing of a motor vehicle in the United Kingdom	Value	**Exemptions from First Registration Fee:** • those first registered and taxed in the 'Disabled Exempt' tax class • historic vehicles previously registered with the old Local Authorities (late conversions) • imported vehicles previously registered under the Personal Export Scheme and New Means of Transport Scheme • Visiting Forces Vehicles • Crown Exempt Vehicles • vehicles registered under the Direct Export Scheme and • off road vehicles

United States	**A gas guzzler** tax is imposed on the sale, use, or lease by the manufacturer or importer of an automobile of a model type that does not meet certain standards for fuel economy. Automobiles imported for business or personal use are subject to the tax. Automobile (including limousines) means any four-wheeled vehicle rated at 6,000 pounds or less unloaded gross weight that is propelled by an engine powered by gasoline or diesel fuel and is intended for use mainly on public streets, roads, and highways. In 2017, the tax applied to motor vehicles that achieved less than 22.5 miles per gallon. The tax was USD 1 000 for automobiles that got between 21.5 and 22.5 miles per gallon and increased in stages, reaching USD 7 700 for vehicles that got less than 12.5 miles per gallon. A tax of 12 percent of the sales price is imposed on the first retail sale of a truck chassis or body, a truck trailer and semitrailer chassis or body, and tractors that are primarily used for highway transportation in combination with a trailer or semitrailer. The tax is known as the retail tax on heavy trucks, trailers, and tractors. **A tax is imposed on taxable tires** sold by the manufacturer, producer, or importer at the rate of USD 9.45 cents (USD 4.725 cents in the case of a biasply tire or super single tire not designed for steering) for each 10 pounds of the maximum rated load capacity over 3 500 pounds. The tax is known as the taxable tire tax.	Fuel efficiency Value Weight Tyres	**The gas guzzler tax is widely applied and must be paid by vehicles sold to the federal government, state and local governments, and non-profit educational organizations. Vehicles used for police, other law enforcement purposes, or firefighting purposes or as ambulances are exempt. Limousines weighing more than 6 000 pounds or designed to carry more than 10 people are exempt.** **Tyres for use on local and school buses or for the exclusive use of the Department of Defence or the Coast Guard are exempt.**

Notes:

1. This table does not include customs duties; specific regimes for second-hand cars (e.g. margin scheme, old timers); diplomatic sales; export/import and transit schemes and insurance premium tax.

2. Israel: The statistical data for Israel are supplied by and under the responsibility of the relevant Israeli authorities. The use of such data by the OECD is without prejudice to the status of the Golan Heights, East Jerusalem and Israeli settlements in the West Bank under the terms of international law.

Table 4.A.2. Taxes on ownership or use of motor vehicles[1]

Country	Taxes	Criteria	Rebates/Exemptions
Australia	**Annual registration fees**. States and Territories levy fees for annual registration, third party compulsory insurance and drivers' licenses. Fees for commercial vehicles are generally higher than the fees for private vehicles. In most States, fees for trucks vary depending on the type of vehicle and the gross vehicle mass. Licence renewal fees vary to reflect validity periods from one to five years.	Commercial/private use Gross vehicle mass	
Austria	**Motor Vehicles Tax**: motor vehicles above a permissible gross weight of 3.5 tonnes: Motor Vehicle Tax based on the weight of the vehicle (from EUR 1.55 to EUR 1.90 per month and ton depending on the weight). Motor vehicles up to and including a maximum permissible gross weight of 3,5 tons: Motor Vehicle Insurance tax based on engine power in kilowatt (cars) or cubic capacity (motorbikes). For cars: gradual tariff from EUR 0.62 to 0.75 per month and kw. For motorbikes: EUR 0.025 per month and by cubic centimetre.	Weight Engine power Cubic capacity	Vehicles used by diplomatic missions and consular offices; armed forces; police; fire brigade; ambulances; mountain rescue; electrically propelled vehicles; self-propelled working machines; trial moving vehicles; taxi services; mopeds and motorcycles with a cubic capacity of maximum 100 CC; vehicle used solely in agricultural production and forestry; vehicles used for disabled persons.
Belgium	**Federal tax**: the use of a company car tax is based on $C0_2$ emissions. The deductibility of expenses, except for fuel costs, related to the use of the car (50 to 120%) is linked to CO_2 emissions. **Annual Road Tax:** **Walloon Region and Brussels** Capital region: the tax rate depends on fiscal hp. and cylinder capacity and is set according to a progressive scale from EUR 80.52 to EUR 2060.92. For vehicles above 20 h.p. (more than 41 cylinder capacity) an additional amount of EUR 112.33 by h.p. is levied. Vehicles of more than 30 years old (25 years old in the Brussels Capital Region) are subject to an annual tax of EUR 36.53. **Flemish Region**: the tax rate depends on fiscal h.p. and cylinder capacity and is set according to a progressive scale from EUR 80.52 up to EUR 2060.92. For vehicles above 20 h.p. (more than 41 cylinder capacity) an additional amount of EUR 112.33 h.p. is levied. Vehicles of more than 25 years old are subject to an annual tax of EUR 36.53. As from the fiscal year 2016 the tax will be modulated depending on the C02 emission, the euro standard and the type of fuel (except for leasing cars). **All the regions**: an "additional annual road tax" is levied on cars entirely or partially powered by Liquefied Gas Petroleum. This tax is based on a progressive scale depending on the engine power from EUR 89.16 to EUR 208. 20 **Kilometre charge**: a kilometre charge is levied in all the Regions on motor	Engine power Cylinder capacity Fuel used Environmental characteristics	**All regions** provide exemptions for cars used by public authorities, vehicles for disabled people and war invalids, agricultural vehicles, rescue vehicles, trial moving vehicles, ships and little boats, taxi services, mopeds and motorcycles with a cylinder capacity of maximum 250 CC. **Flemish Region**: as of fiscal year 2016 a tax reduction of EUR 100 is applicable to cars running on Liquefied Gas Petroleum. Exemption is provided to cars using certain fuels: pure electric, hydrogen-powered, plug-in hybrid (until 2021), CNG/LNG (until 2021).

	vehicles or articulated vehicle combinations intended or used for the carriage by road of goods having a maximum permissible laden weight of over 3,5 tonnes.		
Canada	**Annual fees**. All provinces impose annual fees for the use of motor vehicles. In general, the fees depend on the type of vehicles and in most cases on the weight of the vehicle	Type Weight	
Chile	**Annual Motor Vehicle Tax** (levied by municipalities) for the use of motor vehicles on public roads depending on the commercial value of the vehicle. Lightweight vehicles: depending on the commercial value of the vehicle Passenger vehicles: fixed fee Cargo vehicles: according to loading capacity	Commercial value Fixed fee Loading capacity (trucks)	
Czech Republic	**Road tax** is imposed on all road motor vehicles and their trailers registered and operated in the Czech Republic if they are used by: - taxpayers of corporate income tax (except of vehicles used by public benefit taxpayer for activities which are not subject to corporate income tax); - taxpayers of personal income tax to the activities or in direct connection with that activities from which he has income from an independent activity under the Act on income tax. Vehicles with a total permitted weight above 3.5t registered in the Czech Republic and determined solely for freight transport are always liable to road tax. As regards passenger cars the tax base shall be the engine's cylinder capacity in cubic centimetres, with the exception of electric-driven passenger cars; As regards semi-trailers and other motor vehicles the tax base shall be: the total of the maximum permitted weight on axles in tonnes and the number of axles of semi-trailers; in the case of other vehicles the maximum permitted weight in tonnes and the number of axles. The annual tax rate of passenger cars varies from CZK 1 200 to CZK 4 200 and in the case of other vehicles vary from CZK 1 800 to CZK 44 100.	Cylinder capacity (passenger cars) Type of propulsion Type of fuel Total max. permitted weight on axles and number of axles (semi-trailers) Max. permitted weight and number of axles (other vehicles)	Tax Exemption:vehicles usually with less than four wheels (motorcycles); vehicles used by diplomatic missions and consular offices (where there is a reciprocal arrangement); vehicles ensuring domestic line passenger transport, vehicles operated by the armed forces and civil defence; vehicles which are state mobilisation reserve or emergency reserve; vehicles of the Police of the Czech Republic; fire protection vehicles; ambulances; mining and mountain rescue vehicles; gas emergency service and power engineering emergency service vehicles. Special road sweeping vehicles; special single-purpose vehicles (e.g. vehicles used in road marking) and vehicles belonging to road authorities or to persons authorized by road authorities exclusively used to maintain land communications, except for passenger cars, electrically propelled vehicles, hybrid driven vehicles, vehicles using as fuel either LPG or CNG or vehicles equipped with an engine determined by his producer for combustion of E85. Tax reduction (25% to 100%) for vehicle exclusively used for carriage in the combined transport for which railway transport or inland waterway transport is made use of. The tax rate is reduced for the period of 108 months from the date of the first registration of vehicle (for the first 36 months by 48%, for the next 36 months by 40% and for the next 36 months by 25%.
Denmark	**Passenger cars semi-annual tax**: the tax is based on fuel consumption, with different rates for petrol/diesel. Rates range from DKK 310 (>20km/l) up to DKK 10830 (<4.5km/l) for petrol cars, and from DKK 130 (>32.1km/l) up to 16 100 (<5.1km/l) for diesel cars. **Lorries' annual tax**: Vehicles registered for the first time until 24 April 2007: the charge for private use is DKK 1 060 annually for cars with total permissible	Fuel efficiency Weight (for lorries)	

	weight (tpw) up to 2000 kg and DKK 5 920 annually for cars with tpw between 2000 and 4000 kg. **Charge for private use**. Vehicles registered on 25 April 2007 or after: the charge for private use is DKK 5920 annually for cars with total permissible weight (tpw) up to 3000 kg and DKK 17 590 annually for cars with tpw between 3000 and 4000 kg. For cars used for both private and commercial purposes the rates are 50%. Cars used exclusively for commercial purposes are free of charge.		
Estonia	**Heavy goods vehicle tax**. Varies from 0 to 232,60 (per quarter) EUR depending on the combination of following factors: weight range (12 tonnes to 40 and more tonnes), axel combination (2, 3, 4, 2+1, 2+2, 2+3, 3+2, 3+3), type of suspension (air, other)..	Weight range, Axle combination, Type of suspension	Exemptions apply for Defence Force, Defence League, Enforcement Force and Rescue Service Heavy goods vehicles and Local Authority, NGO, Foundation and Business vehicles intended for rescue operations.
Finland	**The annual tax for passenger cars and delivery vans** is based on CO2 emissions. If the car does not have emission data in the Vehicular and Driver Data Register, the tax is based on the total mass of the vehicle. Tax rates vary from EUR 106.21 for vehicles emitting from 0g CO2/km up to EUR 654.44 for vehicles emitting 400g CO2/km or more. For diesel passenger cars and vans there is a tax on driving power based on total mass of the vehicle. Tax on driving power also applies to other cars and vans using less taxed fuels than petrol. For lorries there is an annual tax based on maximum gross weight, number of axles and use of trailer	CO_2 emissions Weight Number of axles (lorries)	
France	**Tax on business passenger cars**: up to 7 HP: EUR 1130; more than 7 HP: EUR 2440. **Annual tax on polluting vehicles**. An annual tax is payable by owners of vehicles emitting more than CO2 190g/100km. The rate is EUR 190 a year.	Engine power Electric propulsion Type of fuel	**Exemptions**: cars more than 10 years old; cars used for public passenger transport and cars used for leasing or sale; electrically or gas propelled cars (for mixed oil and gas propelled vehicles exemption is reduced by half). Vehicles using both petrol and GPL are exempt at rate of 50%.
Germany	**Motor Vehicle Tax**. For passenger cars being firstly registered since 1 July 2009, the Motor Vehicle Tax is based mainly on CO_2 emissions. It consists of a base tax (according to cylinder capacity) and a CO_2 tax. The rates of the base tax are EUR 2 per 100 cc (petrol) and EUR 9.50 per 100 cc (diesel) respectively. The CO2 tax is linear at EUR 2 per g CO_2/km. Cars being firstly registered before 1 July 2009 are taxed according to their polluting emissions (EURO-Norm) and cylinder capacity.	Polluting emissions Cylinder capacity CO_2 emissions Electric propulsion	Cars with CO_2 emissions below 95 g/km are exempt from the CO_2-element. Only the base tax is due. Exemption for pure electric cars for ten years after the first registration, if the car is registered between 18 May 2011 and 31 December 2020.
Greece	**Annual road tax on private passenger cars** registered for the first time in Greece before 31.10.2010 (as well as those with international initial registration before 2002), and also motorcycles regardless of their date of registration: based on cylinder capacity from EUR 22 to EUR 1 380.For the above category, there is an extra criterion of years of circulation of cars. Private passenger cars and taxis registered for the first time in Greece, after 1.11.2010: based on CO_2	Cylinder capacity CO_2 emissions Electric propulsion Gross weight (trucks) Number of seats (buses)	The main exemptions are: cars used by public authorities, municipalities, ambulances etc., cars used by disabled persons and members of foreign diplomatic services; electric cars, hybrid cars registered until 31.10.2010, with engine displacement under 1.549 cc; private passenger cars, registered after 1.11.2010 with CO_2 emissions under 90g/km Motorcycles up to 300 cc cylinder capacity

	emissions from EUR 0 to EUR 3.72 per gram of CO_2. Annual road tax on trucks based on gross weight and on buses on the number of seats.		used in order to replace old technology ones (replacement should take place up to 31.12.2009). For motorcycles with cylinder capacity over 300 cc used in order to replace old technology motorcycles exemption applies for 5 years only following the date of first registration of the new motorcycle. Cars and motorcycles, registered with a valid permission of circulation, may be imported for a limited period up to six months per year, by the customs procedure of temporary importation.
Hungary	**Motor vehicle tax** levied according to capacity of engine (in Kw) of passenger cars and motorcycles. The tax base for busses, semi-trailers and caravans is the unladen weight of the vehicle. For lorries the tax is based on net weight plus 50 % of cargo weight. The tax rate for passenger cars and motorcycles is from HUF 140/kW to HUF 345/kW depending on the age of the vehicle (the older the vehicle, the less is due). For lorries, busses, semi-trailers the tax rate is HUF 850/100 kg of the tax base, if the vehicle is equipped with road-saving axles. The tax rate for other lorries, trailers is HUF 1380/100 kg.	Engine capacity Weight (for lorries) Type of axles (for high-duty vehicles) Electric propulsion	Exemption for vehicles: owned by budgetary agencies, religious organisations, owned by social organisations, foundations if this organisations do not have to pay tax on profit, used for public transport or fire service, owned by persons seriously disabled or by persons who regularly transport seriously disabled persons of 13 years old or less. The tax exemption is available for one vehicle, if its engine capacity does not exceed 100 kW, passenger cars equipped with environment- saving engine
Iceland	**A disposal charge** of ISK 350 is levied on each vehicle for each six-month period. This charge is payable for fifteen years from the date of the first registration of the vehicle in Iceland, except when the vehicle is already 25 years old at the beginning of the payment year. The charge is an environmental tax that is intended to finance the disposal of the vehicle at the end of its useful life. Once the vehicle is delivered for scrap, a ISK 20 000 refund will be paid to the owner. Motor vehicles fuelled with diesel in excess of 10 tonnes are subject to a special weight/distance tax, calculated on the basis of the weight of the vehicle and the number of kilometers driven. Owners of diesel vehicles that weigh less than 10 tonnes do not pay a weight/distance tax. **A semi-annual road tax on passenger cars** is levied based on the vehicle's carbon dioxide emissions declared by the car manufacturer for combination of city and road driving. Where emission data are not available, the tax rate is based on the weight of the vehicle. The semi-annual road tax is ISK 130 for each gram of carbon dioxide emission for emission above 121 grams, in addition to the minimum fee which is ISK 5 925.	Weight Distance CO_2 emissions	.
Ireland	**Road Tax on private cars** based on CO_2 emissions. Rates vary from EUR 120 (for 0g CO_2/km) to EUR 2350 (above 225g CO_2/km). Tax on commercial vehicles based on net weight: from EUR 333 (<3000 kg) up	CO_2 emissions Weight (commercial vehicles)	Electrically propelled vehicles: EUR 120 flat rate – private and EUR 92 flat rate – commercial not over 1 500kg

	to EUR 5195 (>20 000 kg)	Electric propulsion	
Israel[2]	**Annual licensing fees**: private and commercial vehicles weighing up to 3500 kg total:the vehicles are sorted into seven groups (generally the price). The annual licensing fees are reliant upon the year of vehicle production, and the group the vehicle belongs to The annual licensing fees range between NIS 718 to NIS 4 535. Commercial vehicles above 3,500 kg,motorized by diesel, have a different tariff.	Price Age Category	Vehicles for disabled person, diplomats, United Nations Organisations, specific charity institutions.
Italy	**Annual Ownership Tax**: From EUR 2.58 per KW to EUR 4.95 per KW according to engine cylinder capacity and polluting emissions. Regions are entitled to vary the national rate. A surtax on use of cars and vehicles intended for the transport of persons or goods applies at a rate of EUR 20.00 for each KW exceeding 185 KW in engine power. Such surtax is reduced after five, ten or fifteen years from the construction of the vehicle by 40%, 70% and 85%, respectively	Engine power Polluting emissions Electric propulsion	Exemption for historical vehicles over 30 years old recognised as having special historical or collectors' interest; flat rate road tax on other vehicles over 30. An exemption of 100% from ownership tax is allowed for electric, LPG and CNG vehicles in the first 5 years (from the first registration) and an exemption of 75% afterwards in many regions. 100% exemption also applies to vehicles for disabled persons.
Japan	**Motor Vehicle Tonnage Tax** (National) (N.B. *Commercial vehicles): levied according to weight , the tax rate are for passenger vehicles from JPY 4 100 per 0,5 ton up to JPY 6 300 per 0,5 ton (from JPY 2 600 up to JPY 2 800); for lorries from JPY 3 300 per 0,5 ton up to JPY 6 300 per 0,5 ton(from JPY 2 600 up to JPY 2 800) **Automobile Tax** (Prefecture) (N.B. *Commercial vehicles): levied according to cylinder capacity for passenger vehicle from JPY 29 500 up to JPY 111 000 (from JPY 7 500 up to JPY 40 700); for lorries: (e.g.4-5 tons maximum load) JPY 25 500 (JPY 18 500); for buses: (e.g.41-50 passengers capacity) JPY 49 000 (JPY 17 500). **Light Vehicle Tax** (Local): levied on light vehicles and motorcycles according to cylinder capacity and standards.	Weight Cylinder capacity Impact on the environment	Special measures of reduced Motor Vehicle Tonnage Tax Vehicles with low impact on the environment, barrier-free buses and taxis, trucks with collision damage alleviation brake control device, etc. Special measures of refunded Motor Vehicle Tonnage Tax Used vehicles properly scrapped or destroyed by certain disasters before the expiry date of valid period of inspection certificate. Special measures of reduced Automobile Tax and Light Vehicle Tax Vehicles with low impact on the environment.
Korea	**Automobile Tax**: rates are applicable according to cylinder capacity from KRW 80 per cc up to KRW 200 per cc for non-commercial vehicles; and from KRW 18 per cc to KRW 24 per cc for commercial vehicles.	Cylinder capacity	Full exemption for disabled persons
Latvia	**Annual tax for passenger cars:** cars with first registration after 31 December 2008 and registered in Latvia after 31 December 2016, is based on CO_2 emissions. For cars registered after 2005, the tax is based on gross weight, motor capacity and maximum motor power. Annual tax for passenger cars registered before 2005 is based only on gross weight. **Annual tax for motorcycles**: based on motor capacity, for heavy goods vehicle is based on gross weight and number of axes and type of suspension if gross weight exceeds 12 000 kg.	CO_2 emissions Weight (passenger cars and heavy goods vehicles) Motor capacity (passenger cars and motorcycles) Maximum motor power Number of axes and type of suspension (heavy good vehicles)	The main exemptions are for: -a car, motorcycle, tricycle or quadricycle, the owner, holder or driver of which is a disabled person -a vehicle, the owner, holder or driver of which is a representative of a diplomatic, consular or international organisation or a person who has diplomatic or consular privileges and immunities -an emergency vehicle - vehicles having been registered or being registered with the status of historic motor vehicle

		Electric propulsion	- electric mobiles
Lithuania	**Charge for busses and heavy vehicles** (vignettes). Applicable annual tax rate threshold - from EUR 289 (for busses) until EUR 1158 (for heavy vehicles of more than 12 tonnes of gross laden weight).	Vehicle type, category, class and group, emission class, gross laden weight.	Exemptions: vehicles used by public authorities; vehicles specially designed for the use and (or) transport of disabled persons; vehicles of health care institutions (ambulance and resuscitation cars); buses on local (city and suburban) regular routes.
Luxembourg	**Automobile Tax**: the annual circulation tax is based on CO_2 emissions. Tax rates are calculated by multiplying the CO_2 emissions in g/km with 0.9 for diesel cars and 0.6 for cars using other fuels respectively and with an exponential factor (0.5 below 90 g/km and increased by 0.1 for each additional 10 g of CO_2 /km). Tax on heavy vehicles (also known as "Eurovignette") is levied on vehicles (lorries) with a gross weight of 12 tons or more for the use of motor ways. Tax also varies according to Euro norms.	CO_2 emissions Electric propulsion	Exemptions: vehicles for disabled people; historical vehicles; cars used by public authorities; electrically propelled cars
Mexico	Starting 2012, the tax on ownership was eliminated as a Federal Tax. State governments may impose a tax on ownership and/or periodic registration. Registration fee is MXN 1 365 on average and Tax on ownership usually goes from 2.6% to 25% based on value, type of vehicle and number of passengers.	Value Type of vehicle Number of passengers Electric propulsion	States exempt hybrid and electric vehicles used for public passenger transport; Some states provide exemptions for particular uses. Some states provide a subsidy of 100% for vehicles of any value.
Netherlands	**Motor vehicle tax** is based on the dead-weight and the type fuel used. There is a Provincial surtax. Tax on heavy vehicles (also known as "Eurovignette") is levied on vehicles (lorries) with a gross weight of 12 tons or more for the use of motor ways in the Netherlands. Tax also varies according to Euro norms (diesel category)	For motor vehicle tax: Fuel used Weight Region (province) CO_2 emissions For tax on heavy vehicles: Number of axles Polluting emissions	Vehicles with a CO_2 emission of 0 are exempt. Low-emissions vehicles (CO_2 is not exceeding a level of 50 g/km) pay 50% of the taxes. Other examples of exemptions are: (Animal) ambulances; vehicles used by fire brigades and by the police/defence; funerary vehicles; vehicles used to clean, maintain or construct roads; taxis and vehicles older than 40 years. Other special regimes apply such as reduced tax rate for delivery vans owned by entrepreneurs and used for business purposes for at least 10% and for vans equipped for and used by disabled persons.
New Zealand	**Vehicle license fees**. Most vehicles are required to be continuously licensed in order to operate on public roads. Vehicle licenses are valid for up to 12 months. Fees vary depending on the type of vehicle being licensed. For a private passenger vehicle, the base fee for a 12 month license is NZD 52.11.	Vehicle type	
Norway	**The traffic insurance tax** replaced the annual motor vehicle tax from 2018. Daily tax: NOK 9,15 for diesel cars without factory-fitted particle filter and NOK 7,85 for other cars, NOK 5,46 for motorbikes. NOK 1,27 for moped, tractors etc.	Vehicle type Electric propulsion Particle filter	**Electricity powered vehicles** are exempt from the Traffic insurance tax.
Poland	**Annual Motor Vehicles Tax** levied at municipal level on heavy goods vehicles of maximum permissible gross laden weight over 3.5 tons, road and ballast tractors, trailers and semi-trailers and buses.	Weight Type of vehicle Number of passengers for	Vehicles under possession of diplomatic representations, consular offices and other foreign missions. Transport vehicles constituting mobilisation supply. Special vehicles and vehicles used for special

		busses	purposes. Historic vehicles.
Portugal	**Annual State and municipal tax** due by the ownership of the vehicle, it was reformed on 1st of July of 2007 for passengers vehicles and mixed use cars with gross weight not exceeding 2500 Kg, if registered after the reform, tax rate is based on motor capacity and CO_2 emissions and for vehicles registered since 1981 up to the reform rates vary depending on motor capacity or voltage, date of registration and fuel type. Vehicle excise duty on lorries above 2.5 tonnes used in public and private transport of merchandise.	Motor capacity CO_2 emissions Electric propulsion Weight Number of axels Vehicle type and fuel Type of suspension	Vehicles owned by the State (central, regional or local administration), fire brigades, foreign States, diplomatic and consular missions, international organizations, specialized European agencies and disabled persons; vehicles seized by the State for as part of a criminal procedure. Are also exempt ambulances, passengers vehicles destined to rental or taxi services, tractors, funerary vehicles, non-motorized vehicles that are purely electric or moved by renewable energies.
Slovak Republic	**Motor Vehicle Tax** is imposed only on vehicles that are registered in the Slovak Republic and are used to conduct business activities in the tax period. Rates vary depending on type, weight, cylinder capacity, number of axles (for utility vehicles and buses) of the vehicle and type of engine.	Usage Vehicle type (passenger cars) Weight Cylinder capacity (utility vehicles and buses) Number of axles Type of engine	**Exemption:** vehicles for Diplomats - vehicles used by diplomatic missions and consular offices, vehicles used for emergency services (first aid), vehicles for Public Services - public buses, vehicles used solely in agriculture or forestry. **Tax reduction (50%)** for hybrid motor vehicles or hybrid electric vehicles, vehicles using compressed natural gas (CNG) or liquefied natural gas (LNG), hydrogen-powered vehicles, vehicles which were used for combined transport at least 60 times. The tax rate is reduced for the period of 108 months from the date of the first registration of vehicle (for the first 36 months by 25%, for the next 36 months by 20% and for the next 36 months by 15%).
Slovenia	**Circulation tax** (levied on an annual basis) – an annual fee for the use of road transport vehicles is paid once a year for the use of motor vehicles and trailers in Slovenia by vehicle owners. The fee is paid at the time of renewal of registration certificate. By paying an annual duty a person acquires the right to use a registered vehicle in road traffic for the next 12 months. The amount of tax depends on the category of the vehicle and is proportionate to the duration of the registration period in a certain year.	Cylinder capacity, Engine power, Weight Polluting emissions Electric propulsion Type of suspension Number of seats	Tax exemptions: Vehicles exclusively using electricity for power, tractors and tractor trailers, motorcycles, three-wheeled cycles with engine capacity up to 50 cc and light four-wheeled cycles, light trailers with maximum permissible weight up to 750 kg, motor vehicles registered to the Slovenian Army, Civil Protection, Mountain Rescue Service, Ecological Laboratory with mobile unit, police and fire-fighting vehicles, ambulances, motor vehicles and trailers registered for diplomatic and consular missions, vehicles owned by certain international organizations, and vehicles used for the transport of disabled persons. Tax reduction for low polluting trucks Trucks of category N1: tax reduction for EURO 5 (-25%) and EURO 6 and higher (-35%) and tax increase for EURO 3 (+10%), EURO 2 (+20%), EURO 1 (+30%) and EURO 0 or lower (+40%); Trucks of category N2, N3 and buses (M2, M3): tax reduction for EURO 5 (-25%) and EURO 6 and higher (-35%) and tax increase for EURO 3 (+10%) EURO 2 (+20%), EURO 1 (+30%) and EURO 0 or

			lower (+40%) Tax reduction for buses and trucks with air suspension (-15%) Tax reduction for old-timers (-80%) and vehicles acquired for transport of families with four or more children (-50%).
Spain	**Motor Vehicle Tax** (levied by municipalities) based on engine power for passenger cars, passenger capacity for buses, loading capacity for trucks and cylinder volume for motorcycles.	Vehicle type Engine power Cylinder capacity	**Tax exemptions:** Official vehicles belonging to public bodies of diplomatic offices, ambulances, vehicles adapted to disabled people, public transport vehicles over nine seats, tractors and other vehicles of agricultural use; historic vehicles.
Sweden	**The annual circulation tax** for cars from 2006 and later or, older cars that meet at least Euro 4 exhaust emission standards, is based on CO_2 emissions. Also campers, light goods vehicles and light buses that are taken in to use in 2011 or later are taxed based on the CO_2 emissions. The tax consists of a basic rate of SEK 360 plus SEK 22 for each gram CO_2 the vehicle emits above 111 g/km. If the vehicle can be driven with diesel fuel this sum is multiplied by 2.37. For vehicles that can be driven with alternative fuels, the tax is SEK 360 plus SEK 11 for each gram CO_2 the vehicle emits above 111 g/km.	Weight CO_2 emissions Type of fuel. Electric propulsion	An exemption from annual circulation tax applies to green cars during the first five years. The exemption applies to cars, campers, light goods vehicles and light buses with low emissions of CO_2 in proportion to the vehicles weight. The vehicles emissions of CO_2 shall not exceed a calculated value; (95 + 0,0457 x (the vehicles weight in kg – 1 372)). For alternative fuel vehicles the value is calculated; (150 + 0,0457 x (the vehicles weight in kg – 1 372)). Electric cars shall not consume more electricity than 37 kWh/100 km.
Switzerland	**Cantonal (provincial) tax**. The annual motor vehicle tax depends on the weight or engine volume of the vehicle. **Federal tax**: Use of Swiss motorways (first and second-class motorways) has been generally subject to charge. The charge is levied in the form of the motorway charge sticker, which costs CHF 40. The obligation to display a motorway charge sticker generally applies to motor vehicles and trailers with a total weight of up to 3.5 tons each. This group comprises primarily passenger vehicles, motorbikes, vans, trailers, etc. Motor vehicles and trailers with a total weight exceeding 3.5 tons (so-called heavy vehicles) require a motorway charge sticker if they are not subject to the heavy vehicle charge. These include, for example, heavy utility vehicles (e.g. crane lorries). The performance-related heavy vehicle charge (LSVA) depends on the total weight, polluting emissions and kilometres driven in Switzerland. It is levied on all motor vehicles and trailers that have a total permissible laden weight of more than 3.5 tons, are used to transport goods, are registered in Switzerland or abroad and are driven on the Swiss public road network. The lump-sum heavy vehicle charge (PSVA) is levied in the form of a lump sum on heavy motor vehicles for the following vehicle types that are driven on the Swiss public road network: heavy passenger vehicles, heavy campervans, motor-homes and caravans, vehicles used for transporting passengers	Weight Engine volume Kilometres driven Polluting emissions Electric propulsion	A reduced rate of the motor vehicle tax usually applies to electric and agricultural vehicles.

	(coaches, buses), tractors and motor carriages, motor vehicles for fun fairs and circuses. Other motor vehicles for the carriage of goods and with a maximum speed of 45 km/h.		
Turkey	Motor Vehicle Tax levied on all motor vehicles - based on weight, type and cylinder capacity. Paid as two equal instalments per annum by registered owner.	Weight, Vehicle type Cylinder capacity Electric propulsion	Electrically propelled passenger cars are not subject of the tax
United Kingdom	**Vehicle Excise Duty (VED).** on lorries is set according to the number of axles, weight and type of vehicle. Cars that are presented for registration in the UK on or after 1 March 2001 – and before 01/04/17, on the basis of a type approval certificate specifying a carbon dioxide (CO_2) emission figure, attract a rate of VED according to the amount of CO_2 emitted and the type of fuel used. These cars fall within a 13-banded graduated VED system. The bands are labelled A-M, with band A containing the least polluting vehicles and band M comprising of vehicles that have high CO_2 emissions. Full details can be found at www.direct.gov.uk/Motoring Cars registered on or after 01/04/18 on the basis of a type approval certificate specifying a carbon dioxide (CO2) emission figure, attract a rate of VED for its first vehicle licence according to the amount of CO_2 emitted and fuel used. For the second vehicle licence, vehicles with a list price exceeding GBP 40 000 attract a standard rate of VED plus an additional rate of VED. Vehicles with a list price of GBP 40 000 or less attract a standard rate of VED. For private cars which do not fall into the above graduated VED system there is a two-tier threshold: vehicles not over 1549cc pay an annual rate of duty of GBP 145, and those over 1549cc pay a rate of duty of GBP 230.	Vehicle type CO_2 emissions Type of fuel Electric propulsion	Tax exemption applies to vehicles for disabled people, historic vehicles, which are 40 years old, limited use vehicles, agricultural machines, mowing machines, steam powered vehicles, electrically propelled vehicles, and electrically assisted pedal cycles. Vehicles belonging to public bodies such as ambulances, fire engine, police cars, etc.
United States	**Heavy Highway Vehicle Use Tax** is imposed on the use of trucks weighing 55 000 pounds or above. For those trucks (except logging trucks) weighing no more than 75 000 pounds, the tax is USD 100 per year plus USD 22 for each 1 000 pounds in excess of 55 000 pounds. For those trucks weighing more than 75 000 pounds, the tax is USD 550. For logging trucks, the tax is USD 75 per year for trucks weighing at least 55 000 pounds plus USD 16.50 per 1 000 pounds in excess of 55 000 pounds. For logging trucks weighing more than 75 000 pounds the tax is USD 412.50. A credit may be claimed for the tax in the following year if the vehicle was driven 5 000 miles or less (7 500 miles or less for agricultural vehicles.). **State and local taxes**. State and local governments may impose a periodic registration, operators' license, parking and inspection fees as well as property taxes.	Weight (for trucks)	

Note:
1. Excluding insurance premium tax.
2. Israel: The statistical data for Israel are supplied by and under the responsibility of the relevant Israeli authorities. The use of such data by the OECD is without prejudice to the status of the Golan Heights, East Jerusalem and Israeli settlements in the West Bank under the terms of international law.
Source: national delegates; position as at 1 January 2018

Annex A. Countries with VAT

Almost all countries levy general consumption taxes i.e. taxes on the sale of most goods and services. The general consumption tax applied by the majority of those countries is value added tax (VAT[1]) i.e. a tax collected at all stages of the processes of production and distribution of goods and services, accumulation of the tax being prevented by allowing businesses to deduct the tax they incur on their inputs from the tax they collect on their outputs. Exports of goods and services are generally within the scope of VAT, although they are commonly zero rated. On the other hand, the importation of goods and services is subject to tax to ensure the neutrality of the tax system (see Chapter 1). A minority of countries (and some sub-national entities) apply retail sales taxes, i.e. single-stage taxes on goods and services supplied to final consumers (these are not listed in the table below). All OECD countries levy VAT, except the United States, where resale sales taxes are levied at sub-national level (see Chapter 1).

As of 1 November 2018, 168 countries and territories in the world have implemented a VAT.

Countries and territories operating a VAT					
No.	Country	Implementation	Rates 2018 (%)		
			Standard[2]	Reduced[3]	Increased
1	Albania	1995	20	0, 6	
2	Algeria	1992	19	0, 9	
3	Andorra	2013	4.5	0, 1, 2.5	9.5
4	Antigua and Barbuda	2007	15	0, 12.5	
5	Argentina	1974	21	2.5, 5, 10.5	27
6	Armenia	1993	20		
7	Australia	2000	10	0	
8	Austria	1973	20	10, 13	
9	Azerbaijan	1992	18	0	
10	Bahamas	2015	7.5		
11	Bangladesh	1991	15	2, 4.5, 5, 6, 10	10 - 500
12	Barbados	1997	17.5	0, 7.5	
13	Belarus	1991	20	0, 10	25
14	Belgium	1971	21	0, 6, 12	
15	Belize	2006	12.5	0	
16	Benin	1991	18	0	
17	Bolivia	1986	13	0	
18	Bosnia Herzegovina	2006	17		
19	Botswana	2002	12	0	
20	Brazil	1964	17, 18	4, 7, 12	25
21	Bulgaria	1994	20	9	
22	Burkina Faso	1993	18	0	
23	Burundi	2009	18	0, 10	
24	Cambodia	1999	10		
25	Cameroon	1999	19.25	0	
26	Canada	1991	GST/HST: 5, 13, 15[4]		
27	Cape Verde	2004	15	0	
28	Central African Republic	2001	19	5	
29	Chad	2000	18	0	
30	Chile	1975	19		
31	China (People's Republic)	1994	16	6, 10	
32	Colombia	1983	19	0, 5	
33	Commonwealth of Dominica	2006	15	0, 10	
34	Congo (Dem. Republic)	2012	16		
35	Congo (Republic)	1997	18	0, 5	
36	Cook Islands	1997	15	0	
37	Costa Rica	1982	13	5, 10	
38	Côte d'Ivoire	1960	18	0, 9	
39	Croatia	1998	25	5, 13	
40	Cyprus[5]	1992	19	0, 5, 9	
41	Czech Republic	1993	21	10, 15	
42	Denmark	1967	25	0	
43	Djibouti	2009	10	0	
44	Dominican Republic	1983	18	0, 16	-

45	Ecuador	1970	12	0	
46	Egypt	1991	14	0, 5	15, 30
47	El Salvador	1992	13	0	
48	Equatorial Guinea	2005	15	0, 6	
49	Estonia	1991	20	0, 9	
50	Eswatini (formerly Swaziland)	2012	14	0	
51	Ethiopia	2003	15	0	
52	Faroe Islands	1993	25	0	
53	Fiji	1992	9	0	
54	Finland	1994	24	0, 10, 14	
55	Former Yugoslav Republic of Macedonia	2000	18	5	
56	France	1968	20	2.1, 5.5, 10[6]	
57	Gabon	1995	18	0, 5, 10	
58	Gambia	2013	15	0	
59	Georgia	1993	18	0	
60	Germany	1968	19	7	
61	Ghana	1998	12.5	0, 3	
62	Greece	1987	24	6, 13[7]	
63	Grenada	2010	15	0, 10	20
64	Guatemala	1992	12	0	
65	Guinea	1996	18		
66	Guinea-Bissau	2001	17	10	20
67	Guyana	2007	14	0	
68	Haiti	1982	10		
69	Honduras	1964	15	0	18
70	Hungary	1988	27	5, 18	
71	Iceland	1990	24	0, 11	
72	India	2017	12, 18	0, 5	28
73	Indonesia	1985	10	0	10 – 125
74	Iran	2008	9[8]		12+3, 20 (5 or 10)
75	Ireland	1972	23	0, 4.8, 9, 13.5	
76	Isle of Man	1973	20	0, 5	
77	Israel[9]	1976	17	0	
78	Italy	1973	22	0, 4, 5, 10	
79	Jamaica	1991	16.5	2, 10	21.5, 25
80	Japan	1989	8		
81	Jersey	2008	5	0	
82	Jordan	2001	16	0, 4, 10	26
83	Kazakhstan	1992	12	0	
84	Kenya	1990	16	0	
85	Kiribati	2014	12.5	0	
86	Korea (South)	1977	10		
87	Kosovo	2001	18	8	
88	Kyrgyzstan	1999	12	0	
89	Lao (People's Democratic Republic)	2010	10	0	
90	Latvia	1995	21	5, 12	
91	Lebanon	2002	11	0	
92	Lesotho	2003	14	0, 5	15
93	Liechtenstein	1995	7.7	2.5, 3.7	

94	Lithuania	1994	21	5, 9	
95	Luxembourg	1970	17	3, 8, 14	
96	Madagascar	1994	20	0, 8	
97	Malawi	2002	16.5	0	
98	Maldives	2011	6	0	12
99	Mali	1991	18	5	
100	Malta	1999	18	0, 5, 7	
101	Mauritania	1995	16		18
102	Mauritius	1998	15		
103	Mexico	1980	16	0	
104	Moldova	1998	20	0, 8	
105	Monaco	1968	20	2.1, 5.5, 10	
106	Mongolia	1998	10	0	
107	Montenegro	2003	21	0, 7	
108	Morocco	1986	20	0, 7, 10, 14	
109	Mozambique	1999	17	0, 5	
110	Namibia	2000	15	0	
111	Nepal	1997	13	0	
112	Netherlands	1969	21	6	
113	New Zealand	1986	15	0	
114	Nicaragua	1975	15	0, 7	
115	Niger	1986	19	0, 5	
116	Nigeria	1994	5	0	
117	Niue	2009	12.5	0	
118	Norway	1970	25	0, 10, 15	
119	Pakistan	1990	17	0, 2	18 - 25
120	Panama	1977	7		10, 15
121	Papua New Guinea	1999	10	0	
122	Paraguay	1993	10	0, 2, 5	
123	Peru	1991	16 + 2[10]		
124	Philippines	1988	12	0	
125	Poland	1993	23	0, 5, 8	
126	Portugal	1986	23	6, 13[11]	
127	Romania	1993	19	5, 9	
128	Russia	1991	18	10	
129	Rwanda	2001	18	0	
130	Saint Kitts and Nevis	2010	17	0, 10	
131	Saint Lucia	2012	12.5	0, 10	
132	Saint Vincent and the Grenadines	2007	15	0, 10	
133	Samoa	1994	15	0	
134	Saudi Arabia	2018	5	0	
135	Senegal	1980	18	0, 10	
136	Serbia	2005	20	10	
137	Seychelles	2012	15	0	
138	Sierra Leone	2009	15	0	
139	Singapore	1994	7	0	
140	Slovak Republic	1993	20	10	
141	Slovenia	1999	22	9.5	
142	South Africa	1991	14	0	
143	Spain	1986	21	4, 10[12]	
144	Sri Lanka	1998	15	0	

145	Sudan	2000	17	0	30
146	Sweden	1969	25	0, 6, 12	
147	Switzerland	1995	7.7	2.5, 3.7	
148	Chinese Taipei	1986	5	0	
149	Tajikistan	1992	18	5	
150	Tanzania	1998	18	0	
151	Thailand	1992	7[13]		
152	Togo	1995	18	10	
153	Tonga	2005	15		
154	Trinidad and Tobago	1990	12.5	0	
155	Tunisia	1988	19	0, 7, 13	
156	Turkey	1984	18	1, 8	
157	Turkmenistan	1992	15	0	
158	Uganda	1996	18	0	
159	Ukraine	1992	20	0, 7	
160	United Arab Emirates	2018	5	0	
161	United Kingdom	1973	20	0, 5	
162	Uruguay	1972	22	0, 10	
163	Uzbekistan	1992	20	0	
164	Vanuatu	1998	12.5	0	
165	Venezuela	1993	12	8	27
166	Vietnam	1999	10	0, 5	
167	Zambia[14]	1995	16	0	
168	Zimbabwe	2004	15	0	
169	Barhain[15]	[2020]	5		

Source: F. Annacondia, International - Overview of General Turnover Taxes and Tax Rates, International VAT Monitor (2018), Journals IBFD, cited with permission of IBFD, see http://online.ibfd.org/kbase/, All rights reserved.

Notes

[1] The acronym "VAT" refers to any national tax that embodies the basic features of a value added tax as described in Chapter 1, by whatever name or acronym it is known *e.g.* "Goods and Services Tax" ("GST")

[2] The standard rate is the rate that generally applies, unless the legislation explicitly provides that specific goods and services are subject to different (reduced or increased) rates.

[3] Reduced rates include zero-rates applicable to domestic supplies (i.e. an exemption with right to deduct input tax). This does not include zero-rated exports or other supplies subject to similar treatment such as international transport or supplies to embassies, international organisations and diplomatic missions

[4] **Canada:** additional HST rates apply on the top of the federal 5% GST rate in several provinces (see Table 2.A2.1)

[5] **Footnote by Turkey**: the information in this document with reference to « Cyprus » relates to the southern part of the Island. There is no single authority representing both Turkish and Greek Cypriot people on the Island. Turkey recognizes the Turkish Republic of Northern Cyprus (TRNC). Until a lasting and equitable solution is found within the context of United Nations, Turkey shall preserve its position concerning the "Cyprus issue".
Footnote by all the European Union Member States of the OECD and the European Union: the Republic of Cyprus is recognised by all members of the United Nations with the exception of Turkey. The information in this document relates to the area under the effective control of the Government of the Republic of Cyprus.

[6] **France:** Specific rates also apply in some regions/territories: 0.9/2.1/10.0/13.0 & 1.05/1.75/2.1/8.5 (see Table 2.A2.1)
[7] **Greece:** Specific rates of 4.0/9.0/17.0 apply in some islands
[8] **Iran:** In addition to VAT (at the rate of 6%) an additional levy of 3% is collected and treated in the same way as VAT.

[9] **Israel:** The statistical data for Israel are supplied by and under the responsibility of the relevant Israeli authorities. The use of such data by the OECD is without prejudice to the status of the Golan Heights, East Jerusalem and Israeli settlements in the West Bank under the terms of international law.

[10] **Peru:** in addition to the standard IGV rate of 16%, a 2% sales tax (IPM) is levied at municipal level

[11] **Portugal:** In the Islands of Azores, the standard VAT rate is 18% and the reduced rates are 4% and 9%. In the Islands of Madeira the standard rate is 22% and reduced rates are 5% and 12%.

[12] **Spain:** Rates of 0.0%, 3.0%; 7.0%, 9.50%; 13.50%, 20% apply in the Canary Islands.

[13] **Thailand.** The standard rate should increase to 10% from 1 October 2018

[14] **Zambia** has announced its intention to remove the VAT system in 2019 and to replace it with a sales tax at retail level.

[15] **Barhain** has announced its intention to implementation a VAT on 1 January 2019

Annex B. Exchange rates

Country	Currency	PPP rate[1]	Market rate[2]
Australia	AUD	1.47	1.31
Austria	EUR	0.80	0.89
Belgium	EUR	0.80	0.89
Canada	CAD	1.25	1.30
Chile	CLP	404.19	648.68
Czech Republic	CZK	13.11	23.39
Denmark	DKK	7.24	6.60
Estonia	EUR	0.55	0.89
Finland	EUR	0.90	0.89
France	EUR	0.80	0.89
Germany	EUR	0.78	0.89
Greece	EUR	0.60	0.89
Hungary	HUF	138.89	274.48
Iceland	ISK	140.82	106.82
Ireland	EUR	0.81	0.89
Israel[3]	ILS	3.79	3.60
Italy	EUR	0.72	0.89
Japan	JPY	99.59	112.18
Korea	KRW	877.05	1130.64
Latvia	EUR	0.50	0.89
Lithuania	EUR	0.46	0.89
Luxembourg	EUR	0.89	0.89
Mexico	MXN	9.23	18.87
Netherlands	EUR	0.82	0.89
New Zealand	NZD	1.47	1.41
Norway	NOK	10.17	8.27
Poland	PLN	1.80	3.78
Portugal	EUR	0.59	0.89
Slovak Republic	EUR	0.49	0.89
Slovenia	EUR	0.60	0.89
Spain	EUR	0.66	0.89
Sweden	SEK	9.10	8.55
Switzerland	CHF	1.22	0.99
Turkey	TRY	1.45	3.65
United Kingdom	GBP	0.71	0.78
United States	USD	1.00	1.00

Notes:

1. Purchase Parity Rates (PPP) for GDP 2017. Accessed on 1 July 2018. For further detail see *www.oecd.org/std/ppp*.
2. Average market rates 2017. OECD Monthly Monetary Statistics. For further details see *stats.oecd.org*.
3. Israel: the statistical data for Israel are supplied by and under the responsibility of the relevant Israeli authorities. The use of such data by the OECD is without prejudice to the status of the Golan Heights, East Jerusalem and Israeli settlements in the West Bank under the terms of international law.

Note on exchange rates: Cross-country comparisons of thresholds or tax amounts expressed in national currency require their conversion into one single currency. By convention, the currency used in this publication is the United States Dollar (USD). Two rates can generally be used for converting national currencies into USD: (1) market rates, which are currency exchange rates observed on the markets (the rate used in this publication is the average rate for 2015 as published in the OECD Monetary and Financial Statistics). (2) the purchasing power parity rates (PPP) for GDP, which equalise the purchasing power of different countries by eliminating differences in price levels between them; they show the specified number of monetary units needed in each country to buy the same representative basket of consumer goods and services that costs USD 1 in the United States. PPP exchange rates (for 2015) are used for Tables 1.A1.10 (Chapter 1), 2.A2.3 and 2.A2.7 (Chapter 2) as they provide for a better comparison of the value of VAT relief thresholds. Market exchange rates are used for the other tables as they allow easier comparison of prices and the level of taxes in countries.
Source: OECD.

Annex C. Most sold brands of cigarettes in OECD countries

Most sold brands of cigarettes in OECD countries[1]

Country	Most sold brand 2016
Australia	Winfield
Austria	**Marlboro**
Belgium	Marlboro
Canada[2]	—
Chile	Pall Mall
Czech Republic	L&M
Denmark	Prince
Estonia	Marlboro
Finland	L&M
France	Marlboro
Germany	Marlboro
Greece	Marlboro
Hungary	Marlboro
Iceland	Winston
Ireland	Silk Cut
Israel	Marlboro
Italy	Marlboro
Japan	Mevius
Korea	Esse
Latvia	Winston
Lithuania	Marlboro
Luxembourg	Marlboro
Mexico	Marlboro
Netherlands	Marlboro
New Zealand	Pall Mall
Norway	Prince
Poland	L&M
Portugal	Marlboro
Slovak Republic	L&M
Slovenia	Marlboro
Spain	Marlboro
Sweden	Marlboro
Switzerland	Marlboro
Turkey	Parliament
United Kingdom	Mayfair
United States[2]	—

1. Data as at 1 July 2018.
2 No most sold brand is available for the United States and Canada as an average price weighted by consumption in each State/Province was used.
Source: World Health Organisation.

ORGANISATION FOR ECONOMIC CO-OPERATION AND DEVELOPMENT

The OECD is a unique forum where governments work together to address the economic, social and environmental challenges of globalisation. The OECD is also at the forefront of efforts to understand and to help governments respond to new developments and concerns, such as corporate governance, the information economy and the challenges of an ageing population. The Organisation provides a setting where governments can compare policy experiences, seek answers to common problems, identify good practice and work to co-ordinate domestic and international policies.

The OECD member countries are: Australia, Austria, Belgium, Canada, Chile, the Czech Republic, Denmark, Estonia, Finland, France, Germany, Greece, Hungary, Iceland, Ireland, Israel, Italy, Japan, Korea, Latvia, Lithuania, Luxembourg, Mexico, the Netherlands, New Zealand, Norway, Poland, Portugal, the Slovak Republic, Slovenia, Spain, Sweden, Switzerland, Turkey, the United Kingdom and the United States. The European Union takes part in the work of the OECD.

OECD Publishing disseminates widely the results of the Organisation's statistics gathering and research on economic, social and environmental issues, as well as the conventions, guidelines and standards agreed by its members.

OECD PUBLISHING, 2, rue André-Pascal, 75775 PARIS CEDEX 16
(23 2018 49 1 P) ISBN 978-92-64-30902-9 – 2018

www.ingramcontent.com/pod-product-compliance
Lightning Source LLC
Chambersburg PA
CBHW061211240926
51846CB00006B/1183